Dissonant Records

Media Origins

Edited by Elizabeth Losh and Jacqueline Wernimont

Numbered Lives: Life and Death in Quantum Media, Jacqueline Wernimont, 2018
Sex Dolls at Sea: Imagined Histories of Sexual Technologies, Bo Ruberg, 2022
Dissonant Records: Close Listening to Literary Archives, Tanya E. Clement, 2024

Dissonant Records

Close Listening to Literary Archives

Tanya E. Clement

The MIT Press
Cambridge, Massachusetts
London, England

© 2024 Massachusetts Institute of Technology

This work is subject to a Creative Commons CC-BY-NC-ND license.

This license applies only to the work in full and not to any components included with permission. Subject to such license, all rights are reserved. No part of this book may be used to train artificial intelligence systems without permission in writing from the MIT Press.

The MIT Press would like to thank the anonymous peer reviewers who provided comments on drafts of this book. The generous work of academic experts is essential for establishing the authority and quality of our publications. We acknowledge with gratitude the contributions of these otherwise uncredited readers.

This book was set in Stone Serif and Stone Sans by Westchester Publishing Services. Printed and bound in the United States of America.

Library of Congress Cataloging-in-Publication Data

Names: Clement, Tanya Elizabeth, author.
Title: Dissonant records : close listening to literary archives / Tanya E. Clement.
Description: Cambridge, Massachusetts : The MIT Press, 2024. | Series: Media origins | Includes bibliographical references and index.
Identifiers: LCCN 2023052594 (print) | LCCN 2023052595 (ebook) | ISBN 9780262548724 (paperback) | ISBN 9780262379236 (epub) | ISBN 9780262379229 (pdf)
Subjects: LCSH: Hurston, Zora Neale—Archives. | Ellison, Ralph—Archives. | Sexton, Anne, 1928–1974—Archives. | Anzaldúa, Gloria—Archives. | Literature—Archival resources. | Sound archives—Social aspects. | Literature—Research. | Listening—Social aspects. | Intermediality.
Classification: LCC CD973.2 .C58 2024 (print) | LCC CD973.2 (ebook) | DDC 929.1072—dc23/eng/20240402
LC record available at https://lccn.loc.gov/2023052594
LC ebook record available at https://lccn.loc.gov/2023052595

10 9 8 7 6 5 4 3 2 1

For John Barton

Contents

Series Foreword ix
Preface xi

    Introduction: Records and Resonance in the Archives 1
1 Amplify: Close Listening to Silencing and the 1921 Tulsa Race Massacre 23
2 Distortion: Authority, Authenticity, and Agency in Recordings of Zora Neale Hurston's Black Folk 45
3 Interference: Silence and the Ideal Listener in Ralph Ellison's American Novel 69
4 Compression: The Entelechy of Records in Anne Sexton's Poem "For the Year of the Insane" 91
5 Reception: Conocimiento in Gloria Anzaldúa's Spirituality Tapes 111
    Coda: Distant Listening and Resonance 149

Notes 161
References 191
Index 215

Series Foreword

Media Origins is a venue for interdisciplinary, humanistically informed research that recovers and interrogates the origin stories of contemporary media technologies. The titles address a range of cultural objects in the history and prehistory of computation. The series explores the politics of design and labor, role of economics more broadly imagined, and cultural frameworks of shared meaning making that undergird not only innovation but also maintenance, consumption, and disposal. Such origin stories often examine precomputational precursors to understand the larger social patterns, values, and beliefs behind a given medium's trajectory into the contemporary technological milieu. Volumes in the series may deploy feminist, postcolonial, queer, or antiracist theory to foster deeper conversations about the framing narratives of innovation.

The Media Origins series cautions that in its obsession with the new, "new media" have developed an alarming ahistoricism that puts media studies at risk of losing valuable and largely undocumented accounts, particularly when cultural memory resides in rapidly aging witnesses, or records that are precariously stored in informal or neglected archives. Rather than reinforce assumptions about the technological survival of the fittest based on market metrics, the series excavates foundational platforms that have been all but ignored due to their perceived lack of commercial success.

Media Origins was launched to counter historical narratives that tend to emphasize the "inventor myth," crediting a lone auteur. Unfortunately, overtelling one origin story usually comes at the expense of often-marginalized groups and participants that were instrumental at inception or adoption. Equally damaging to understanding media origins can be the reification of artifacts with little attention to the larger discursive contexts of their invention, manufacture, and adoption. In looking at the interactions between actors and objects, books in the Media Origins series may revise existing views about the dynamics of power and control, specialization and distribution of labor practices, or systems of credit.

Preface

Sound archives of all kinds are underrepresented in scholarship, teaching, and the public imaginary. Listening happens less often than reading, especially in literary study. My primary concern in this book is to make possible new studies of different stories in literary history by listening. By listening closely to archival recordings, I uncover archival practices and processes that continue to pose barriers to increasing forms of access and expression with heard and unheard audio. I am concerned with the silences that surround these artifacts in the archive because, as I explain in the coming chapters, silence does not always mean lack of presence, but rather silence can suggest the absence of a cosounding with the perceptions, experiences, and memories of historical and present-day listeners. Silence is sometimes the absence of resonance.

Dissonant Records: Close Listening to Literary Archives is a form of advocacy for the continued, responsible use of historical audio artifacts in literary study. The Council on Library and Information Resources and the Library of Congress has warned that libraries and archives will not continue to preserve sound recordings if they are not used (2012). As of April 2023, the international digital library platform Europeana includes 55 percent images and 43 percent text objects, but only 1 percent sound and 0.6 percent video objects. The Digital Public Library of America has 27 percent images and 50 percent text, with fewer than 1 percent sound objects and moving image objects combined. The Internet Archive, which allows the community to upload artifacts, reports that its collection—still mostly comprising text—has 37 percent books and texts, 13 percent audio, 8 percent video, and 4 percent images.[1] It seems that what matters in brick and digital libraries is text.

Dissonant Records demonstrates that the complexities of preservation, access, and use go far beyond digitization and online discovery. Long before the decision is made to digitize a collection, library and archives must contend with archival recordings that are often damaged, exist on disintegrating media, or are restricted to the public due (rightfully) to privacy or concerns about cultural sensitivity. Once the decision to create access has been made, protocols for access might be disparate or confusing within and across institutions. The shifting landscape around rules and regulations means professional archival and library practices change among professionals from one generation to the next. Language barriers, cultural traditions, and limited resources make creating access for global communities a challenge, especially in postcustodial archives cautiously trying to approach these concerns responsibly.[2] In archival reading rooms, historical recordings are often dressed up as other media, text documents, or books. Copies of the original recordings that used to be on glass or metal discs, reel-to-reel tapes, or audio cassettes are often now reproduced and made available on CDs that are reformatted copies of copies. I have received archival recordings on CDs tucked in the same manila folders, filed away in the same gray repository boxes, as manuscript letters. The boxes were delivered to my reading room table on a metal rolling cart alongside a CD player, which, out of date, was missing a cord. On a different visit, another CD player was delivered to me with broken headphones. In a third reading room, there were no headphones at all. I listened to the recordings on the lowest volume at which I could still understand so as not to disturb the other researchers. If you are able to listen to archival recordings, it might entail hundreds of hours of exploration and close listening, because the metadata that librarians and archivists create is often based on the limited information they find on old, incomplete, confusing, or wrong and unverified labels.[3]

bell hooks asserts that personal, small details are "often what grabs people," what "makes theory seem as it does for me, to have concrete application" (Olson and hooks 1994).[4] Yet, listening to details can be a slippery method. Listening is messy, inexact, and trying to listen for meaning—no matter who or where you are, no matter the subject, the topic, or the medium—is a method of interpretation that requires repeating listenings: stopping the recording, scrubbing back over what's been heard—if the old CD player you're using even lets you do that—and listening again. Even when discs, tapes, and records are made accessible, their meanings may remain difficult to discern. Recordings can be hard to "read." Listening for how social and material dissonance resonates in archival records is slow work—especially when the audio records in question have been considered by previous scholars to be less important, uninteresting, irrelevant, beside the point, or nonevidential "hearsay." Trying to browse or skim while listening is a sure means to miss something important. Spoken words happen in real time, sequentially, and sampling such sounds for meaning is like choosing a random page of a book to reconstruct the synopsis of its plot—the devil of the plot is in which details, not in any details.

I have often had to stop a recording or rewind because I am convinced I misheard what I thought I heard or what I thought they said. I listen to short snippets at a time because I remember more precisely what has been said in the silence after a phrase is spoken before a new phrase begins. Words spoken are sometimes muted voices under water or a fast cackle or swiftly released breath, and crying, smoking, vomiting, singing, or the loud roar of an air conditioner can blur words for a listener. Giggling, whooping, and eating nuts with friends can obfuscate who is speaking and when. Voices in historical recordings can sound like coughing or the roar of an animal; they often overlap, with multiple people speaking at once; they can be too quiet or too loud and confused by the sounds of an audience, a car passing by, or the warp and wow of the recording or playback device. What *was* that in the background? Where *are* these people? Some recordings are distorted or lost, some were never saved, and many more moments, peoples, and events were never recorded in the first place.

Indeed, this book considers *mis*listening to details appropriate, expected, and, in some cases, preferred. I know that my ideas about what I am listening to will influence what I think I heard *and* saw. I also know that when I am transcribing, I add words that were not spoken or were spoken in a different order than I might choose.[5] I have ideas about a speaker I've read about before they speak and as they speak even before I understand what they are saying. If I listen to hours of recordings for voices I think will be there, it is to understand their presence when they are, but silence also impresses itself on me as an active absence rather than simply nonattendance. And how does one accurately capture in words the pure joy of chortling or the sadness of crying, moaning, sarcasm, or derision? And what about the powerful vocality of silence? Ultimately, something is lost in translation and over space and time and in both listening and writing about listening. Out of context and now, it's pretty hard to get a joke spoken in 1984 that has been recorded on cassette tape and then repeated on paper in this book. What can we learn from these mislistenings about scholarship in the archives more generally?

Being aware of the inexactitudes that make up a human's experience of human experience is productive. My hope is that describing small, confusing, or dissonant details that bely the situated social and technical processes behind recording and playing back historical audio collections will grab readers of this book and make the theory of resonance that I describe in the first chapter seem like a worthwhile approach for incorporating audio recordings in literary study. I acknowledge the "listening ear" that Jennifer Lynn Stoever (2016) suggests as a figure indicating that dominant listening practices accrue through social and political contexts, but I am also cautious about creating false binaries that divide hearing and seeing in what Jonathan Sterne (2015) calls the audiovisual litany: "hearing is concerned with interiors; vision is concerned with surfaces," "hearing involves physical contact with the outside world; vision requires distance from it," "hearing places you inside an event; seeing gives you a perspective on the event," "hearing tends toward subjectivity; vision tends toward objectivity," and so on (66–67).[6] I try to avoid these binaries by orienting my intervention toward the extent to which *intermedia*—described in the next chapter as an awareness that all media are interpolated through other media—invites scholars to question perspectives and power in scholarship with any medium.

Material, contextual, and political details of audio recordings that have historically garnered little interest are made to matter in this book, but I do not presume to give voice to the voiceless. The writers I discuss here—Zora Neale Hurston, Ralph Ellison, Anne Sexton, Gloria Anzaldúa—are well-known literary figures. They and the many scholars who have brought them to mainstream literary study have fought to be heard. I have chosen these authors as my focus in this book *because* they are known, but also because their histories are complex. I admire how they have pushed past social boundaries in landscapes that they had to navigate with care and creativity. By close listening to their archives, my goal is—first and foremost—to demonstrate a research practice with audio archives, but to do so in order that these authors' lives and works are experienced in the fullness of their complexities, experienced in terms of their voicings as well as their silences. By focusing on close listening as a method, I seek to redirect attention toward a kind of listening in which details around artifacts, events, and technologies (and thus peoples and communities) that have been obfuscated by the practices and protocols of cultural heritage institutions are made resonant and meaningful to literary scholars.

Karen Barad writes that "mattering is simultaneously a matter of substance and significance" (2007, 3), and throughout *Dissonant Records* I build a theory of resonance by including situated anecdotes describing my experiences using these materials—my joys, frustrations, and mistakes. To amplify a resistance in the materials is provocative because it heightens questions around authority, agency, and materiality in the archives. Each chapter shows that voicing cultural history is as much about the context, the process, and the intermedial aspect of the telling as the telling itself. In an attempt to create new points of access and to inspire further discovery by new listeners, I have also created accompanying online audio "editions" of recordings from each chapter with annotations linked from my website at http://tanyaclement.org/dissonant_records.

I owe many thanks to friends, colleagues, students, and family who have generously given me their time and expertise, improving this book in so many ways and helping me be a better listener by listening to me. Amelia Acker, Zoe Bursztajn-Illingworth, Casey Boyle, Melanie Feinberg, Nicole Furlonge, Jennifer Guiliano, N. Katherine Hayles, Heather Houser, AnaLouise Keating, Michelle Niemann, Samantha Pinto, and Jonathan Sterne all read drafts, sometimes multiple times, and gave me invaluable feedback. Graduate students Bethany Radcliffe and Ali Gunnells provided me significant hours of dialogue during independent studies, where we dove into archives of sound together, learning collaboratively. Linda Gray Sexton has continued to give me generous permission to work with her mother's materials and many kind words along the way. Librarians and archivists could not have been more supportive, especially during the pandemic, when it seems that many of them stuck around, keeping the lights on and the reel-to-reels spinning, helping desperate researchers like me get access to digital files even as the library doors stayed closed. In particular, I want to thank Carla Alvarez at the Benson Latin American Collection Rare Books and Manuscripts Reading Room, Tamar Brown at the Schlesinger Library on the History of Women in America, Christina Davis and Mary Graham from Harvard's Woodberry Poetry Room, Todd Harvey at the Library of Congress,

Sheena Perez at Oklahoma State University at Tulsa Libraries, and Lauren Walker at the Harry Ransom Center at the University of Texas. A fellowship at the Harry Ransom Center, a library grant at the Schlesinger Library, and a book workshop funded by the English Department at the University of Texas offered me incredible support for my research. In addition, I've had the great fortune to be involved in multiple, sponsored digital humanities projects throughout writing *Dissonant Records*, which have served to keep me abreast of evolving trends in technologies and practices for creating access to and doing research with audio collections. I have been incalculably lucky to lead a team of amazing researchers in the AudiAnnotate Extensible Workflow and AVAnnotate projects, which have been generously funded by the American Council of Learned Societies and the Mellon Foundation, and which include incredible partners at the American Folklife Center at the Library of Congress, Library of Congress Labs, the Furious Flower Poetry Center at James Madison University, the Fortunoff Video Archive for Holocaust Testimonies at Yale Library, the Harry Ransom Center, the Woodberry Poetry Room, and the SpokenWeb Consortium. AVAnnotate could not have happened without my friends and colleagues Sara and Ben Brumfield at Brumfield Labs, Bert Lyons and Shawn Averkamp from AVP, and the many students I have had the pleasure to work with, including Liz Fischer, Kylie Warkentin, Evan Sizemore, Luke Sumpter, Kayleigh Voss, and Trent Wintermeier. I am also thankful to be part of the SpokenWeb Consortium project, led by the ever-patient Jason Camlot and funded by the Social Sciences and Humanities Research Council in Canada. I consider myself extremely fortunate to be able to call so many interesting and pleasurable conversations work. Much, much thanks to the folks at the MIT Press, including Liz Losh and Celia Pearce, who got this project started, and Noah Springer, who was an encouraging and thoughtful editor.

My deepest gratitude is to my family—John, Isabela, Margaret, and Thomas who often had to wait patiently—for something to do, somewhere to go, something to eat, someone to listen—while I wrote a book.

Introduction: Records and Resonance in the Archives

> This silence promotes denial. And how can we organize to challenge and change a system that cannot be named?
> —bell hooks (2004, 25)

In a 1994 interview, American author, professor, feminist, and social activist bell hooks audibly eats a Butterfinger. An audio recording of the interview available online from the University of North Texas Digital Library includes hooks unwrapping her candy bar for a snack. On the UNT library's website, hooks's name appears under "Creation Information" alongside the year of the recording, and the fact that the recording is part of a larger collection about writing and rhetoric centered on issues of *JAC: A Journal of Composition Theory*. The description also lists the interviewer—scholar of rhetoric, culture, and literature, Gary Olson. The moment during which hooks takes a break to eat her snack and share a paper cup of Olson's Sprite (trying as she was that day to avoid caffeine or drink too much soda) resonates with my work in this book. The snack provides an unscripted opportunity for a third, unidentified, voice to intervene. I can hear this person, who has not been named on the website where I found the recording, moving through the room and asking Olson and hooks if they would like something to drink, offering to pay for it, and then leaving, the door closing behind them. Their physical proximity to the interview participants, and their familiarity with Olson are audible in their actions (a close brushing, a swishing, an amplified voice) and their tone (comfortable, amused). Without a word, but audibly unlatching and then returning to unlock the door, this third person also seems familiar with the layout of the building; they know where to find the soda machine without asking. At first listen, they seem to belong in the interview room, and then later, in the interview discourse.

The snack exchange does not appear in the transcript of the interview "bell hooks and the Politics of Literacy: A Conversation" that Olson published in the winter 1994 issue of *JAC*, but on the recording, Olson calls the third voice "Betsy when he's talking to hooks"[1]

Olson: Audience is an important consideration for a lot of us in the field. In "Breaking Bread" you say, "I've never focused on publishing my literary criticism"—something Betsy asked you before—"to the degree that"—you stole my question—"that I have"—or was it your question that you restole (*laughs*)?

Third voice: My question.

hooks: ... I called it "Altars of sacrifice: remembering Basquiat" and had a quote from a black church song "you're all on the altar of sacrifice laid." Again, that convergence for me of motifs of spirituality and cultural criticism.

Olson: Great answer

Third voice: Really!

Olson: (*coughs*) Um.

Third voice: I'm not allowed to participate, but I can (*laughs*).

Olson: That's not true.

hooks: You can even be our "Amen." (Olson and hooks 1994)

At the time of the recording, Elizabeth Hirsh was an assistant professor in the English Department at the University of South Florida, where Olson was a more senior colleague. This is the same Elizabeth Hirsh who in 1995, a year after the *JAC* interview with hooks was published, coedited with Olson the acclaimed *Women Writing Culture*, which included interviews with Sandra Harding, Donna Haraway, Luce Irigaray, and Jean-François Lyotard, and another transcript of the same interview with bell hooks. An endnote in Olson's journal article gives tribute to "Elizabeth Hirsh, for extensive assistance in preparing for and conducting this interview" (Olson 1994, 19), but for the book publication, Olson and Hirsh must have thought it was appropriate—perhaps even ethical, given the goals of *Women Writing Culture*—to finally list Hirsh as one of the interview's coauthors. Due to the lack of metadata, we can only assume Hirsh is "Betsy" on the online recording.

Dissonant Records: Close Listening to Literary Archives is about absences and silences in historical materials, the making of archives and evidence, the writing of history, and the hermeneutics of media. I use *resonance* as a theory and *close listening* as a method, and I seek to teach how, while incorporating audio archives into literary study, scholars become better close listeners to archival *inter*media. I organize the chapters in *Dissonant Records* around audio technology terms that can help conceptualize opportunities for exploring meaning making in the archive because, by and large, the technological means by which I accessed the recordings for this book have shaped what I have heard and what I write about what I've heard (or misheard). Like *resonance*, these technical terms are also cultural keywords—*amplify, distortion, interference, compression,* and *reception*—that can guide the discussion of meaning making "along the archival grain" (Stoler 2009)[2] of archival audio and away from metaphors often deployed in knowledge production that call forth primarily visual, empirical, and objective epistemes.[3] With these keywords, I am signaling that there is a permeable boundary between the notion of archival records as fact or historical evidence and the media of those artifacts, between objective and subjective knowledges, and between reason and affect.[4] Starting with an imperative (Amplify!), I am suggesting that modes of reproduction, storage, and dissemination based on privileged epistemes have participated in silencing practices that critical theorists have sought to amplify within institutional structures of power.

Primary questions that I ask in *Dissonant Records* are who, what, and how are we not studying in our cultural histories? Why? Why not? *Dissonant Records* is an intervention that considers the expanded role literary study can play in media studies as a means of articulating how meaning making matters within and beyond established institutions built on heteronormative sociotechnical systems of authority that at once facilitate and preclude access to significant people, places, and events.

Records

Dissonant Records joins prevailing discourse around the role archival records and media play in constructions of authenticity, authority, evidence, and objectivity in the archives.[5] Archives and records management literatures demonstrate that perceived affordances of the record have been heavily influenced by media concepts that privilege the concept of the record as a written text. Historically and typically, archival records are texts. Based on extensive study of the literature, Geoffrey Yeo defines *records* generally as "persistent representations of activities by participants or observers or their authorized proxies" (2007, 342), and, in Western culture in the twenty-first century, it is a definition that is media specific: a paper, written document often defines a record of evidence (Gitelman 2014). The paper document is a "prototype" for the nature of the record in the minds of professionals in archives and records management. As a prototype, the paper record becomes a conceptual, mental mapping that Yeo argues shapes principles, practices, and infrastructures around making cultural records (2007). Even in the digital age, newer informational systems are developed under the assumption that records are textual and documentary, an assumption that reifies the paper document prototype in the practices and protocols of authoritative institutions that house, preserve, and create digital access to records.

Consequent to the affordances that paper record prototypes seem to uphold as information and evidence, print prototypes have become powerful tools for maintaining the ideologies of those in power. This is especially true when a trauma is perceived to be at the hands of the same authoritative institutions that use records to afford "memory, accountability, legitimization of power, a sense of personal or social identity and continuity, and the communication of such benefits across space and time" (Yeo 2007, 330). Scholars of disability, immigration, and LGBTQ studies and many others have shown that an insistence on paper favors those processes that toe the line of the status quo in institutions. As a result, when archival scholars discuss how to address the misrepresentation of communities in the archives, issues of verity, representation, and authority become entangled with modalities and media.[6]

Audio media, such as those discussed in this book that record meetings and conferences, performances and oral histories, therapy sessions and conversations among friends, might seem to fit the prescribed form and function of the record (persistent and authorized), yet such media when not in print still often play a marginal role in record keeping (Yeo 2008, 124). Consequently, the media objects I include in *Dissonant Records*, often dismissed as untrustworthy based on genre—because like diaries, letter, memoirs, and fiction, they are not considered sanctioned representations of an event—are also deemed unreliable witnesses due to media type.[7] As cultural records, these literary artifacts are considered *un*authorized proxies.[8]

Printed and manuscript objects may take evidential prominence in systems of cultural authority, but audiovisual technologies are also implicated in how these sociopolitical systems of power shape who and what is represented in the archive.[9] Examples suggest that classifying, organizing, standardizing, and authenticating cultural artifacts based on media format reduces representations of culture(s) to that which can be communicated and saved by that media type. In other words, writing in print about sound cultural artifacts based on their paper or print-like characteristics foreshortens the range of discussion one can have about that sound artifact. Further, Jonathan Sterne (2003) argues convincingly that those in positions of power produce media and media devices that reflect what they consider is most important to perceive. He uses the history of sound technologies to demonstrate where the emergence of audile technique is based on privileging the reproduction of sounds that are considered worthy of attention, such as amplifying voices or music over static or surface noise (25). Similarly, Mara Mills (2011) considers how phonetics and deaf education coincided with the emergence of "communication engineering" in early twentieth-century telephony and identifies how hearing and sight ableism influenced the provisions of telephonic, technological innovation. Hochman (2014) further describes how innovation, experimentation, and use of audiovisual technologies have deep ties within academic and cultural heritage institutions with early twentieth-century movements to document races, cultures, and languages that were perceived to be dying and in need of established institutions for their safeguard.

Both pursuits—representation and long-term archival storage—have the potential to maintain hegemonies in knowledge production, no matter the media. When Ralph Ellison tells a Brown University Library audience in 1979 that Americans are "notoriously selective in the exercise of historical memory," he indicates a biased selectivity for print media in the archive as a root cause for history's bifurcation into "two basic versions of American history: one which is written and as neatly stylized as ancient myth, and the other unwritten and as chaotic and full of contradictions, changes of pace, and surprises as life itself" (1995, 598). More recently, Diana Taylor has described the "rift" between the written and the spoken word in the archive as medium-specific: it is "between the archive of supposedly enduring materials (i.e., texts, documents, buildings, bones) and the so-called ephemeral repertoire of embodied practice/knowledge (i.e., spoken language, dance, sports, ritual)" (2003, 19). She explains that a repertoire that "enacts embodied memory" is "ephemeral, nonreproducible knowledge" and typically considered less significant in scholarly study (20). But Ellison also recognizes that all types of recordings must be considered with capaciousness, caution, and care. Ellison tells his library audience that in contrast to the US culture as represented in officially sanctioned, "written and neatly stylized" histories, Americans "live in a constant state of debate and contention" and "do so no matter what kinds of narrative, oral or written, are made in the reconstruction of our common experience" (1995, 599).[10] In each case, an attempt at a "true" representation of culture indicates that "no medium has a single, particular logic" (Gitelman 2014, 9).[11]

To uncover media absences in literary scholarship and suggest that such cases can, instead, signal moments of agency and resistance, I cast a wider net in my readings of literary texts than the paper documents that are usually taken to define what counts as objective, factual records in the archives. While the focus in *Dissonant Records* is primarily on audio recordings, I understand media as *inter*media that cut across different communicative modalities, technologies, and scholarly practices. I use the term *intermedia* throughout *Dissonant Records* to signal an understanding of media in the archives as ontological and political phenomena, synthetic fusions of different modalities, media forms, and media devices that form a feedback loop within a spatially and temporally situated sociotechnical context.[12] By using intermedia to foreground a consideration for the synthetic, political, and ontological nature of media in the archives, I consider if or how media-specific materialities presuppose definitions.[13]

Media-specificity in literary analysis is a significant "mode of critical attention which recognizes that all texts are instantiated and that the nature of the medium in which they are instantiated matters" (Hayles 2004, 67). Media specificity has included innumerable and largely productive examinations of varied media as objects of literary study, including book jackets (Genette 1997), the page (Bornstein 2001), magnetic tape (Sayers 2011), cassette tapes (Hayles 1997), the interface (Emerson 2014), word processing software (Kirschenbaum 2016), and bitstreams (Kirschenbaum 2021), among others. These and other studies demonstrate that no media apparatus sounds out without intermedial echoes, even in especially text-heavy fields of inquiry.[14] Consequently, posing intermedia as dissonant records of study is a means to amplify, pay attention to, and create feedback across archival media in literary study and to turn up the volume on varied material and social registries of cultural histories, even as literary scholarly analysis has typically been focused on *mono*media-specificity—a consideration for paper, print, *or* audio rather than paper, print, *and* audio.[15] A theory of resonance in *Dissonant Records* begins with an understanding of audio, print, and digital media in the archives as intermedia and an invitation to question what epistemological practices are othered as these media clash within institutional processes that facilitate knowledge production, preservation, and reception.

Resonance

If—as hooks suggests in the quote that begins this chapter—silence promotes denial, then naming the systems of power that enculturate identity through our cultural register encourages change. When an unnamed Elizabeth Hirsh speaks during the hooks interview, I perceive a provocation that I seek to address in *Dissonant Records*: How do scholars make meaning of signals in the cultural record that are dampened by that register? In this case, a simple answer might be to listen, but as an active scholarly practice, listening is not just hearing or perceiving. Listening is shorthand for meaning making, and not just by humans. The register by which scholars gain access to sound artifacts is defined by personal registers ("one's mind, heart, or memory"), as well as by the apparatus of machines and institutions that "record" or "set down (facts, names, etc.) in writing, esp. accurately or officially" in a historical register.[16] By both definitions, the import is clear: a particular technical and sociopolitical context influences how and why artifacts *resonate* as culturally significant. When I hear someone say that a person, place, thing, or event resonates with them, I understand the term as a placeholder for a sense or a feeling of meaning for which the variables of causation are too numerous or too complex to articulate exactly, but for which the speaker has a presumed sense of matter and of what matters, of significance. Consequently, I use *resonance* as a capacious theory to help identify properties of meaning making in how and why the literary media archive registers. As a cultural hermeneutic, a theory of resonance in the archives may seem multitudinous,[17] but it can also proffer ambiguity as an invitation to articulate what role agency can play in the context of archival media in literary study. Resonant properties—materiality, dialogism, and entelechy—can provide traces of agential intra-actions that have shaped ideas about being, knowing, and doing; of ontology, epistemology, and ethics; and of fact and value in the archive.[18]

A first and primary aspect of resonance is a reminder that the material particularities of the apparatus always matter. Resonance is a material condition. It occurs when an event creates sound waves that match a receiving object's resonant frequency or the rate at which that object naturally vibrates.[19] The resonant frequency can be the vibration of the larynx or the bell, but it is also the gravitational pull between orbiting bodies in space or between complex clusters of electrons: at a certain resonant frequency, a child's swing will push higher or a bridge will collapse. While there is no sound without resonance, these latter examples demonstrate that there can be physical resonance without sound.[20]

Resonance is a reminder of the extent to which meaning making in the archive is determined by understandings of the materiality (and the ephemerality) of the media with which scholars engage.[21] As "electrical signals representing sound," audio's material condition in the archive is evidenced by its mediation through technologies.[22] When the narrator of Ralph Ellison's *Invisible Man* (1952)—a novel about US racial conflicts in the first half of the twentieth century—concludes his story, he uses a sonic metaphor to ask the reader to be aware of the power dynamics that shape what we are receptive to perceiving: "Who knows but that, on the lower frequencies, I speak for you?" (581). He imagines the presence of a resonant cultural register where voicing and listening happen as low-frequency vibrations out of the perceptual range of the dominant white culture. With this metaphor, he is able to express his concern with how meaning registers in the mind, heart, and memory as well as how the apparatus affords meaning making through the electrical currents that record sound's measure and broadcast its potentiality within (and without) a range of cultural perceptions. What is resonant or significant—what matters to whom—is ontologically inseparable from a consideration of substance (matter) or, in the case of literary audio archives, what is recorded and how (Barad 2007, 127–128).

A second, property of resonance suggests that meaning making is dialogic. The *Oxford English Dictionary* defines resonance as the power to evoke "images, memories, and emotions" and *to resonate* as "to respond in a sympathetic or corresponding manner; to react emotionally or positively."[23] As a situated response to the complex world in place and time, a feeling of resonance can mark a personal and situated mode of meaning making but resonance also indicates an aurally relational mode of understanding that is often paraphrased as "this speaks to me," "I hear you," or "I feel you."[24]

At the 1949 Macy Conferences on Cybernetics, anthropologist Margaret Mead described the interpersonal properties of resonance in scientific research. During a panel discussion entitled "Possible Mechanisms of Recall and Recognition," the panelists use *resonance* as shorthand for an analyst's inability to be objective due to physical and psychological similarities that become apparent in the relationship between the analyst and their patient (Pias 2016, 128–129). Mead, anticipating the later work of Sandra Harding (1986) and the politics underlying feminist epistemologies to dismantle value-neutral claims in scientific practice, explains why such resonance between analyst and patient can be a significant tool for understanding how scholars are themselves instruments within the process of observation:

> There is one other point that was made here, which I don't think should be allowed to drop.... It is not a question of minimizing resonance. It is a question of using resonance. It is a question of getting a sufficient training and control of the particular relevant resonant factors so that man becomes an accurate instrument in this interpersonal situation ... as if anybody could sit and record day after day this sample of the patient's behavior without themselves becoming intricately refined into a specialized instrument. (Pias 2016, 128–129)[25]

For Mead, resonance invites theories of interpersonal interpretation that are mediated across space and time, through and with technology, and in context with other people. Likewise, within the audio archive, evidence of the person recording, the person recorded, the listener to the recording (then and now), the institutions and other media and media devices where the recording, processing, storage, and playback environments happen provide traces of how resonance (meaning and matter) is cocreated through the apparatus of the archive. Resonance is not just personal. Resonance is not just about "I feel." It's dialogic; it's "I feel you."

In a third aspect, resonance is entelechic. It is meaning making premised by a coconstructed field of potential meanings in archival study that are processual and fluid rather than static. The field of potential meanings in the archive is proscribed by shifting entanglements of materiality and dialogic intra-actions that dictate a field of potential meanings in a recursive loop.[26] Michel-Rolph Trouillot contends that history "reveals itself through the production of specific narratives" in a particular context (1995, 25) but that scholars must take into account the fluidity between perceptions of history as a social process and history as knowledge, a fluidity that invites some ambiguity (22–23).[27] I imagine this ambiguity as an invitation to making many meanings. It is a shifting field of possible resonances like an acoustic space in which material-discursive practices and causal intra-actions influence sound dynamics.[28] This field of possible resonances would be like hooks's church, where what resonates is dictated by singers and the piano, by the number of bodies in the congregation and how loudly they sing, which in turn is influenced by the properties of the church walls, the thickness of the stained-glass windows, and the material of the pews and flooring, but also the convergence "of motifs of spirituality and cultural criticism" that is a factor of hooks's personal and situated history as a young, Black, female church member who was writing poetry in 1950s segregated Kentucky.[29] Further, what has potential resonance for me when I listen to the hooks recording with which I began this chapter likewise depends on the history I bring as a person and as a scholar of literature, archives, textuality, and sound. The technical apparatus and the social and political history that undergird the cultural register of the interview also matter to what resonates with me, including the published *JAC* transcript and the book *Women Writing Culture* that Hirsh and Olson published together in 1995, UNT library's online access to the original audio recording, and its incomplete metadata.

When hooks tells Hirsh during the interview that Hirsh can be the "Amen" to hooks's conversation with Olson, the comment might go unheard by the listener of the archived recording—unregistered in the mind, heart, or memory. (In fact, the reader of this book may have to read the transcription at the beginning of this chapter again to remember the comment.) Without knowledge of the larger context of hooks's own experience in the Black church, where call and response between the preacher "on stage" and his congregation is a proscribed and situated power dynamic in how meaning making happens, the remark "You can even be our 'Amen'" could go unremarked. If Hirsh is recognized and heard as Hirsh, this moment during which the participants break for a snack and hooks tells Hirsh that she is integral to the dynamics of the interview can also mark Hirsh as part of an interpersonal power differential already at play. On record in the remark (with the recognition) are traces of hooks's own history as well as Hirsh's relationship to Olson, Olson's relationship to hooks, and hooks's relationship to Hirsh. And, what about the listener? I am also participating in the moment's potential resonance in this book: it is my choice to include the hooks recording because Hirsh goes unrecognized.[30]

Agency

Resonance is an indicator of the complex self and how world making and identity construction are agential acts realized in conversation. bell hooks writes that her ideas about "talking back" and her movement toward subjecthood developed in her childhood experiences as part of a community: "Moving from silence into speech is for the oppressed, the colonized, the exploited, and those who stand and struggle side by side, a gesture of defiance that heals, that makes new life and new growth possible. It is that act of speech, of 'talking back,' that is no mere gesture of empty words, that is the expression of our movement from object to subject—the liberated voice" (2014, 9). hooks learned that both speech and silence were agential practices of 'talking back' and "that it was important to speak but to talk a talk that was in itself a silence" (hooks 1986, 125). hooks explains:

> Taught to speak and yet to beware of the betrayal of too much heard speech, I experienced intense confusion and deep anxiety in my efforts to speak and write. Reciting poems at Sunday afternoon church service might be rewarded speech. Writing a poem (when one's time could be "better" spent sweeping, ironing, learning to cook) was luxurious activity, indulged in at the expense of others. Questioning authority, raising issues that were not deemed appropriate subjects, brought pain, punishments. (hooks 1986, 125)

In her efforts at self-expression, hooks uses her domestic and church experiences to ask about the possibilities of expression as she has experienced and developed them in dialogue with her community. In her awareness of "the betrayal of too much speech," hooks demonstrates that listening for resonant dissonances is less a metaphor for intersubjective availability than it is—as the recordings in this book will demonstrate—about people using listening in ways that may be more about denying intersubjectivity and defending against vulnerability. In other words, listening may be less about an openness to alterity and more about the complex negotiations of being with others in the world.

Dialogue and agency are not always about speaking. Agency can be performed through listening and silence. Scholars typically understand "having a voice" as agency enacted, but hooks writes that "for black women," agency "has not been to emerge from silence into speech but to change the nature and direction of our speech, to make a speech that compels listeners, one that is heard" (2014, 6). She describes listening to a "black male preacher whose speech was to be heard, who was to be listened to, whose words were to be remembered" in contrast to listening to "the voices of black women—giving orders, making threats, fussing" that "could be tuned out, could become a kind of background music, audible but not acknowledged as significant speech" (6). The ongoing agential cuts required to activate listening and resonance—to activate being heard and making meaning—are discussed in the *JAC* interview when hooks describes her own situated process for creating an opportunity for resonance with an audience. She explains, "As a person on the lecture circuit, I used to just bring the lecture that I had been told to give, but there were times when I would have an audience that really wasn't open to what I had planned to talk about" (Olson and hooks 1994). The talk she had been invited to give at Tufts University the day before the *JAC* interview serves as an example: she had been invited to speak on representations of Black women but was told by the professors who had invited her that they'd rather have her speak on cultural diversity. "But then I had dinner with students and talked with a lot of them," she explains. "When I came to the talk, I sensed that they really wanted me to talk about Black women. And I felt that I would lose a whole dimension of listening if I switched the topic, especially because the other lecture started with a white male and my relationship to the white male" (Olson and hooks 1994). There are multiple variables at play when considering "the whole dimension of listening" or what resonates with a particular audience and why. Thus, when hooks chooses what lecture she is going to give at Tufts and how she is going to give it, her sense of its potential resonance is shaped by the interpersonal nature of her and her audience's histories and experiences and their senses of identity (racial, gendered, classed, abled). She is also mindful of the sociopolitical context these factors might engage at the place and time of her talk. In these cases, "having a voice" and "being heard" is not an issue of speech versus nonspeech. It is an issue of potential resonances, differentially articulated and triangulated by a social apparatus that includes multiple agents and marks the circulation of meaning between speaker and listener in space and time.

My agential cuts in *Dissonant Records*—the entry points to articulating what I consider meaningful or resonant in the archive—are material and dialogic aspects of media that invite a listening ear to epistemological practices. As a book that focuses primarily on recordings from the United States, *Dissonant Records* takes into account the "infrastructural purpose" that materiality and significance share in the recording apparatus on the scale of a national media history (Mattern 2015), but it is the nature of media's material and historical complexities—their potentially dissonant properties in literary culture—that create a possibility for resonance that speaks to me and this project. The different modalities of print and sound recording invite competing agential cuts around reason/affect/knowledge/absence. Consequently, I attend to the semiotics of sound alongside those of print and to the role of the listener and aurality with as much care as I consider the entextualized voice of the speaker.[31] This is not a history of the archive, media, or technology so much as a consideration of potentially understudied social and material modes of dissonance and resistance in literary culture that have been silenced by theoretical and practical norms.

Dissonance

On the one hand, studies based on audio objects, the history of the ear, and associated technologies seem to invite alterity and the possibility for paradigmatic changes. Veit Erlmann's *Reason and Resonance* (2010) positions theories of reason from René Descartes' *L'Homme* (Antoine-Mahut and Gaukroger 2017) to Martin Heidegger's *Being and Time* (1962) within the context of developing understandings of the workings of the human ear to tell an alternate history of modernity through the "Age of Reason." Erlmann describes how Enlightenment principles that are based on reason, observed evidence, and authority are simultaneous with but in contrast to the historical trajectory of principles around resonance. Sterne (2003), Mills (2010, 2011), Siegert (2013), and Stoever (2016) have well detailed how early information scientists' understandings of the ear (and by synecdochic extension, human perception) were shaped by deaf culture and education, experimental phonetics, psychoacoustic communities, and Black music and literature, and how, in turn, these scientists influenced commercial, military, and science research-based practices. On the other hand, concerns about the institutions and technologies that govern the histories of media in US literary culture inevitably invite questions about whether it is possible to change scholarly paradigms and study archival media with different filters.[32] It is useful to consider Alexander Weheliye's *Phonographies*, in which he cautions that Afro-modernity in ethnographic studies may be an invitation to think about issues of temporality, spatiality, and community as a function of research methods or "the foundations upon which these distinctions are routinely administered" (2005, 14), but it is also important to note that scholars like Weheliye and Katherine McKittrick argue that a commitment to anticolonial thought in the study of Black music (for example) must go beyond staid disciplinary boundaries or "normative academic logics," because such commitments can represent Black creative and intellectual lives as a priori oppressed (McKittrick 2021, 45, 51). Certainly, Weheliye does not care to position more abstract, proposedly "valid" methods of research versus empirical, historical, or ethnographic methods. The "easy opposition of the 'theoretical' and 'cultural'" against these more empirical methods is a "tension" for which he admits he has little patience (14).

While I cannot answer to all the above concerns, it is important to acknowledge that these tensions between normative logics in scholarship on records and media and postcolonial perspectives exist. As a literary scholar, I have been trained to read for significance by looking for differences like these. Therefore, when I listen for resonance, I also perceive dissonance. In common parlance, consonance typically represents stasis and resolution while dissonance connotes what is jarring, unsettling, and upsetting. Like consonance, dissonance is a subjective categorization of resonance, dependent entirely on context. The tritone, for instance, might be considered dissonant in church music, but it is essential in the twentieth-century avant-garde and in the form of a passing note in jazz.[33] Dissonance is a reminder that resonance can encompass discomfort, inequality, and contest. Listening differently in literary study can be generative for a postcolonial consideration of cultural registries where resonance and dissonance indicate an alternative fields of possible meanings produced by a shifting triangulation of agential forces, both human and material.[34]

Dissonant Records

There is a resistance in the materials discussed in this book. Currently, not all the recordings mentioned are digitized and only a portion are freely available online. The diary entries, conference proceedings, field recordings, letters, oral histories, therapy sessions tapes, and tarot and other spiritual readings I write about are considered accessible in the reading rooms of large and well-funded libraries in the United States,[35] but in some cases, the recordings are distorted, truncated, missing parts, or mislabeled. All of these artifacts are described in different ways, with different institutional and professional standards, with more and less information in finding aids that make them more and less discoverable through metadata and search engines. In other cases, even when the archival audio recordings have been digitized, institutional protocols safeguarding privacy and copyright keep the recordings boxed in rooms with limited visiting hours that are long distances away for many scholars. As a result, prolonged, sustained listening is challenging in the best of times and almost impossible during institutional closings—like those endemic to the COVID-19 pandemic, for example,—that shuttered libraries and archives along with businesses, schools, and public spaces during the writing of this book. These material and situated histories and contexts, the politics of the time, the available resources and tools, and the interest of faculty, staff, donor families, and the public all have bearing on what gets acquired, processed, digitized, discovered, and studied.

Nevertheless, in the next chapters, I investigate a variety of archived media. These media include what Black Tulsans have produced to mark the 1921 Tulsa Race Massacre because these artifacts had been kept by Ruth Sigler Avery, a local white activist and unpublished historian whose works were collected as a sidenote to her father-in-law's collection at the Oklahoma State University–Tulsa Special Collections and Archives.[36] I listen for Zora Neale Hurston on 1935 field recordings originally made on acetate disks, shipped from the Library of Congress to the recording site in Florida and then sent back to Washington, where they were transposed in 1986 onto reel-to-reels and then digitized in 2007. I listen for silences in 1953 recordings of Ralph Ellison at a Harvard Summer School conference that a Woodberry Poetry Room curator discovered in a subbasement of Houghton Library near a stack of books while looking for something else (Ireland

2014).[37] I read an Anne Sexton poem for audible resonances with her therapy recordings, which she allowed her therapist to share because "the tapes provided a historical record of the processes by which a human being had survived a mental illness by turning her treatment into an education in the service of art" (Middlebrook 1991b, 26)—though Sexton's doctor, her daughters, and her biographer faced public pushback saying sharing them was an infringement of her privacy.[38] I also listen to and read signs of listeners in the spiritual writings and recordings that Gloria Evangelina Anzaldúa made of herself and her friends. Acquired by the Nettie Lee Benson Latin American Collection at the University of Texas at Austin (where Anzaldúa felt alienated by the white-dominated university and unhappy with the Chicano and feminist movements), the tapes have been digitized by a graduate class in the library school and are also available on CDs, most of which are nearly inaudible on the old computer station set up in the reading room.

These stories are not a detail of grievances so much as an acknowledgment that working with intermedia for *Dissonant Records* became an opportunity for me to consider how listening for dissonance can amplify situated, multimodal, technical machinations through which knowledge production (expression, dissemination, and reception) happen in the archives. These experiences invited, for me, an intersectional consideration of contested issues around class, gender, nationality, and sexual orientation within sociotechnical systems that often facilitate identity and knowledge production. Avery's interviews of 1921 Tulsa Race Massacre survivors, which directly inform current representations of the event, and Ellison's writings about the 1921 massacre and speeches about race during the years of the *Brown v. Board of Education* hearings are infrequently cited.[39] Hurston's *Mules and Men* (1935) is essential reading for understanding Black lives in the Reconstruction-era South, yet her participation in the 1935 recordings that documents her field work goes largely unremarked. Sexton's poetry is a window into white gender roles during the cult of domesticity in the 1950s and 1960s, but scholars rarely read her poetry in the context of the therapy sessions where she learns to lay out her personal concerns. In interviews, Anzaldúa talks about the role spiritual activism and dialogue play in her writings about the borderlands yet her tapes of tarot and palm readings she gave and received are seldom mentioned.

Listening for dissonance in these intermedia archives amplifies the material conditions of what matters and what is excluded from mattering in literary study. In some of these cases—especially with Sexton's therapy tapes and Anzaldúa's spiritual recordings but also regarding the surveillance of Black lives on which I touch in the chapters on the Tulsa Race Massacre, Hurston, and Ellison—the use of recordings may feel voyeuristic or like an unwitting replication of the colonialism or racism that the authors' associated literary work challenges. I try to be transparent about these issues even when I feel clumsy. I believe that these authors are particularly insightful about their work and lives and that articulating the permeable boundaries between the different modalities of print and sound recordings in their archives is a way of interrogating what is considered fact, what is contested, and what is silent, absent, or intentionally unsaid. These matters must be addressed to understand their work in all its complexity.

The first chapter, "Amplify: Close Listening to Silencing and the 1921 Tulsa Race Massacre," is a guide to the rest of the book, establishing the important role that close listening can play as a methodology for articulating resonance in literary archives. The tension between scholarly notions of paper as record and sound as ephemeral "hearsay" is a central topic of this chapter's discussion of historical and fictional representations of the 1921 Tulsa Race Massacre. Mainstream rhetoric around the event describes the massacre as "untold," but this discourse surrounding its censorship in history poses an assumption about freedom, speech, and silence that goes unexamined in stories of the massacre. I show how listening to archival recordings of survivor oral histories in Avery's archive that have formed the basis of historical and fictional accounts over time and various media amplifies silences in how the history of the event has been told in mainstream histories.[40] Close listening to nonverbal, paratextual moments (such as silence, laughter, and tone) in Avery's oral history collection is a method for amplifying what Wendy Brown (2005) refers to as "modalities of silence." I trace how the amplification of these modalities serves to reinforce as well as to refuse prevailing narratives of silence and create alternative, possible modes of agency for Tulsa Massacre survivors in traditional and popular histories such as the award-winning 2019 HBO series *Watchmen*, and the novels *Magic City* (Rhodes 1998) and *Fire in Beulah* (Askew 2001). Titling this chapter with a sonic metaphor as an imperative, I describe in "Amplify" how close listening to intermedia across genres is a necessary and urgent methodology for historical, reparative, archival work in literary study.

In the second chapter, "Distortion: Authority, Authenticity, and Agency in Recordings of Zora Neale Hurston's Black Folk," I listen for social and technical distortions in two sets of recordings: approximately seventy-five brief "tracks" or recorded songs, stories, and explanations from a folklore recording trip Zora Neale Hurston took in 1935 to Florida and Georgia for the Library of Congress[41] and three longer recordings recorded on June 18, 1939, at the Federal Music Project Office in the Jacksonville, Florida, office of the Work Projects Administration (WPA).[42] As primary materials for Hurston's publications,[43] these recordings are important cultural artifacts for better understanding her production of Black folk in the United States. Close listening for audio distortions introduced through the process of recording and digitizing the original reel-to-reel tapes exposes how inaudibility and indiscernibility prevail over fidelity in the recording apparatus of her 1930s fieldwork. Hurston's work resists a fidelity to the real and to notions of "the author," "the text," and "the object" of study on which protocols for preservation and access in academia, anthropology, and government are based. Distortions mark Hurston's acts of "dark sousveillance" (Browne 2015) and are part of a repertoire (Taylor 2003) that amplifies Black epistemologies of self-making that challenge these traditional modes of authority, authenticity, and subjectivity and create resonant possibilities for imagining new transgressive formulations of identity.

I introduce the acoustical term *interference* in chapter 3, "Interference: Silence and the Ideal Listener in Ralph Ellison's American Novel," as a means of articulating and identifying audio as a thematic trope that influenced how Ralph Ellison discusses morality and the novel in American literature. From Ellison's perspective, the very possibility for silence or revelation in history making is part of an active process influenced by conflicting moral imperatives. As a cultural record, the novel must deal with the moral tension that runs particularly high in US culture where a diverse population constitutes a "culture of cultures" that is "always in conflict as they repel and attract and blend, each with the other" (Ellison 1995, 468). American literature (and its archives) can also reflect moments of affective resistance, especially in a culture of change. Social and political conflicts and counteracting silences are evident in recently discovered recordings of Ellison's participation in the 1953 Harvard Summer School Conference on the Contemporary Novel. During the ongoing hearings on segregation in *Brown v. Board of Education*. The recently discovered reels of the 1953

Introduction

discussions suggest a means of introducing how Ellison uses sound and audio technologies to articulate the collective power that the novelist and the audience have in cocreating resonant records of US culture. I introduce "interference" as a phenomenon described in acoustical theory that occurs when two sound waves occur simultaneously, creating "live spots" and "dead spots" in an acoustical environment. This concept helps me to articulate the tensions that Ellison notes in US literature when he claims that the strongest moments of resonance are live spots, but interference also helps me to describe dead spots I hear on the recordings, where the collision of moral frequencies has a neutralizing effect and resonates as silence.

Close listening to Anne Sexton's therapy recordings in chapter 4, "Compression: The Entelechy of Records in Anne Sexton's Poem 'For the Year of the Insane,'" invites a new rationale for considering compression in intermedia textuality. In Sexton's papers at the Arthur and Elizabeth Schlesinger Library on the History of Women in America at the Radcliffe Institute for Advanced Study are several hundred recordings of her personal therapy sessions. At the Harry Ransom Center at the University of Texas at Austin, there are four handwritten and typed journals in which Sexton wrote responses after or while listening to the taped sessions. Even though Sexton listened to the tapes as she wrote the journal entries in real time, they are now housed in quite separate institutions with different policies for access and delivered on very different playback platforms, including CD players and external hard drives. In this way, a physical, geographical separation; different analog and digital formats; and disparate sociotechnical infrastructures comprise the social condition of Sexton's therapy text, a text that itself brings to bear issues of privacy, ownership, presentation and performance, gender, and disability. What I call Sexton's "therapy text," which comprises her tapes and her journals, requires an engagement with intermedial modalities and devices—it is an intermedia text.[44] I define *compression* in this chapter as a foundational element of textuality that is essential for reading the therapy text's cultural conditions as well as the tension between Sexton's desire for a transcendent, imagined self and that goal's inevitable failure. Close listening to her therapy text reveals that the compression practices engaged in her recorded practices of self-realization had a profound impact on Sexton's sense of self-expression and therefore on her project to condense thought and language in poetry. In a close reading of her popular poem "For the Year of the Insane," I describe how the intermedial production of Sexton's therapy text encouraged an experience and expression of identity that influenced her evolution from a desire to write poetry that prescribed a "true" self to writing poetry that includes an assumption of finitude as a provision for expressing an always mediated self.

In chapter 5, "Reception: Conocimiento in Gloria Anzaldúa's Spirituality Tapes," I listen to Anzaldúa taping herself and friends reading tarot cards to each other. With the interviews, there are approximately forty of these "spiritual recordings" archived in her papers at the Nettie Lee Benson Latin American Collection at the University of Texas in Austin. There is evidence on the recordings that the taping scenario—the equipment setup, the recording process, the saving, the sharing, the relistening—influenced how Anzaldúa articulated her spirituality.[45] The recordings tell us about the recording context and amplify the material, situated nature of Anzaldúa's listenings and her dialogic process of identity construction, what she calls *conocimiento*. In this chapter, I listen to Anzaldúa's "sighs, sniffs, whistles, clicks"—a shorthand for describing the sounds in the recordings of everyday language "that borde[r] on the linguistic," because linguists consider these "liminal signs" as vague, equivocating "between showing and saying, giving off and giving, symptoms and symbols" (Dingemanse 2020, 191). Yet, the act of listening to these liminal signs correlates with a productive aspect of conocimiento Anzaldúa would call *nepantla*, a "liminal zone" where one is "in a constant state of displacement—an uncomfortable, even alarming feeling" (Anzaldúa and Keating 2002, i). These recordings make audible how the process of intermedial-produced dialogue influenced Anzaldúa's ideas about receptivity, critical awareness, and identity.

In *Dissonant Records*, I focus on audio recordings in literary study to heighten interest in these archival artifacts and how scholars interpret them. Listening to Hurston and Ellison differs from listening to Anne Sexton and Gloria Anzaldúa listening to themselves. Amplification, distortion, interference, compression, and reception are technical terms and cultural keywords that function as levers to pry open the technological and sociopolitical practices that create a possibility for resonance. Working with audio can be messy. Beyond the difficulties around access due to copyright restrictions and privacy concerns and the difficulties inherent in listening to time-based media, there are overlapping infrastructures that comprise originary and remediated formats, and conflicting information infrastructures in the form of metadata and authority control in the cataloguing and description process. Perceived as inconsistencies, these are archival dissonances, which are often impugned in the pursuit of authenticity, authority, and validity generally in literary study and—as I describe in the brief coda, "Distant Listening and Resonance"—in computational and machine-learning research.

The principles of resonance I have laid out here are contingent on the central premise that this materiality and personal situatedness as well as the technical and the social practices surrounding the recording scenario in space and time matter. Listening for dissonance provides a positionality that can help scholars better understand how differing interpretive frameworks, practices, and understandings of culture—objective/subjective, material/abstract, time-/stasis-based, and process-/product-driven—can coexist in clamorous superimposition (if not always harmony) without canceling each other out. The presence of dissonance is a reminder that scholarly work in liminal spaces feels precarious and produces vulnerability and discomfort. Yet, if scholars listen closely, differently, for resonant dissonances, we may hear how recorders and record players "aimed to control the apparatus of documentation rather than acquiesce to getting played by it" (Brooks 2021, 137), and we may learn to perceive silences in the archival record not as absences but, perhaps, as traces of "the betrayal of too much heard speech" (hooks 1986, 125). Listening for resonances is an attempt to mark the situated, entanglement of matter and meaning and to indicate an agential world building where relational agents engage in practices that shape and change the potentialities of knowledge production. *Dissonant Records* marks why and how meaning making in the audio archive matters.

But the **point** here **is** that by pushing significant details of our experience into the underground of ***unwritten*** history, we not only overlook much which is positive, but we blur our conceptions of ***where*** and ***who*** we are . . . by overlooking the blending and metamorphosis of cultural forms which are so characteristic of our society, ***we misconceive our cultural identity***.
—Ralph Ellison, "Going to the Territory," address given on September 20, 1979, at Brown University. Emphasis added by Father John B. Wolf and read on May 31, 1987, at the All Souls Unitarian Church in Tulsa, Oklahoma (Ellison 1995, 599; quoted in Charles Johnson, Avery Collection box 3, "Sermon")

1 Amplify: Close Listening to Silencing and the 1921 Tulsa Race Massacre

On May 30, 1921, an African American named Dick Rowland from the Greenwood District in Tulsa, Oklahoma, allegedly assaulted a white woman named Sarah Page. By dawn on June 1, Greenwood would be burned to the ground with almost 300 people killed, including over 200 African Americans. In addition to the deaths, 35 square blocks of nearly 1,300 homes and almost 200 Black-owned businesses were destroyed and approximately 12,000 residents were rendered homeless (Oklahoma Commission 2001). Survivors say that the massacre was instigated by an editorial with the headline "To Lynch Negro Tonight," published on the front page of the May 31 afternoon edition of the *Tulsa Tribune*. Less than a month after Greenwood was in ruins and so many United States citizens had lost their lives—a grand jury of twelve white men meeting under the demand of Oklahoma governor James B. A. Robertson and attorney general S. Prince Freeling decided that the Greenwood residents were at fault and had instigated events. They called the massacre the Tulsa Race Riot.[1]

The May 31 editorial enraged the Black community to come to arms and the white community to respond with murderous, catastrophic results. Unsettled by sickness and violence, Tulsans in 1921 were still reeling from the reintegration of World War I soldiers and the outbreak of the 1918–1919 H1N1 flu pandemic, which infected a third of the world's population. Adding to these anxieties were two conflagratory elements: the success of the Greenwood district, an established and thriving Black business and living community, and an increasingly active local white supremacist Ku Klux Klan contingent that hosted thousands in local parades and festivals. Soon after the editorial's publication, crowds of both Black and white Tulsans converged on the courthouse where Rowland was jailed. Shots were fired, giving rise to the massacre and the eventual destruction of the Greenwood district. William D. Williams recalls the editorial in his 1978 interview with historian Scott Ellsworth,[2] and Dr. Hobart Jarrett remembers it in his interview with Eddie Faye Gates (Gates 2003, 81). Local historian Ruth Sigler Avery says that many of her interviewees, including a former principal at Booker T. Washington High School told her the same.[3] Yet, the editorial itself remains missing. There is no physical evidence of its existence, the page having been torn from all remaining editions in newspaper archives.[4] An article in *Tulsa World* on May 31, 2002, explains that "what the Tribune really said, didn't say and may have said" is still up for debate because "the best witness, the newspaper itself, is unavailable" (Krehbiel 2020). The editorial remains a significant artifact in the cultural register. It has a real presence in the memories of the massacre survivors despite there being no material evidence of its existence.

The erasure of the Tulsa Race Massacre in US history has been reiterated in fictional and historical accounts.[5] Time and again, histories written about the event begin with the question, "How could we not have known about such a thing?" (Madigan 2001, xv). When the city of Tulsa planned a surge of activities in 2021 to commemorate those who died in the 1921 massacre, they called the anniversary tribute an opportunity for the world to "experience history too long untold" (1921 Tulsa Race Massacre Centennial Commission). In contrast to this discourse, community dialogue and materials in local archives demonstrate that primarily Black communities have told, retold, recorded, shared, and preserved stories from the Tulsa Race Massacre across various media and genres for over a hundred years. Stories from Tulsa Massacre survivors come from a multigenerational community of African Americans in text, in still and moving images, and in sound through newspapers, magazines, pamphlets, and books of poetry, fiction, and memoir; dramatic and documentary films; oral histories, songs, and theater works; not to mention lesson plans. These told and retold stories of trauma and resistance are what have kept the history of the event present and answerable in Tulsa, moving the survivors to seek reparations in a case that progressed to the Supreme Court. Yet, the discourse around silencing endures, despite the avid and impassioned *re*telling that has continued to keep pace. Why? Who and what does the narrative about silencing serve? What role do media in the archive play in why and how this discourse endures and what alternate narratives about the Tulsa Race Massacre could scholars amplify instead if we read and listen to its intermedial artifacts differently?

Juxtaposing close listening and close reading of different archival media, this chapter models the basic methodology behind the objective of *Dissonant Records*: to listen closely to archival audio recordings and throw into debate questions about what is worthy of attention in the archive, by what means, and by whose authority, and to create new possibilities for resonance and meaning making in literary study. Absent a rich archive of print documents (from missing newspaper articles to missing government records), the history of the Tulsa Race Massacre is based on oral history recordings and other archival media, which become entangled in the discourse around speech, silence, and identity in its retellings. In this chapter, I first amplify how silencing functions in discourse about the massacre and how "modalities of silence" (Brown 2005) serve to reinforce prevailing narratives about freedom, oppression, and victimhood surrounding the Tulsa Race Massacre today.[6] In the second part, I listen to oral histories with Tulsa Massacre survivors and read closely documents and other ephemera of community events in Ruth Sigler Avery's archive at the Oklahoma State University Library, paying attention to the stories people tell (and occlude) but also what they convey through tone, cadence, velocity of speech, the material environment, media, genre, and "off the record" silences among other "noises."[7]

When imposed silences are broken, it is assumed that "what emerges is truth borne by the vessel of authenticity or experience" (Brown 2005, 83), but Ralph Ellison and others question the role of stories in which African American stereotypes are projected as the "easily dominated minority . . . not so much to crush the Negro as to console the white man" (1995, 96–97). Perhaps worse, stereotypes of Black victimhood and reparation "may feed the powers it meant to starve" through the depoliticization of underlying social conditions and by increasing public exposure, regulations, and even violence for those who are most impacted by these conditions (Brown 2005, 84, 85).[8] In this chapter, I show how listening "along the archival grain" (Stoler 2009) of intermedia in the archive can suggest new readings of fictional accounts of the Tulsa Massacre as stories that resist prevailing narratives in which Black Tulsans are simply the subjects rather than the agents and authors of their history.

The Massacre in Print

The *Tulsa Tribune* editorial was only the first instance of what became a "missing," suppressed, and biased run of media coverage around the massacre. The mainstream local *Tulsa World* and the *Tribune* both published "virulently racist editorials" blaming Black Tulsans for the events (Walker 2021),[9] while only a few national and international news outlets ran stories that covered Tulsa's "shame," including Oklahoma City's major Black newspaper, the *Black Dispatch* (Dunjee 1921, 4). Tulsa's two Black newspapers, the *Tulsa Star* and the *Oklahoma Sun*, were destroyed during the fires. In general, national and international coverage waned fairly quickly.[10] It did not help matters that after the grand jury impugned the Greenwood residents, it also disparaged general news media coverage by claiming such reporting was singularly biased—against the jury's findings:

> We condemn the exaggerated and untrue reports of the press, purporting to give the facts, both as to the cause and result of the riot, the information on which came from excited minds, for the time unreliable. We feel that judgment based on such reports is not only unfair to one race but to both; not only unfair to Tulsa and Tulsa county, but to the entire state as well as the nation. While we recognize the apparent necessity of giving reports of happenings while it is "news," we further feel that the findings of the court of inquiry should be given equal publicity in correcting misstatements of the press and wrong impressions created. (Quoted in Gill 1946, 91–92; Halliburton 1975, 40)

Soon after the grand jury's charges, officials on Tulsa's Executive Committee of the Board of Public Welfare passed a resolution to suppress further discussion in the media, noting the bias against the local militia and government in particular, and "asking every person to refrain from criticism and to leave to the grand jury the function of declaring who was to blame" (quoted in Gill 1946, 88). After this time period, there was little to no media reporting of the massacre for decades.[11]

Fifty years later, local white historians would reveal the role that local officials played in the massacre and begin to articulate a conspiratorial plot to hide or destroy documents. Ruth Sigler Avery became fascinated with the massacre, which she witnessed as a young white girl from the safety of a Tulsa hilltop. Documents in her archive tell multiple accounts of her seeking "missing" government evidence for her manuscript project "Fear, the Fifth Horseman: A Conspiracy of Silence."[12] On one manuscript page where

Avery describes her struggle to recount Dick Rowland's history through official records, she notes that "to trail him through local records and district court files you come to a dead end. In this town, where the tragedy occurred, the morgue file of the Newspaper shows the original story has been torn out from its front pages as though in anger—or fear. Microfilmed records of the Central Library show the newspaper accounts in the same condition." (Avery Collection, "Fear").[13] A 1976 letter to Avery from Ed Wheeler—a member of the Tulsa County Historical Society and the author of "Profile of a Race Riot" (1971)—includes a long anecdote about a 1970s government official who found 1921 documentation of hundreds of dead African Americans that far exceeded the official tally and how he still refused, fifty years later, to expose the records.[14] These and other accounts in Avery's archive suggest nefarious acts of hiding and cutting that were, perhaps, not officially sanctioned by local officials but also went uncorrected.

Consequent to the absence of archival newspaper and government records, the history of the Tulsa Race Massacre as published today has been based largely on the availability of survivors' archives comprising oral histories, personal writings, photographs, and ephemera from memorial events.[15] Early accounts came from Black and white Tulsans. Just days after the event, Mary Elizabeth Jones Parrish, a local Black journalist, was the first to collect and transcribe survivor stories. Her "Events of the Tulsa Disaster" was limited to fewer than two dozen copies, but it was likely limited and never published because, while it exposed white Tulsa's culpability, it had been commissioned by Tulsa's Interracial Committee, which was committed to upholding Black blame for the event (Messer 2011).[16] In contrast, ten years after the event, white author Frances W. Prentice published the event's first fictional portrayal in a short story called the "Oklahoma Race Riot" in the popular journal *Scribner's* in 1931, and it was disseminated widely. Prentice's story, which catalogs a woman's perspective of the happenings from the "white side of the tracks," was subsequently reprinted in 1939 in *Tellers of Tales: 100 Short Stories from the United States, England, France, Russia and Germany* (Prentice 1939, 1526). For decades, Black locals Mozella Jones, W. D. Williams, and Henry C. Whitlow kept their unpublished writings and photographs of the massacre in personal notebooks, ready to use in the classroom or during community events.[17] Nearly eighty years later, Greenwood survivor and historian John Hope Franklin and local school teacher Eddie Faye Gates, both members of the Oklahoma Commission to

Study the Tulsa Race Riot of 1921, would help author the commission's 2001 report based on these accounts. In 1999, Gates interviewed 200 survivors and 300 of their descendants for her *Riot on Greenwood: The Total Destruction of Black Wall Street* (2003).

After Parrish's first interviews on paper and before Gates's 1999 recordings, most of the oral histories forming the basis of historical accounts were conducted by white interviewers. On the fiftieth anniversary of the event, Ed Wheeler's "Profile of a Race Riot" (Wheeler 1971) was the first widespread publication to rely heavily on interviews with African American survivors.[18] Wheeler in turn inspired Avery, who went on to record over eighty hours of interviews with Tulsa Massacre survivors in the 1970s and 1980s, including the only recording of Dick Rowland's foster mother and the first narrative to tell his side of the story. After Wheeler and Avery, Scott Ellsworth conducted interviews in the 1970s for a dissertation project with many of the same survivors, the result of which was *Death in a Promised Land: The Tulsa Race Riot of 1921* (Ellsworth 1982), the first long-form historical treatment of the event.[19] Preserved in state-run archives and made freely available to the public, Avery's and Ellsworth's interviews would inform most of the later histories and fictional accounts of the massacre,[20] including Tim Madigan's extremely popular 2001 history *The Burning: Massacre, Destruction, and the Tulsa Race Riot of 1921*—which would form the basis of Damon Lindelof's Emmy Award–winning 2019 *Watchmen* series.[21] Most recently, the *New York Times* ran an extensive multimedia (no audio) essay on the massacre, describing Dick Rowland's activities in minute detail and crediting Ellsworth and Madigan. The article does not mention Avery, even though Madigan explicitly writes that his information on Rowland "is drawn largely from the transcript of Avery's interview with the shoeshine boy's caregiver" (Parshina-Kottas et al. 2021).[22]

There is a kind of irony in assigning "voicelessness" to oppression and reiterating that premise again and again via a singular media and mode (paper and print) when so many traces of the event's history and the voices of its survivors have been recorded on other media. The authors of these massacre histories and fictions are often outspoken about why including oral histories in their research process was the necessary consequence of a degradation of American democratic ideals, an essential loss of freedom that they sought to ameliorate.[23] Avery, in line with many social historians in the 1970s and 1980s who were committed to the importance of oral history as a means of capturing the "everyman" version of events, scrawled across a manuscript page of her history, "How can you analyze a major tragedy of America's twentieth century unless you study at least some of its thousands of participants?" (Avery Collection, "Fear"). Similarly, Ellsworth remarks in his interview with survivor Seymour Williams, "No one has really written about it. I'm trying to find people, particularly black people who remember the event and who I can sit down and talk to because to me, the black perspective on it is the most important and it's something you can't get if you go down to the library or something like that."[24] In such accounts, the failure of US institutions such as the mainstream media and government to record the event becomes a failure that cuts to the core of American democratic principles. In his 1976 letter to Avery, Wheeler writes that "it is incredible to me that in a modern American city, fear of those who may have participated in a disaster of more than five decades ago still exists.... Until such fear is overcome and faced with the courage necessary to defeat such movements, the freedom of everyone is in jeopardy" (Avery Collection).

These interviews became important and influential historical accounts. As a result of the many interventions from the 1970s to the early 2000s and the rise of public consciousness around the details of what happened, the Oklahoma government changed the name in 2018 of its commission and all other official references from the "Tulsa Race Riot" to the "Tulsa Race Massacre." And, in 2020, just shy of the event's hundredth anniversary, the Library of Congress accepted a proposal from the Oklahoma University Librarians and Archivists to change the official subject heading to refer to the event as a "massacre" instead of a "riot." Yet, listening closely to the recorded interviews is important because there is a danger in using oral histories to "give voice" to groups that are politically and socially marginalized from the powers of mainstream culture. The voicing can have the opposite effect than intended, reifying the victimization of survivors.[25]

The Massacre in the Archives

The silences, absences, and fears reiterated in the discourse about government records and mass media in published and unpublished histories of the massacre underscore the significance of other media sources in the archives, though not perhaps for obvious reasons. In some cases, the well-intentioned white authors listed above conducted oral history interviews that, on close listening, provide a portrayal of the events that tells just as much about the social politics of media and the interviewing scenario as it does about the massacre itself. Examining the interviews is necessary work as it provides insight into the interviewer and the process of historiography.[26] When Avery and Ellsworth conducted their interviews, they were amateur researchers interviewing primarily Black survivors. Both interviewee and interviewer had lived through decades of legalized segregation and racially prejudiced US institutions with which their families (on both sides of the interview) may have also been associated in some capacity. Listening to the survivors' recordings creates an opportunity to amplify how power and modalities of silence work within the larger discourse about speech and freedom in the event's history.

There are three recordings and multiple documents in community scholar Ruth Avery's archive at the Oklahoma State University Library that reveal how modalities of silence function in historical discourse around the event. In one recording, on March 8, 1971, Avery interviews Verna Prince.[27] On the recording, the dynamic between the two women sounds comfortable and easy. Avery begins the interview and introduces Prince's history by reading aloud an excerpt from the *Dallas Express* from September 3, 1932, on the death of Barney Cleaver, a former US marshal, the first Black deputy sheriff in Tulsa, and Prince's uncle. Prince and Avery sit in Prince's family home on Greenwood Street, about which there had apparently been an article in the *Tulsa Tribune* entitled "Elegance in Tulsa History," from which Avery reads at the conclusion of the interview. The article discusses the house's history and style, including its location near the Frisco tracks that once separated white from Black Tulsa and how the house burned during the 1921 massacre.[28] Avery begins the conversation by establishing a comfortable familiarity with Prince on common ground: she compliments Prince's home while also describing her own long-standing heritage in Tulsa. Prince responds with equal cordiality and the dialogue forms into a very polite conversation.

It is a seemingly innocuous easiness, but the tone of the discussion masks the complexities of relationships between whites and Blacks in Tulsa. The interview takes place just a month shy of the Supreme Court's ruling in *Swann v. Charlotte-Mecklenburg Board of Education* on April 20, 1971, that it was legal to use bussing to achieve desegregation in schools, a ruling that would spur Tulsa to finally desegregate that same year. [29] The city's ongoing racial power differentials are subtly revealed when Avery turns to question Prince about her activities on the night of the massacre and how Prince got to McNulty Park. The park is where Black Tulsans had been detained by the American Legion during the massacre, which was the beginning of a much longer detainment for countless African Americans who were kept in armed detention camps for months and released only with the signature of a white sponsor. Given the authority her uncle was granted by Tulsan officials, Prince would likely have been given preferential treatment or, at the very least, would have had a sense of security or safety with white Tulsans that her neighbors may not have shared. Prince recalls being taken to the McNulty fields by car and adds, "You know a lot of them were marched along the railroad tracks to the Convention Hall" (Avery Collection, Prince interview 1971). That Prince uses "them" instead of "us" could mark her own sense of her elevated status and difference from the many Black Tulsans who were rounded up that night.

During the interview, Avery and Prince laugh together quietly and easily when they can't remember some detail or when they both remember the same things at the same time, including how hot and humid June in Tulsa can be. Avery steers the conversation, asking the questions and interrupting Prince to correct her recollection of small details around what events happened during the massacre and when. Prince does not protest when Avery corrects her. When Prince speaks, Avery says, "Uh-huh," encouraging her to continue. The conversation continues civil and relaxed, each woman easy in her role. Toward the conclusion of the recording, Avery monopolizes the conversation to tell Prince about her own experiences and connections in Tulsa and about her book project to document the massacre. Prince shows a mild, courteous interest. "Is that so?" she says and, "You don't say?" Prince's tone is cordial when she prompts her interviewer to continue, which Avery does in a quicker cadence, happy it seems for Prince's interest. While they sit in Prince's elegant home, two women of the same age chatting, a train rumbles past Prince's house with a low whistle, a reminder of the past that marks the separate yet connected histories of these interlocutors from opposite sides of the train tracks. Listening to the interview in which Avery easily talks more than Prince and talks over Prince, it is not clear who is controlling the narrative—Avery with her speech and questions or Prince with her marked, polite silences. Prince has revealed very little that Avery does not seem to already know.

In comparison to the interview with Prince, Avery's conversation with two white men has a different tenor. William R. Holway, Walton Clinton, and Avery represent long-standing, white Tulsa families and institutions, and there is rarely a pause between these interlocutors. The speakers are friendly and familiar, but not necessarily polite, and in contrast to the previous interview, they laugh at moments of unease, at moments of conversation that might be perceived then and today to many audiences as reprehensible rather than laughable. There is a power dynamic apparent in the volume of the men's voices. The men's voices are brash, louder than Prince's, though the recording equipment is likely the same. Sometimes the laughter is an abrasive cackle such as when, during his interview, local developer William R. Holway tells Avery and her colleague Arthur Wade, "Of course they burned hundreds of homes in the Black section. Funny thing was the white folks woke up the next morning to find out they own the mortgages on all the houses and all the pianos and [Holway laughs] everything they have."[30] In another interview, Walton Clinton, the son of a local doctor, describes his recollection of the detainment of Black Tulsans at the McNulty Park. In his view, the American Legion was doing the Greenwood community a service detaining Black Tulsans who needed white direction and authority: "They fed them and took care of them and looked after them," Clinton recalls. Then, he immediately tells a joke to illustrate his point describing a Greenwood resident who approached Fred Johnson, a member of the American Legion on duty at McNulty Park. Clinton uses a higher, ridiculous falsetto when he says the lines spoken by the woman:

> This woman came to Fred, and she said, "Can I see my husband?"
> And Fred Johnson said, "Well, what's his name?"
> She said, "Well I don't know." She says, "You know we've just been married a short time." [Avery laughs] And said, "you know I just call him 'ole big boy.'" [Avery, Settle, and Clinton laugh]
> So, he said, "Well now would you know your husband if you see him?"
> "Oh, I sure would!" [Avery, Settle, and Clinton laugh]
> He said, "Well come on in here with me then." So, Fred Johnson has this woman, and he took her in.
> She says, "There's ole big boy!" [Clinton laughs].[31]

Clinton unwittingly describes the woman's confusion as humorous ignorance rather than conscious subterfuge. Fact or fiction, there are many reasons the interviewee might not want to tell Fred Johnson the name of her husband, including the potential danger she might face from white volunteers.[32]

Both Prince's interview and this story illustrate tactics that Saidiya Hartman might call "acts of defiance conducted under the cover of nonsense, indirection, and seeming acquiescence" (Hartman 1997, 25, 8). The men's overt racism is amplified by the context created by Avery, which depends on a community-based empowerment that is likely long-standing in a racially divided town like Tulsa. Their rapport is easy for the most part, but Avery, who seems to control the conversation with Prince by interrupting her, takes on the role of supplicant with the men, speaking less and more deliberately, and letting them shape the conversation. At times, it seems her choice of questions is meant almost to invite their hate speech. She draws out their experiences and, unlike in her conversation with Prince, she does not correct them. When she asks Clinton about the Klan activity in Tulsa, for example, Clinton recalls that "churchgoing" Tulsans who belonged to the Klan were trying "to clean the town up" and that they had a big meeting space in the center of town called Beno Hall. "You know what I was told?" Avery asks. "They called it Beno Hall? Be no N[—]. Be no Catholic. Be no Jew." Clinton chuckles in response. "That's a good story," he says. The empowered perspectives in both interviews, which shape an idea of Black personhood and experience as a shallow, silly caricature at the service of a false white superiority, is buttressed by the undertones of an assumed white privilege that has afforded that power in the first place. Their laughter seems to tell its own story about how the silencing of individuality, subjectivity, lived experiences, and racism can occur. Listening for what is covered up, under the radar, and perceived as speech and silence in these interviews may provide more information about the interlocutors, their positionalities, and how they shape historical narratives than listening for an authoritative, accurate, or authentic history of the massacre.

Beyond the oral history recordings in Avery's archive, other artifacts tell stories about the daily lives of massacre survivors: notecards of conversations had in a car on a ride home from a gathering alongside video recordings of television programs; poetry; newspaper clippings; reports; books; trials; police reports; photographs; correspondence; telegrams; memorandums; newsletters; chamber of commerce meeting minutes; the transcript of a television program, *Science of Murder*, that highlights the massacre; and materials related to a community event titled "Song of Greenwood: A Musical about Tulsa's Past Told by Tulsa's Future" that took place at the Greenwood Cultural Center from May 29 to June 1, 1998.[33] There is also a typescript sheaf of seven pages with a title page and the rusty marks of a, now absent, paper clip. The title page says that on Sunday, May 31, 1987, Tulsa's All Souls Unitarian Church held a memorial service at which interim minister Charles E. Johnson gave a sermon titled "No One Is Dead, until They Have Been Forgotten," and the senior minister, John B. Wolf, performed a reading from "Native Oklahoman" Ralph Ellison's *Going to the Territory*, an address that Ellison gave at a festival in his honor at Brown University in 1979.[34] The document's origins are indeterminable, but Avery, who indicates in her manuscript "Fear, the Fifth Horseman" that she was at the church that day, either recorded and transcribed the notes herself or she received the original pages from Wolf, a course of events that seems most likely given the emphasis marks included for its performance.

According to Ellison, a pluralistic society where there is a more complex understanding of the power dynamics underlying freedom and oppression or speech and silence requires a pluralistic historical representation across media, form, and message. The idea that identity in the US is expressed through the everyday practices of democracy would seem to resonate with an audience at Tulsa's All Soul's Unitarian Church in 1987 to memorialize the massacre. Italicized and bolded phrases on the transcript indicate where Wolf must have emphasized certain of Ellison's points about the silencing powers of history, media, democratic ideals, social reality, and personal agency. Wolf's transcript begins with a quote that is a direct allusion to the silencing of histories of Black trauma in US history: "Considering the ironic fact that Americans continue to find themselves stumbling into (as well as over) details of their history," Wolf says, "tonight's is a most **American** occasion" (Ellison 1995, 597; quoted by Johnson, Avery Collection, box 3).[35] The emphasis indicates that complexity rather than ideals are the foundations of the lived experiences of US democracy and that an articulation of how history is constructed is central to an understanding of how a multitudinous history is formed. Wolf concludes the reading by emphasizing Ellison's assertion, quoted at the start of this chapter, that communicating "unwritten" history is a moral imperative when articulating a US "cultural identity" that includes both shared bloodlines and cultural traditions of expression: "In spite of what is left out of our **recorded** history," Wolf quotes, "our **unwritten** history looms as its obscure alter ego, and although repressed from our general knowledge of ourselves, it is **always** active in the shaping of events" (Ellison 1995, 598, quoted in

Johnson 1987). Wolf adds with emphasis that "by overlooking the blending and metamorphosis of cultural forms which are so characteristic of our society, *we misconceive our cultural identity.*" That Wolf highlights such a misconception is a suggestion for his congregation to let go of ideals and embrace the difficult practice of being American. Wolf concludes, "It is as though we dread to acknowledge the complex, pluralistic **nature of our society**, and as a result we find ourselves **stumbling** upon our *true national* identity under circumstances *in which we least expect to do so"*—circumstances that Wolf implies relate to the Tulsa tragedy (Ellison 1995, 599, quoted in Johnson 1987). This evidence of a smaller, more intimate 1987 event in a church sits in contrast to Tulsa's broadly publicized, citywide anniversary commemoration and its claim to facilitate an experience of "history too long untold" (1921 Tulsa Race Massacre Centennial Commission).

The Massacre in Fiction

Like the histories before them, the fictional accounts of the massacre might seem to conflate ideals about speech and freedom or reinforce narratives around oppression and victimhood for Black Tulsans. Ellison claims that the difference between "reportage" and literature includes a "deep personal necessity" for the reader of literature to identify "with those who are indeed defeated," but he goes on to explain that literature "with unconscious irony . . . advises stoic acceptance of those conditions of life which it so accurately describes and which it pretends to reject" (95).[36] Rilla Askew, who calls herself "a citizen-novelist," is deeply concerned in *Fire in Beulah* (2001) with representing the complex lives and perspectives of "ordinary" Tulsans left out of early published histories.[37] Her motivations to write *Fire in Beulah* include elevating the stories of Black and indigenous communities and their mode of history making. "But black people knew," Askew writes. "The story of the riot was handed down orally in black families . . . in direct contradiction to the complicit silence in white communities" (Askew 2017, 36). Similarly, the novel *Magic City* (1998) is Jewell Parker Rhodes's "praise song to those black men," she writes. "It is a praise song, too, to women who speak disturbing truths—who give birth, prepare the dead for burial, and in between sing the songs and speak the stories which can uplift communities" (Rhodes 2017). Fears around the precarity of US freedoms coupled with shame at being part of a collective system of societal values where Black perspectives had been muted[38] likewise compelled Damon Lindelof to develop *Watchmen* (2019) around the Tulsa Race Massacre story. In an interview, Lindelof explains that when HBO called for a third time to ask him to produce an updated version of the *Watchmen* comic, he had recently been watching the August 2017 white supremacist "Unite the Right" rally unfold in Charlottesville, Virginia, and reading Ta-Nehisi Coates's 2014 article in *The Atlantic*, "The Case for Reparations," where Lindelof first learned of the Tulsa Massacre: "the way that [Coates] wrote about it . . . it felt like the destruction of a world to me" (Mazin and Lindelof 2019). Inspired to read Tim Madigan's popular history *The Burning* (2001), Lindelof recalls,

> I was just astonished by this story on every single level, most of all because I'd never heard about it, and I felt shame and embarrassment, and I would talk to other people. Like, I'd talk to other people of color and they'd go, "oh yeah" and I'd talk to white people and they'd go "What?" and then I'd start explaining "Oh, this is what happened" and I would see them start to feel, get embarrassed and then disconnect, which is what we do when we think we are supposed to know something and we don't know it. (Mazin and Lindelof 2019)

Like the historians above, Lindelof likens the real destruction of house, home, and loved ones to the destruction of his worldview, which is based on an American democratic ideal in which speech, the act of voicing, and the powers of knowledge production (in the form of the US historical record and published registry) equal freedom.[39]

Though the narratives surrounding freedom and its loss are subtle and complex in Askew's novel *Fire in Beulah*, Rhodes's novel *Magic City*, and Lindelof's series *Watchmen* (2019), all three authors tend toward recapitulating scenes shared in survivors' oral histories and amplifying key moments when Black Tulsans are victimized by US institutions that normally safeguard individual rights and personal safety. These scenes include:

- French propagandists telling Black US soldiers that they are fighting for freedom they themselves do not possess (Askew 2001; Lindelof 2019; Rhodes 1998),
- white crowds assembling to block ambulances from the first Black man shot in Tulsa, left lying in the street (Askew 2001),
- Black men shooting from a burning church (Askew 2001; Lindelof 2019; Rhodes 1998),

- a white man walking down a chaotic, smoke-filled street in a woman's leopard skin coat and other white men and woman rolling pianos away from burning Black homes (Askew 2001; Lindelof 2019),
- a white boy shooting a well-regarded Black doctor who has raised his hands in compliance (Askew 2001),
- Black bodies being dragged behind cars and stacked in piles on truck beds by white men (Askew 2001; Lindelof 2019).

These moments, based on real accounts, are scenes that represent violences committed against Black bodies. Used by the authors to underscore occasions when the basic tenets of freedom for Black Tulsans were compromised, the scenes can be read as "terrible spectacles" used for enjoyment and the dramatization of "the origin of the subject" in US culture (Hartman 1997, 3).[40]

In contrast to this reading, tracing silence and speech in the archive can provide significant resources for understanding fictional representations in different terms than those in which Black Tulsans have become represented as an "easily dominated minority" (Ellison 1995, 96).[41] The oral histories and other archival artifacts reveal how fictional accounts can also invite counternarratives about speech, silence, freedom, and oppression surrounding the massacre. For instance, the unspoken complexities that underly the quiet cordiality between Avery and Prince and the overt expressions of power in Avery's conversation with Holway and Clinton point to similar modalities of silence that Rilla Askew uses to express interdependent racial identities in *Fire in Beulah*. In that novel, Althea Whiteside, her husband, and their housekeeper Graceful live in the Whiteside house. Even as their respective identities (Black, poor, young, pregnant versus white, rich, nearing middle-age, childless) create seeming differences, Althea and Graceful—from white Tulsa and from Greenwood—have a shared heritage. The reader learns at the beginning that Althea's husband and Graceful share the last name Whiteside, implying that slavery connects their families in the past through Althea's husband's family. The cycles of violence continue as rape connects them in the present narrative when Althea's brother attacks Graceful, who becomes pregnant.

As in Price and Avery's circumstances, Althea and Graceful's story is told less through the words they say to each other (or to the reader) and more through the intimate actions that amplify the codependence of Black and white Tulsa. The primary story about Althea and Graceful is given in the third person. First-person narratives of unnamed characters also occur, appearing with a different typeface to mark their status outside the main storyline of the text. They are co-present but not directly related to the Whitesides. In these narratives, Askew gives voice to an unnamed white woman in a Black church, an older Creek woman who had helped with births in the white community, and a white man who participates in the massacre. Like the oral histories where a violent racial history sits quietly behind every story, these first-person narratives have the potential to redefine and redistribute authority behind who is given agency to tell the event but the potential for these characters to shape the story is forestalled by the copresence of the story between Althea and Graceful. In its contrast to the first-person narratives, the third-person perspective sets Althea and Graceful up at a distance from the reader, each other, and the broader community of unnamed, everyperson, first-person narrators. In comparison to these narrators, Althea and Graceful are disempowered to speak "out loud"; a silence stands in for what they think. Over the course of the narrative, the women come to depend on each other—Graceful for Althea's money and protection, and Althea for Graceful's comfort and solace. Askew's depiction of the two Tulsan women evinces a deeply entwined community, where oppression, dominance, and Black and white heritage can take on more complex valences than those represented in whitewashed news items and coded personal stories.

It is important to hear the racist undertones of the above recordings as they are associated with and dependent on traditional institutions (the American Legion; the local, municipal authorities; old, established family ties) in order to listen for alternative acts of personhood and power that do not arise wholly in answer to the power negotiations relegated by these traditional strongholds of white privilege.[42] In contrast to the narrative of victimhood and dominance signaled by Holway and Clinton, Jewell Parker Rhodes is inspired in *Magic City* by the resilience of massacre survivors "who stood firm in the face of overwhelming odds" (Rhodes 2017). The moments Rhodes uses to portray her characters are situated in individual, everyday moments of magic and spirituality that mark, like the African praise songs, a rite of initiation into becoming the self. Heralded by declarations of personhood that are framed by a repeated question—"Who do you think you are?"—dreams, folk tales, and the Black church guide the spiritual awakenings for characters' experiences and help them express their emotions as they struggle for self-definition. Through the "extraordinary magic of ordinary people," Rhodes portrays subjectivity in ways that biased media coverage of the event and interviews with white Tulsans like Holway and Clinton cannot (Rhodes 2017).[43] The facts (and white Tulsa) say that her main characters, Mary and Joe (stand-ins for Sarah Page and Dick Rowland), started a riot and a massacre, but Rhodes gives spiritual identities to Mary and Joe and the agency to change the narrative that has shaped their identities in history.[44] Joe is a Houdini admirer who performs magic tricks and sleights of hand and has long conversations with his dead brother, who appears to him. Mary experiences memories of her deceased mother that are less about the facts of what happened than the feelings about womanhood that these encounters evoke. These identifying moments happen during incidents of great personal unease to the characters, when what is happening and how they behave—Joe getting apprehended by the white sheriff, Mary's beloved brother Jody siding with her rapist—is in direct conflict with each character's evolving identity and their resistance to traditional societal mores. *Magic City* amplifies the lives of ordinary Tulsans to subvert stories like Holway's and Clinton's and provides a counternarrative in which everyday acts—acts often disappeared by official records—suggest the pluralistic and lived experiences of Black and white Tulsans.

Histories of the massacre frame it as a past event for Black Tulsans, but untold futures, a central premise of Damon Lindelof's *Watchmen* series, are equally important. In *Watchmen*, history is not relegated to a set past. Aired in October 2019 as a new HBO series based on the 1980s comic of the same name,[45] *Watchmen* links the Tulsa Race Massacre, its messy media history, and the event's complex portrayal across history and fiction as a marker of a dystopian United States where the ideals central to democracy have always been and will always be in conflict. As the show progresses, a backstory evolves that is shared with the comic (1986–1987), the graphic novel (1987), and the less successful 2009 *Watchmen* film. The pre-2019 versions are set in a 1985 cold war dystopia in which the United States has won the Vietnam War under a third-term President Richard Nixon. Nixon, who had deployed Doctor Manhattan's powers (the comic's most powerful superhero) to win the Vietnam War, now has the United States on the brink of World War III with the Soviet Union. The original comic's creators used multimedia and disrupted (and disruptive) chronologies to make a point about the making of history as a messy process of potentialities. In the graphic novel *Watchmen* (1987), a cacophony of media to make the case for situated human embodiment, chance, and choice in how history is told: pictures and text, speech acts in bubbles, facial and hand gestures, bodies in costumes, governmental and doctor reports, scrapbooks, letters, clippings from newspapers, notes from a production company, photographs, company letters, notes, memorandums, desk calendars, and magazines. Like the many media that make up an intermedia archive, the novel *Watchmen* engages these various media—with their coffee and ink stains, paper clips and staples, rips and tears, highlights and redactions—to depict real-world events that become altered as a result of the sudden and disruptive appearance of modern-day superheroes. Readers are invited to ask, What if the United States had won the Vietnam War? What if there had been a third world war, Nixon was in office, and superheroes were real? What if vigilantism (in this case, acting like a masked superhero) is outlawed in the United States and superheroes are the bad guys? What if we tell history with cartoons, superheroes, and through coffee stains?

Based on this alternative past, the future the *Watchmen* series inhabits is Tulsa in 2019, where reparations sanctioned by the US government for Tulsa Massacre survivors and their descendants are the central cause of social and political disruption. The reparations have given rise to what Wendy Brown describes as unemancipatory "techniques of subjugation" that, instead of ameliorating the intergenerational suffering caused by the massacre, establish new regulatory norms for its Black citizens (2005, 84). The main character, Angela Abar, is the granddaughter of a Tulsa survivor and a former detective who has ostensibly left the police force to avoid violent antipolice attacks and to focus on her home life, but the increasing violence compels her to become the masked vigilante Sister Night. The primary antagonists are "the 7th Kavalry," a white supremacist organization responsible for the "White Night" attack, during which the organization targeted Black police officers in their homes on Christmas Eve. The Kavalry, which includes corrupt representatives of the state, wear the mask of Rorschach, a complex, fan-favorite "antihero" in the original *Watchmen* comics, who participated in brutal acts to solve the murder of his friend.

In *Watchmen*, reparations have thrown Tulsa 2019 into chaos again, and the citizens live with the future that Avery and Ed Wheeler predicted, where no white or Black Tulsan is safe. As a result, all the characters, including the superheroes, become antiheroes: Doctor Manhattan obliterates everyone—the Kavalry, corrupt senators and police, the scientists behind a plot to kill him, and, in the final blow to the US government, himself, their best weapon for peace. Only Abar survives and the final point of *Watchmen* seems to be that superheroes are real, but reparations, peace, and freedom remain conceits based on US ideals that ultimately end in latent violence and chaos. The series season ends with Abar baking at home in her kitchen, saddened by the Doctor's death but seemingly at peace with her children's newfound safety, when she drops a carton of eggs. One egg remains intact, and she realizes that Doctor Manhattan has left it for her as a means to share his super strength. In the final scene, Abar breaks and eats the egg and places a tentative toe out over a still, blue pool to see if, as the Doctor had once promised, his transferred powers would give her the ability to walk on water. Abar's future portends to be a remediation of the past with the same quest for peace and potential for chaos that heralded Greenwood's destruction in the first place. *Watchmen*'s themes are reminiscent of Ellison's point that democracy and freedom comprise a "blending and metamorphosis of cultural forms" in a racialized society in which cultural identity is a complex and pluralistic process across time (Ellison 1995, 599).

There is another egg in *Watchmen*, an "Easter egg" that anticipates the central themes of this book about agency and the significant role intermedia and fiction can play when amplified in the cultural register.[46] The opening scenes show a wealthy business district of an early twentieth-century city, well-heeled residents on foot and in fine carriages or polished, black Model T Fords. The people are under siege. Armed militia with World War I machine guns are shooting at them from the ground and from low-flying, single-engine bombers by air. The scene—men, women, and children running, falling, screaming; buildings burning and smoking; brown-metaled, monstrous machines roaring low overhead—is chaos. While mass, wartime destruction in the early twentieth century is not an unsurprising or particularly innovative opening scene for a movie or a television show, this particular portrayal feels different. It is not a scene set in a war torn European village or beachfront. Horses and cars careening, people screaming, airplanes growling low overhead—the camera zooms in on a newspaper sweeping across the dusty road and then caught briefly center screen. It is a momentary view like one frame in a comic book, there to set the stage and tell the viewer where we are, when, and why: "Tulsa Oklahoma, May 31, 1921" the newspaper headline says, and then the editorial title beneath it adds, "To Lynch Negro Tonight."

The appearance of the missing editorial in *Watchmen* is not evidence of a confirmed fact. Instead, its appearance is a fiction amplifying resonant truths. It is a reminder that resonant truths can become matter that signifies, can become history. The particularities of the Tulsa tragedy—an event steeped in racial hatred, police brutality, government corruption, and, later, reparations—struck a chord with a mainstream audience watching the *Watchmen* HBO series, who had just seen wide media coverage of the violence in Ferguson, Missouri, over the police shooting of Michael Brown, the deadly Unite the Right rally in Charlottesville, Virginia, over the removal of a statue of Robert E. Lee, and the virulent protests in response to President Donald Trump's first impeachment and George Floyd's death. To viewers who began to watch the show at the height of its popularity in 2020, *Watchmen* likely seemed prescient of the Black Lives Matter protests in the United States, the conflicts around voting fraud allegations in the US presidential election, and the anxiety of a worldwide pandemic. A Greenwood man in *Fire in Beulah* identifies the particular clang of the bell that this headline tolls and says why it still resonates today: "This ain't about Dick Rowland," the man says, "this about every black man in this country" (Askew 2001, 287). Likewise, *Watchmen*'s premise—a government-supported massacre of a Black community, government-sanctioned reparations, and a conspiracy involving the local police and a KKK-like militia—must not have seemed too farfetched. In mass media, the public record, and the cultural imaginary, Black Tulsans are no longer held solely responsible for the most destructive act of domestic terrorism experienced in US history, but they are still the victims of its telling. It is important to understand what role archival media and fiction had and have in how we understand their stories.

* * *

This chapter concerns silences in the historical record and how no media are free from obfuscation, but it is also about paying attention across media to identify clues for understanding history differently. In the introduction, I define resonance as interpersonal, of matter, and agential or world making. This chapter serves as an introduction to close listening as a methodology for articulating resonance in literary study by what is amplified in the intermedia archive. To amplify is "to make large; in space, amount, capacity, importance, or representation."[47] It is to increase in material and significance, to make more matter and to make things, people, places, and events matter more. Technically, amplification happens across multiple devices: a transducer such as a microphone or the needle stylus on a record player translates sound into a low-voltage signal that it relays to an amplifier. The amplifier modifies the signal for an output device such as a speaker. The needle on a record player is a transducer that converts a sound wave into a signal, but a pen, a typewriter, a computer keyboard could also be considered part of an amplification process, converting thoughts and ideas or spoken sounds into media to be shared and made large in the public imagination.[48] Just as the process of sonic amplification is a situated process that involves more than a string of devices, more than a wave of matter transferring from one medium to the next, cultural amplification is a situated process of matter and meaning. Someone in a place and in a time must situate the microphone, drop the needle, ink the typewriter ribbon, print the page, and turn up the volume.

In the remaining chapters of *Dissonant Records*, I position close listening as a method that can be used alongside close reading to expose new patterns of meaning in the cultural record. To listen closely to audio recordings for meaning in literary study is to listen to "sound as material, where sound is neither arbitrary nor secondary but constitutive" of meaning (Bernstein 1998, 4). It is listening to "what you would *think* of as noise" (Brathwaite 1984, 17).[49] Close listening is a choice to amplify a speaker's style, tone, and on- and off-the-record silences as well as an audience's reaction in the form of laughter and applause (or silence), the technological environment through distortions among other "noises," and/or the lived context—for example—when a train rumbles by. It is listening to the proximity of the tracks and reading how that proximity might play out on the page. Close listening to dissonant records is an invitation to amplify new modes of interpretation in the archive and redefine what is worthy of attention in literary study.

Zora Neale Hurston: Just a minute. It's coming out like I like it now because if you're leading, you got to come out.

Man's voice: What's going on? Go ahead.

Zora Neale Hurston: Go on.

—"See Day Dawning," Alan Lomax, Zora Neale Hurston, and Mary Elizabeth Barnicle (Expedition Collection, 1935, 336 B)[1]

2 Distortion: Authority, Authenticity, and Agency in Recordings of Zora Neale Hurston's Black Folk

An ethnographer, novelist, and dramatist, Zora Neale Hurston was also a collector, speaker, performer, and recorder of other people's stories and her own Black folklore. She was trained at Barnard College in the 1920s under the supervision of anthropologist Franz Boas and completed ethnographic fieldwork in Alabama, the Bahamas, Florida, Georgia, Haiti, Jamaica, and New Orleans.[2] In the 1930s alone, Hurston wrote numerous short stories, journal articles, books, and musicals based on her early life in Eatonville, Florida. She was awarded a Guggenheim fellowship, appeared on multiple radio programs, was read and translated widely nationally and abroad, received generous patronage, and was hired by universities and the US government to record, write about, and perform Black culture. From Alice Walker's work "Looking for Zora"[3] in the 1970s to more recent discussions "complicating Zora" (Carpio and Sollors 2011), many scholars have written about Hurston's work, describing it as both a politically polarizing and a representationally complex expression of Black folk.[4] Fittingly, Hurston writes in her autobiography *Dust Tracks on a Road* (Hurston 1942) about African Americans in the United States: "There is no *The Negro* here. Our lives are so diversified, internal, attitudes so varied, appearances and capabilities so different, that there is no possible classification so catholic that it will cover us all except My people! My people!" (192).

Because of its intermedial forms, its multigenre expressions, and general lack of fixity, Hurston's work also resists current modes of archival preservation and categorization, making her creative process difficult to study. Unpublished manuscripts of plays, stories, and essays by Hurston are few and rough, and her working field notes do not exist.[5] She has famously described how her own recording methods are entangled in the community's practices of folk: "I just get in the crowd with the people if they're singing and I listen as best I can and I start to joining in with a phrase or two and then, finally I get so I can sing a verse and then I keep on until I learn all the song, all the verses, and then I sing them back to the people until they tell me I can sing them just like them." Asked if this was the same way she collected the songs she published in the journals and her book *Mules and Men*, Hurston says, "I learned the song myself and I can take it with me wherever I go."[6] She reminds us in these comments that her methods of recording folklore comprise a complex process of trying to represent a culture that actively resists dominant means of representation.

Very few scholars have written about the recordings that are the main concern of this chapter, which include approximately seventy-five brief "tracks" or recorded songs, stories, and explanations from a folklore recording trip Hurston took in 1935 to Florida and Georgia with Alan Lomax and Mary Elizabeth Barnicle for the Library of Congress, as well as three longer recordings put online by the Florida Memory Project from a June 18, 1939, session at the Federal Music Project Office of the Work Projects Administration (WPA) in Jacksonville, Florida, with Carita Doggett Corse, Herbert Halpert, and Stetson Kennedy.[7] One primary reason for the silence in scholarship about these recordings is that close listening for Hurston on both the 1935 and 1939 recordings is difficult work. It must be preceded by acts of preservation and access that include transposing the original acetate disks onto reel-to-reel tapes and then digitizing them. Access for scholars is determined by how the original catalogers described (or did not describe) her work and how those descriptions influence metadata and online curations that still rely on that information today. Additionally, while the 1939 recordings are online, most of the 1935 recordings are still not freely available outside the reading rooms of the Library of Congress. That few have written about the 1935 recordings also signals the fact that close listening is a slow, daunting practice that happens in real time and requires meticulous and repeated listening sessions. Perhaps most importantly, distortions on the recordings might seem to scholars to render them inauthentic, non-authoritative, and poor evidence of Hurston's ethnographic and creative work. In contrast, I argue that these recordings and their distortions, which disrupt how institutions preserve recordings and make them discoverable, are important traces of Hurston's early work in the field and how she came to shape her writings on race and identity.

Reading Hurston

Hurston struggled with the gendered and racialized politics of ethnographic professional practices. In a 1928 letter to Alain Locke—a scholar sometimes called "the father of the Harlem Renaissance"—Hurston criticizes the recently published *Negro Workaday Songs* (1926), collected by white ethnographers Howard Odum and Guy Johnson. "Fearful lest they had beat us to it in the matter of songs," she bemoans to Locke, "cheap white folks are grabbing our stuff and ruining it. I am almost sick—my one consolation being that they never do it right and so there is still a chance for us" (Hurston 2002, 120, 126). In particular, she criticizes the authors for miscategorizing songs and cutting into pieces others that had been part of something larger: "Heavens knows," she writes, "there has never appeared one genuine Negro bit on there" (120). Hurston then complains to her benefactor, American socialite and philanthropist Charlotte Osgood Mason, "white people could not be trusted to collect the lore of others" (Hurston 2002, 121). Her experience with white ethnographers did not improve. In a 1937 letter, Hurston accuses Alan Lomax, the lead ethnographer on their trip for the Library of Congress, of "pettiness and trickery and lies":

> There was you with your lies about everything that I showed you. One day you had never heard of it . . . But bless me gawd a week later, you were an authority on it. You and your papa [John Lomax] had found it in Texas. I see you tell that lie again in your book. And there was Barnacle [sic], looking like a mammy walrus with a sunburned nose who had heard the identical thing in a medieval miracle play or something of the sort. It was just too funny assuming that white skin could fool black brain. (Cappetti 2010, 610)

Even after becoming well known in the Harlem Renaissance as an ethnographer, writer, and creative, she is still frustrated. In 1944, she writes a letter to novelist Claude McKay about being asked on a radio program to write a "kind of Amos and Andy thing":

> They wanted my name to give the air of authentic Negro to it. I have always refused to take a part in things like that. If they want to do it, okay. But I am not going to go on record as saying that it is real. I may even think that it is funny at times, but not Negro humor. If we keep on sanctioning that kind of thing, there will be no place for either Negro actors nor writers, for the whites can do that well enough themselves. (Hurston 2002, 499)

Constantly checked by white academics, socialites, publishers and producers, Black male writers, and, eventually, the National Association for the Advancement of Colored People (NAACP),[8] Hurston would learn to reject how these imposed authorities would position her and "her people" for white culture, a perspective she would hold throughout her life.

Hurston recognized that the politics that complicated what she wanted to achieve were largely unavoidable. While writing her first book, *Jonah's Gourd Vine* (1934), she describes her sense of writing "what was expected of me" as "off-key":

> What I wanted to tell was a story about a man, and from what I had read and heard, Negroes were supposed to write about the Race Problem. I was and am thoroughly sick of the subject. My interest lies in what makes a man or woman do such-and-so, regardless of his color. . . . But I said to myself that that was not what was expected of me, so I was afraid to tell a story the way I wanted, or rather the way the story told itself to me. (1942, 171)

Some of Hurston's most scathing reviews for her best-known and highest acclaimed work, *Their Eyes Were Watching God* ([1937] 2006) came from black male writers like Richard Wright who accused Hurston of playing to white sensibilities and treating Black lives as spectacle for white entertainment. "Miss Hurston," Wright writes, "voluntarily continues in her novel the tradition which was forced upon the Negro in the theater, that is, the minstrel technique that makes the 'white folks' laugh. Her characters eat and laugh and cry and work and kill; they swing like a pendulum eternally in that safe and narrow orbit in which America likes to see the Negro live: between laughter and tears" ([1937] 2006, 25). Saidiya Hartman has similarly argued of white authors that normalizing scenes of violence against Black bodies with such "terrible" spectacles "displace[s] the hideous with the entertaining" and "den[ies] the presence of violence by characterizing it within the context of the socially endurable," making them "an opportunity for white self-reflection" on the human condition (1997, 34).[9] In contrast to Richard Wright's similar critique of Hurston's work, however, there is an argument to be made that Hurston's ability to "make white folks laugh" with folk tales and songs was a subversive mode of world making.

Hurston learned to work within ethnographic practices of knowledge production to disrupt them. On a basic level, she believed that recording dynamic Black lives on paper and on tape to "save them from cultural obscurity" could not adequately define, represent, and preserve the complex identities of "my people" (Hemenway 1977, 80). As anthropological practices were oriented toward the representation of monolithic, authentic "facts" about African Americans for white culture, Hurston instead described her recording process differently for different audiences—a method that is exemplified by the following accounts, one written for a fellow Black literary writer and the other for her white professor of anthropology. For instance, in April 1929, she writes to Langston Hughes about her dual goals for presenting Black lives in her field work and writings:

> I not only want to present the material with all the life and color of my people, I want to leave no loop-holes for the scientific crowd to rend and tear us. . . . I am leaving the story material almost untouched. I have only tampered with it where the storyteller was not clear. I know it is going to read different, but that is the glory of the thing, don't you think? (2002, 138–139)

A little over six months later, she again describes her method for capturing her "material" in a letter to her mentor, professor Franz Boas:

> I have tried to be as exact as possible. Keep-to the exact dialect as closely as I could, having the story teller to tell it to me word for word as I write it. This after it has been told to me off hand until I know it myself. But the writing down from the lips is to insure [sic] the correct dialect and wording so that I shall not let myself creep in unconsciously. (2002, 150)

Similarly, while her biographer Robert Hemenway calls her the "master of ceremonies" (1977, 166), Hurston paints a more complex picture of her own agency in the dual role she takes on when staging Black folk in her writings. She asserts in one of her first published pieces, *I Love Myself When I Am Laughing . . . and Then again When I Am Looking Mean and Impressive*, "I am not tragically colored. . . . It is quite exciting to hold the center of the national stage, with the spectators not knowing whether to laugh or to weep" (1979, 153).

To document Black folk, then, Hurston attempted to render the inherent complexities of the "folk process" and the folk "manner of rendition" differently than what was expected by her anthropology colleagues (Hemenway 1977, 82; Ward 2012). Hurston famously wrote to Hughes that she was dedicated to recording authentic Black culture and folklore "using the vacuum method, grabbing everything I see" (2002, 129), but she did not necessarily believe in recording as a simple process of duplication (Dorst 1987; Hill 1996). For Hurston, folklore was an ongoing process of community making that resisted colonialist practices, including long-term and static modes of authenticity, originality and authorship, and preservation. "Negro folklore is not a thing of the past," Hurston writes, "It is still in the making" (1981, 56). To represent this process of being Black folk, she experimented with multiple tactics. In a letter to Langston Hughes during her first collecting trip in August 1928, Hurston writes that she was simultaneously working on "1 volume of stories. 1 children's games. 1 Drama and the Negro 1 Mules & Men a volume of works songs with guitar arrangement 1 on Religion. 1. on words & meanings. 1 volume of love letters with an introduction on Negro love" (2002, 124), and her final manuscript was a history of Herod the Great (Hemenway 1977, 4). She used drama and irony to present everyday life and her repertoire crossed a multigenre "literariness" that lent itself to mixed media of expression (Hill 1996).[10] As a result, her autobiography reads like fiction, her folktales read like autobiography, and her fiction reads like the truth. Hemenway would describe Hurston's repertoire of folk tradition as "performed interpretations of the world which influence action—and it does not easily transfer to a print-oriented tradition that conceives of art as something fixed" (Hemenway 1977, 80–81).[11]

Watching Hurston

Situating Hurston in the Jim Crow South surveillance culture is significant for understanding the role audio recording played in her work. Alan Lomax and Stetson Kennedy both recall the "trouble" they had with police due to their involvement with Hurston and the Florida workers in 1935. According to Lomax's biography, Hurston advised Lomax and Barnicle to darken their faces with walnut oil to avoid difficulties with local police as they traveled through African American neighborhoods. Nevertheless, Lomax was picked up at least twice by local authorities for simply being with Hurston and talking to the Black workers (Szwed 2011, 81–82).[12] Kennedy also recalls how during their 1939 fieldwork, Hurston would be compelled to sleep in her car when hotels would not welcome her and how Black turpentine camp workers would put sentries on the lookout for camp guards before they would answer Kennedy's questions. In these situations, Kennedy noticed the men using singing as a form of subterfuge. He recalls interviewing some camp workers about their living and working conditions when one man said, on noticing an approaching supervisor, "Sing something quick, here comes the man." Kennedy further observed that segregation "was enforced by police car, vigilante, peer group, Ku Klux Klan or whatever—you could get killed lighting someone's cigarette or shaking hands, both parties, white and black. They did get killed" (National Public Radio 2002).

Understanding Hurston as both surveillant and *sous*veillant is an acknowledgment of how she inserted herself into the complex subjectivation process that was inherent in 1930s anthropological fieldwork of Black folk. In a surveillance culture like the Jim Crow South, *sousveillance*—the act of recording the recorders—could become "a site of critique as it speaks to black epistemologies of contending with antiblack surveillance," much as "the tools of social control in plantation surveillance or lantern laws in city spaces and beyond were appropriated, co-opted, repurposed, and challenged in order to facilitate survival and escape" (Browne 2015, 21). In *Mules and Men* (1935), Hurston imagines what the surveilled Black man would say when asked about "the theory behind our tactics" for resisting "the white man . . . always trying to know into somebody else's business": "'I'll set something outside the door of my mind for him to play with and handle. He can read my writing but he sho' can't read my mind. I'll put this play toy in his hand, and he will seize it and go away. Then I'll say my say and sing my song'" (1935, 3). Hurston's "tactics" recall Simone Browne's contention that "dark sousveillance" is "a way of knowing" that "speaks not only to observing those in authority (the slave patroller or the plantation overseer, for instance) but also to the use of a keen and experiential insight of plantation surveillance in order to resist it" (2015, 22).

One of Hurston's tactics was to make herself indispensable. In a letter sent to the Lomax family from New York before they left for their Southern collecting trip on May 15, 1935, Barnicle writes that inviting Hurston on the trip "seemed such a good opportunity for us to have a negress—trained anthropologically, artistic by nature and as hoppity-skippity-crazy-mad as we are about folk song and folk dance." Barnicle relates that it was Hurston's suggestion where they should go and that they should get two cars. "Her idea," Barnicle writes, "is that she could be scouting around in one of the cars while we are recording, carrying on meetings"—an arrangement that Lomax later admitted kept their journey with Hurston above the law's reproach in the deeply segregated South.[13] It was Hurston who often determined which songs and stories, when, and whom they would record. After the first trip on August 3, 1935, Lomax writes to Oliver Strunk, then head of the Music Division of the Library of Congress, that Hurston's leadership "had been almost entirely responsible for the great success of our trip." Hurston, Lomax tells Strunk, was "our guide and interpreter in Florida and Georgia . . . had led us into fields we might never have found alone . . . had generously helped us to record songs and negroes she had herself discovered" (Lomax and Lomax Papers). Similarly, for the 1939 recordings, Kennedy describes sending Hurston ahead "as a scout into the communities," to "identify people who had something to give and send us a list with addresses and so on. And sometimes she would wait and take part in the recording. Sometimes she would go ahead to the next place" (National Public Radio 2005).

Acutely aware of her hypervisibility as a Black woman leading a white "expedition" into her hometown and other Black communities, Hurston would equivocate in her role as insider and outsider to Black culture to conform to and disrupt white expectations.[14] Narrating as herself in her first collection of Black folk, *Mules and Men* (1935), she describes a background that would allow her more local authority than her white counterparts. "When I pitched headforemost into the world," she explains, "I landed in the crib of negroism. From the earliest rocking of my cradle, I had known about the capers Brer Rabbit is apt to cut and what the Squinch Owl says from the house top" (1). Born in Notasulga, Alabama, in 1891, she says in the 1939 WPA recordings that she is thirty-five and born in Eatonville, Florida, both "facts" about date and location that Hurston would also set down in writing in her 1942 autobiography, *Dust Tracks on a Road*.[15] Perhaps Hurston did not know the exact details of her origins given the poor documentation around African American births at the time, but in these contexts, she may have also been trying to substantiate her credibility as an authority on the songs they had been collecting from Eatonville by establishing herself as native-born. Hurston would also position herself as an outsider to Black culture with the authority to objectively present or translate Black folk for white audiences. This outsider character in her writings is like any other ethnographer struggling to gather Black folklore: "Very little was said directly to me," the narrator of *Mules and Men* complains on arriving in Eatonville, "and when I tried to be friendly there was a noticeable disposition to fend me off . . . here was I figuratively starving to death in the midst of plenty" (Hurston 1935, 60). Later, around the fire with others at a party, she adds, "I stood there awkwardly, knowing that the too-ready laughter and aimless talk was a window-dressing for my benefit" (62).

Listening for Hurston

On the 1935 and 1939 recordings, audible and discernible distortions index Hurston's sousveillance work. Distortions are a twisting awry or out of shape. They are what Hurston would identify as "off-key" from an expectation (1942, 171). Figuratively, distortion is a word misapplication, a "perversion of words so as to give to them a different sense"; in sound, it is "a change in the waveform of a signal by an electronic device such as an amplifier or during transmission from one point to another, usually impairing the quality of its reproduction."[16] Distortion happens during the process and production of use, but distortion is also a perception. An audio engineer listening for and expecting a certain audio quality could describe listening to a distorted signal as having "a little sense of unease" or a feeling that "things aren't quite right" while an inexperienced or uncritical listener might not sense an aberration (McGowan 2014). Similarly, a person with a limited vocabulary might not perceive that a word has been used incorrectly. Besides, distortions are not without their pleasures. Sound distortions in music can be expressive, malapropisms can be illuminating, and both can be on-key for the situation. A diverted expectation can be an opportunity for reflection and for reconsidering the processes by which perceptions of what is "right" occur.[17]

The social and technical distortions in Hurston's 1935 and 1939 audio recordings are traces of how her early work pushes against the classification and cultural legibility of Black folk on what Paul Gilroy calls a "lower frequency" of resistance (1993, 37). Gilroy describes this low-frequency resistance as performed "under the very nose of the overseers" by "deliberately opaque means" such as singing, dancing, and acting, revealing a "politics of transfiguration" that reflects community needs for solidarity that is "magically made audible in the music itself and palpable in the social relations of its cultural utility and reproduction" (37).[18] In *Mules and Men*, Hurston describes similar tactics about the experience of collecting Black folklore: "Folklore is not as easy to collect as it sounds . . . the Negro, in spite of his open faced laughter, his seeming acquiescence, is particularly evasive. You see we are a polite people and we do not say to our questioner, 'Get out of here!' We smile and tell him or her something that satisfies the white person because, knowing so little about us, he doesn't know what he is missing" (1935, 2–3). Distortions in Hurston's recordings resist sociotechnical processes of authority, authenticity, and subjectivation on which traditional forms of cultural representation in the archive still rely.

June 1935

In June 1935, Hurston took a recording trip for the Library of Congress with Lomax and Barnicle to Frederica, Georgia, and to Belle Glade, Chosen, and Eatonville in Florida.[19] The "Traditional Music and Spoken Word Catalog" from the Library of Congress's American Folklife Center notes more than 700 tracks from the trip, each a few minutes long (American Folklife Center).[20] Information included in the catalog and subsequently in the online metadata comes from a trip log, which was almost certainly written by Lomax.[21] Lomax's log comprises contextual information about the 1935 tracks, including the technical quality and the circumstances of their making, the performers, the type of performance, and the context—such as when it was a group of all men or all women, and when a third party participated in what was being collected. The catalog derived from Lomax's log lists only seven tracks with a specific role for Hurston. Five of the seven tracks are labeled "card playing songs" or "work songs" (American Folklife Center, Traditional Music and Spoken Word Catalog). Lomax's log has similar information but often includes more detailed notations. On his log, "Can't You Line It?" ("Shove it Over," 3136 A) and "Some Old Cold, Rainy Day" (362 B) include the notation "sung by A. B Hicks, trained by Zora Hurston," and the tracks "O Lula" (364 A01) and "Going to See My Long-Haired Baby" (364 A02) are labeled with "sung by A. B. Hicks, under the direction of Zora Hurston"; "Let the Deal Go Down" is a "card playing song, sung by A. B. Hicks, trained and taught this song by Zora Hurston for her folk-opera, A Day in the Section Gang"; "Bella Mina," a round-dance recorded in Chosen, Florida, includes a notation that reads "Miss Hurston had to lead this song because the Negroes had forgotten it" (Todd Harvey, email to the author, September 17, 2020). In the "Traditional Music and Spoken Word Catalog," "Bella Mina" (377 B01) is the only 1935 song credited to Hurston in which she is a "performer" (American Folklife Center). In accordance with Lomax's log and the "Traditional Music and Spoken Word Catalog," the searchable online Library of Congress catalog labels Hurston (along with Barnicle and Lomax) as "recordist" and "collector" for the remainder of the 1935 Florida and Georgia recordings, except for the seventh recording, "Interview with Wallace Quarterman," a former slave interview for which Hurston and her

Distortion 55

colleagues Barnicle and Lomax are also identified as "interviewers" (Hurston, Lomax, and Barnicle 1935).

Listening closely to the recordings and in contrast to what was listed by Lomax and the Library of Congress, Hurston was not only recording or performing in the field: on at least seventy-five of the 1935 recordings, she can be heard consistently and actively participating by directing, gathering information, and otherwise engaging the performers. In the recording of the sea shanty "See Day Dawning," for example, Hurston stops the singers to redirect their song: "Just a minute," she says. "It's coming out like I like it now because if you're leading you got to come out" (336 B). In addition, there are five game songs performed by an "unidentified group of children" collected in Frederica, Georgia, during which Hurston can be heard organizing and directing the children. In the song "All Around the Maypole," Hurston says, "all the children," as if urging them on, and then later directs them to "get up" and "come on" (309 A01). In another game song titled "Steal Miss Liza Jane," she encourages that someone "steal somebody," as per the rules of the game (349 B02). In the spirituals "How about You" and "Coming Home Some Day," Lomax's notation says that "Three little girls between 4 and 8" sing, but I can also hear Hurston guiding them at the beginning and end of the recordings: "Alright," Hurston says to encourage them to begin the first song. She then talks to them when they conclude their singing, prompting them to say their names, and says "okay" to mark the end of the recording session (329 A; 329 B). At the end of "Coming," Hurston can be heard discussing with the girls (or possibly with a colleague) about "singing it over again" (329 B).

When not actively directing the performances, Hurston is engaging with her participants by singing along and generally encouraging them as an audience participant. Hurston is particularly enthusiastic on some of the tracks recorded in her hometown Eatonville, presumably with people she knows or with whom she feels especially familiar. On the track "Careless Love," she joins into the raucous song and sings the line, "Never love a married man" (318 A01). On the spirituals "Leaning on the Lord" and "Sangaree," Hurston can be heard laughing, singing, and clapping (320 B01; 323 B01). On "Sangaree," her tone is both mischievous and merry when she introduces the singer as "John Davis, the big cock, leading Sangaree" (323 B01). Similarly, when the same John Davis is telling the tales "John and his Rival," "John Whips the Giant," "John and the Bear," and "John and the Coon," Hurston responds encouragingly, laughing, sometimes almost screeching with hilarity (347

A02; 348 A01; 348 A02; 348 B01; 348 B02). During "John and the Bear," she says, "John was always tall talking, wasn't he?" During "John and the Coon," she confirms with the storyteller, "He must have been telling fortunes beforehand" (348 B01; 348Bb02). On other recordings, Hurston is concerned with the recording logistics, such as when she asks on "Chain Gang Holler" to the loud group before she gets cut off, "Now everybody on the porch could you please not . . . ," and when she enquires of Lomax, "Alan, you ready?," at the beginning of the shanty "I Ain't Going to Hurt Nobody" (337 A; 335 A).

There are both social and technological distortions behind why Hurston's participation in these performances is not well represented in the Library of Congress catalogs. In the first instance, Hurston's influence was not recognized as authoritative by her white collaborators. The ultimate goal on these trips was to create an "unbiased" verisimilitude of Black folk tales and songs (Roulston 2019), and Lomax would have wanted to capture influences in his recording log that he perceived might influence an event's authenticity. Hurston's absence from Lomax's descriptions means he did not find her role in the recordings substantial enough to note.[22] Secondly, the continued silencing around her participation in the online metadata is, in part, the legacy of Lomax's choices. The information originally collected by Lomax is mapped into the MARC (Machine-Readable Cataloging) standard, which has been the schema used to describe and catalogue cultural artifacts, including these recordings, for digital representation in the Library of Congress since the 1970s. The "relator terms" in the MARC standard, which identify the roles that participants play in a recording, are restricted to traditional roles of influence. As such, there are no terms that correspond to collaborative roles that demarcate the kind of "director," "active audience member," or "enthusiast" that Hurston would have occupied (Network Development and MARC Standards Office 2021). Instead, in MARC, terms like "stage director" are reserved for "a person or organization contributing to a stage resource through the overall management and supervision of a performance" (Network Development and MARC Standards Office 2021). For Lomax and the subsequent catalogers (who may or may not have listened to the recordings), Hurston's activities did not fit the schema for prescribed roles of influence either in the social world of Lomax and his fellow ethnographers or within the MARC standard. The presence of these distortions prompts the questions: Who and what has authorized which and how historical artifacts are made available for scholarship? Through and by which technologies?

Technical distortions also mark why the recording log, the metadata, and prevailing scholarship for these artifacts elide the complex and influential roles that Hurston played during these recording sessions. The recording machine used for the 1935 and the 1939 trips appears to be the same Soundscriber Field Recording Machine built by Lincoln Thompson of Sound Specialties, loaned in 1939 to Florida's WPA program by the Library of Congress's Archive of the American Folk Song (later the American Folk Center).[23] The Library of Congress description for both the 1935 and the 1939 collections explains why the quality of the recordings is sometimes low:

> The field recordings were made on acetate disks, usually recorded at 78 rpm (although occasionally at 33 rpm). Because these disks were shipped from Washington DC to Florida, then to the recording site, and then back to Washington, these disks often were not of the highest sonic quality. Several had surface scratches, and many had various recording speeds. In 1986, the FFP staff made copies of many of these recordings onto reel to reels for inclusion to the Florida Folklife Archive. (Federal Writers' Project of the Work Projects Administration for the State of Florida.)

This description correlates with notes in Lomax's log that describe errors in the recording process, including "Bad Strip Spoiled by Failing Battery" and "Bad Strip, spoiled by changing turn-table speed" (Todd Harvey, email to the author, September 17, 2020). Digitization notes kept later by the Library of Congress during digitization in the 1980s indicate other causes for audio distortion, including that the recordings were often "overmodulated" or the grooves are "poor," "bad," or "collapsed," causing the needle to skip (Todd Harvey, email to the author, September 17, 2020).

Distortions on the recordings may result in sound that is missing or garbled, or it may introduce noises that the audio engineers decided to smooth over or delete. Distortions on all the tracks of "John Henry" stories told by John Davis present as clicks and static on the recording. The digitization notes on the "John and the Rival" track indicate that a "slight mistracking midway through recording results in noisy playback" (347 A02) and the "last groove skips" on "John and the Bear" (348 B01) (Todd Harvey, email to the author, September 17, 2020). On playback, the loud static makes the stories almost inaudible or difficult to discern, especially when Davis is animated and expressing a rise in tension between the characters John and Massa. The more emphatic Davis becomes—raising his voice and quickening his speech—and the more laughter he encourages from his audience (who seem to be sitting very close to the microphone), the more the cacophony of sounds—different voices, different laughter, and static—blend together. At such moments, it becomes difficult or impossible to distinguish the words Davis is saying from the surrounding noise. In another example, notes about the recordings where Hurston is speaking to and singing with the little girls playing games mark a "bad strip." The voices wow and warble on these recordings, warping into a higher pitch such that everyone sounds like a small child (309 A01; 309 B02; 310 B01; 310 B02). The same is true when Hurston joins in on the line "Never love a married man" and sings on "Leaning on the Lord"—for these recordings the digitization log notes that the original recording is "overmodulated" or recorded too loud (Todd Harvey, email to the author, September 17, 2020). Again, on these spiritual tracks, the pervasive flutter makes the timbre of Hurston's voice almost indistinguishable from the other female singers.

In some cases, the choices that sound editors made to ameliorate these distortions and to create a "cleaner" preservation copy in the transference from disc to digital included deleting some of the audio that the engineer considered superfluous. For the song "He's a Dying Bed-Maker" the notes say, "Last 15 seconds difficult to transfer. Tried several passes until successful. Digitally edited different passes together to preserve content" (Todd Harvey, email to the author, September 17, 2020). The notes for the "John Henry" stories generally specify that there is "skipping between cuts" and that the audio engineer "reduced skipping with digital editing." On the extant digital recordings, there are numerous instances of background conversations cut off in mid-speech. These kinds of edits could easily have deleted incidences of Hurston's voice. She often speaks before a performance, such as asking, "Alan, you ready?"; in between songs or stories, such as in the background on "He's a Dying Bed-Maker"; or, as when she can be heard introducing the speakers in "See Day Dawning," after a performance (336 B). There is no way of knowing if audio editors seeking to diminish the presence of what they perceived as distortion and to preserve what they considered more authentic or significant "content" deleted incidences of Hurston's voice from these recordings.

Distortions introduced in how the 1935 recordings were cataloged, edited, and digitized diminish the means of authenticating Hurston's voice and the stories as "the same" as those in Hurston's published texts, but also transform the recordings into interrogative texts and their production into an invitation to question how scholars engage with Hurston's work.[24] There are four tracks titled "John and Old Mistis' Nightgown," "John and his Rival," "John and the Bear," and "John and the Coon" that also appear as "collected" by Hurston in *Mules and Men* (1935) and in *Every Tongue Got to Confess: Negro Folk-Tales from the Gulf States* (2001).[25] On listening to the recordings, the evolution of the tales from what the storyteller says to what Hurston has published is unclear because there are few audible words that can act as an indicator to the written text.[26] Words like "bear," "panther," "coon under the tub," "on the clothesline" are audible among other phrases, but, more often, distorted voices make trying to track how those words and concepts correspond to the texts difficult. Mostly what is audible is the storyteller's exuberant barking, cat calling, whooping, and raucous laughter. The words are indiscernible, but the tone is discernibly joyous, especially that of an unnamed woman in the background (Hurston?) who cackles on and on as though the idea of John outwitting Massa is the funniest thing she's ever heard.

As Hurston writes in her 1934 essay "Characteristics of Negro Expression," "It is obvious that to get back to original sources is much too difficult for any group to claim very much as a certainty" (1981, 58). At the same time, the distortions resonate with Hurston's own ethnographic practices precisely because they introduce complexity and a pluralism of meanings, forcing scholars to suspend more traditional notions of authenticity and authority. "Is this Hurston or not?" becomes a less productive question than "How are authenticity and authority functioning both in the moment of the recording and in current scholarship around Hurston's Black folk work?" These shifts in perspectives bring an analysis of these recordings closer to Hurston's own practice of "deconstructive ethnography," which includes "confront[ing] the plays of power in our processes of interpretation" (Visweswaran 1994, 9).

June 1939

On June 18, 1939, Hurston participated in a recording session for the Federal Writers' Project (FWP) at the Federal Music Project Office of the Work Projects Administration (WPA) in Jacksonville, Florida, with Carita Doggett Corse, Herbert Halpert, and Stetson Kennedy.[27] The session was part of Herbert Halpert's nine-state fieldwork tour of the South between March 12 and June 30, 1939, and included a wide range of people from the community sharing their songs and stories. That day, Halbert recorded Hurston, but also Cuban musicians (including Art Pages), African American workers from the camps including (Harold B. Hazelhurst), an African American preacher (Rev. H. W. Stuckey) and congregant (Irene Jackson), as well as two African American women (Alabama Singleton and Maggie Fulton) and two white women (Beatrice Lange and Evelyn Werner). The Florida Memory Project of the State Library and Archives of Florida digitized the June 18 reels and made three available online. Additionally, to highlight Hurston's performances on the reels, the Florida Memory Project extracted them into an online playlist of twenty brief tracks collectively titled "Dust Tracks" (Hurston, "Dust Tracks").[28]

Resonant with Wright's criticism of Hurston's folklore writings, the "Dust Tracks" playlist gives a singular impression of Hurston's performance of Black folk as spectacle. Many of the stories and songs that Hurston performs in 1939 were performed by Black men and women she had met in the 1920s and 1930s who worked in Florida sawmills and turpentine camps, and who laid down tracks as part of the Florida East Coast Railway. These workers were part of a system formally known as penal servitude and peonage, or "debt slavery," in which an employer compelled a worker to pay off a debt with work.[29] In the songs that Hurston performs, workers describe their conditions in the camps, including where they sleep, what they eat, how physically difficult the work is, and how "Boss" treats them. Their songs and stories often portray how slaves making cartoonish attempts to mimic white society are consequently punished (often physically) or how a slave named John, often under the threat of a lashing or a hanging, eventually outwits "Ole Massa" to escape punishment.[30] Other songs and stories include sexual relationships, where men deceive women and women respond with physical violence or vice versa. The folklore Hurston performs on "Dust Tracks" is often bawdy, sardonic, or witty and seems, when extracted from the longer reels, to elide the suffering that is clearly the physical and psychological stress that the men and women represented in Hurston's Black folk faced in their daily lives.

In contrast, close listening to these performances in the context of the "between-story conversation and business"—included on the longer reels but not included in "Dust Tracks"—amplifies how Hurston's performances went beyond mere spectacle to create a complex subjectivity for "my people" that she would later realize in her writing.[31] Hurston was not a sole performer on these tapes. The larger recording context included Cuban artists, African

American workers, and other Black and white women singing songs and telling stories. On one track, WPA director Carita Doggett Corse marvels at how "interesting" it is "that we have influences from the West Indies as well as the rural South in our Florida Negro folklore," even as Hurston reminds Corse that the songs are sung as a means of "African survival" and that their international roots are tied to a slave trade where tribes were mixed. In contrast to a unified "Florida" folklore, Hurston explains that folklore has a complex sociopolitical and geographic history that is by nature difficult to categorize as regional. Hurston and others sing songs that are "sung in Key West and Miami and Palm Beach and out in the Everglades where a great number of Nassaus are working in the bean fields and whatnot." When asked where she learned what she will perform for the recording, Hurston responds, "I'm going to sing, oh I guess, all the tune is the same. I'm going to sing verses from a whole lots of places." Moreover, after singing "Mule on the Mount," she notes that "the tune is consistent but the verses, you know how things, in every locality you can find some new verses, everywhere."[32] When Halpert later asks who taught her the song "Halimuhfack," Hurston describes its origins as communal in nature, emphasizing how the construction of authenticity around origins can be antithetical to how folklore is created: "I don't remember. I was in a big crowd, and I learned it in the evening during the crowd. And I'm just, don't can't exactly remember who I, who did teach it to me, but I learned it from the crowd most exactly more from one." This sentiment is repeated when "a Latin group now playing at the Cuban Club in Tampa Florida" begins singing traditional Cuban songs. Halpert asks the group's pianist, Art Pages, where and how one of the songs has been learned and he answers that "there is no way of tracing it to its author or its originality. It has just been picked from one generation to the other."[33] Of multiple origins, the varied folk art and performers on the longer recordings point to folk art as a live art, created dynamically and differently each time a song or story is performed.

In contrast to listening to the "Dust Tracks" playlist and much more in line with reading Hurston's folklore in *Mules and Men*, the longer recordings invite a listening experience in which Hurston's performances are juxtaposed with other interviews in which participants narrate their own stories. The comparison between Hurston's performance and the interviews with the other women is essential for understanding how Hurston performs what Lynda Marion Hill (1996) calls "a radical inauthenticity of subject" by conveying a sense of cultural alterity through an "encounter with an alien Other" (309). For example, Maggie Fulton, Irene Jackson, and Alabama Singleton, who are Black, sing children's songs and describe children's games from their youth, explaining the context in which the children sang and played (at church, around the maypole, or at the market). The stories and games are reminiscent of those that Hurston has collected in her writings, where children are joyfully mimicking the daily habits of their elders. Laughter marks their performances. When Halpert asks Singleton to pat her hands like the children whose songs she sings, she laughs. Irene Jackson also laughs when Halpert asks her to sing her song like she did when she was a child, without instruments such as the guitar she wants to play for him. It's not clear what Halpert asks Fulton when she sings a childhood song, but she giggles lightly when she replies, "Just a little barnyard play."[34]

In comparison to the Black participants, Beatrice Lange and Evelyn Werner do not talk about their own lives. Instead, they tell stories that have been passed to them from land- and slave-owning families, marking their privileged lineage. Lange's stories were told to her by the son of a rice plantation owner from Georgia who was in turn told the story by "this old negro of his" who "belonged to his father." Using different voices for different Black characters, Lange performs an old slave's speech with a whiny tone of voice and poor grammar, making him sound like a recalcitrant child. She insists on reading from a paper in her hand, even though Halpert extols her to "tell it" rather than "read it." Lange continues to resist Halpert's prompting to perform the narrative without her written script, saying "Well, I'll kind of glance at it," and then more assertively, "Just let me glance at it." She laughs nervously each time she gives this response. Lange, focused on getting through her written material, hastily rushes over the "punch line" of one story to launch into the next one before Halpert can correct her again. Werner, who "studied voice in Chicago" and was told her story "by one of the heirs to the Reed Plantation," also uses her voice to differentiate the white and Black characters to dramatic effect. She tells the story of a newly freed Black mother who offers her troublesome child back to her master's wife, and when she concludes her "punch line," she stops abruptly, laughing nervously and saying, "That's all." When Werner concludes her story, Halpert asks Dr. Corse to "please explain why did we ask to have this record made?" Ostensibly, the request is made in order that they provide a record of the ethnographic process: Corse promptly responds, "This record was made for the purpose of recording the annunciation of an educated Southern white voice." Someone in the background, in a voice that could be Hurston's, clarifies the description by adding in an almost inaudible, under-the-breath comment, "educated white woman."[35]

Like this sidenote, Hurston's performances are a comment on how authority and authenticity function in the other (Black and white) women's recorded sessions. Hurston is both the authoritative narrator and the narrativized, the insider and the outsider, the subject and the object of study. In general, she is comfortable, even enthusiastic, with the interviewing process and knowledgeable about the recording objectives, explaining her observations with comfortable enthusiasm. When she is performing for Halpert a song about how working men rhythmically strike railroad lines while singing, she is all the while banging a stick on a table. She often laughs and guffaws in joy. She is perceived by her white counterparts to be an intellectual (and fun!) asset to the project. Typically, when Hurston sings these songs on the recordings, she is personally absent from the narrative; she is the impartial observer. These are songs she has simply "learned from the crowd," she says. Her positionality and dual subjectivity in the interview process offers possibilities for altered modes of enunciation for the other participants.[36] It is possible the white women laugh awkwardly in chagrin or distress because Hurston is in the room taking on the responsibilities of the ethnographer and disrupting how they think Black women should behave. It is also possible that Singleton, Fulton, and Jackson are, like Hurston, laughing because they feel empowered, "not tragically colored," but quite excited "to hold the center of the national stage" (Hurston 1979, 153).

Hurston's own laugh provides yet another reading. Traces of the boundary between Hurston's dual roles as insider and outsider and consequently the precarity of her position as a Black female authority performing authentic Black folk material are marked with her own awkward laugh when she sings a "jook" song for Halpert. In Hurston's experience, the jook houses—which she explains in a letter to Langston Hughes as a "baudy [sic] house in its general sense" (2002, 143)—were establishments on the camps where men and women would play and listen to music, dance, love, and brawl, free from white observation. The songs reflect the complex tenor of the establishments for Black women by combining a disrespect for white laws that govern Black bodies with lewd songs about women. When Hurston sings "Tampa," for instance, it includes these lyrics: "Thought I heard someone says 'nasty butt, stinky butt, take it away. I do not want it in here. Oh, I'm so glad the law has changed. The women in Tampa got to wipe their ass. Oh I do not want it in here . . . hold up the window, let the stink go out . . . nasty butt, stinky butt, take it away. I do not want it in here.'" In "Po Boy," she sings: "Laid in jail, my back turned to the wall. Coming a time when a woman don't need no man. . . . Mistreat me you mistreated more than this gal"; and in "Mama Don't Want No Peas No Rice," she sings about a wife and a mother who cannot perform these roles because, as her husband laments, "All she wants is Whiskey Brandy all the time." It is when Hurston sings "Uncle Bud"—a song about his being aggressive with women, his "shitting turds," and how low his testicles hang—that Halpert interrupts her performance, questioning her on a more personal level. Halpert asks, "Is it sung before the respectable ladies?" Hurston responds quickly in a raised pitch and an emphatic tone, "Never! It's one of those jook songs and the woman that they sing Uncle Bud in front of is a jook woman." Halpert rebukes her, teasing, "I thought you heard it from women." Laughing, Hurston answers more slowly with a lowered voice and a softer tone, "Yes, I heard it from women." The laugh points to Hurston's changed subject position from impartial observer and professional anthropologist to an observed member of a marked group of Black women who are signified as "jook women." She, like the other Black participants, is suddenly put into a positionality that sits in contrast to the "educated white women" and "the respectable ladies" in the room.[37] Her laugh, like the other women's laughs (Black and white), signals their precarious worth in relation to white and male privilege.

Hurston's laugh can be heard differently again based on her performance in 1935 in "See Day Dawning"—the recording with which this chapter begins. On the tape, Hurston suddenly does something curious. This is the only recording in which she purposefully breaks the fourth wall to talk to an invisible audience. After Henry Blue and "an unidentified male group" stop singing, there is a 15 second pause broken only by the *wow, wow, wow,* of the audibly turning disc, and then Hurston does her usual routine, reciting the song's genre, the singer's name, where it was sung, and the date: "This sea shanty sung by Henry Blue in St. Simon Island, May 11, 1935," she says (336 B). A sea shanty was cheering, as Herman Melville describes it in *Redburn* (1849), and a means by which the men kept up their progress and their spirits while hoisting the sail, but it was also a method by

Distortion

which the sea captain kept the men in line. In *Redburn*, a seaman notes that "with such a cheering accompaniment, I am sure the song was well worth the breath expended on it," but also that "some sea-captains, before shipping a man, always ask him whether he can sing out at a rope" (1849, 43). Perhaps it is because of the same dual role the songs played for the workers on the train tracks, the turpentine mills, and the fields that Hurston blurts after the pause in a raised, aggressively happy, sing-songy, carnival auctioneer's voice: "All the men are pulling on a rope and singing for all their worth, folks!" (336 B). In any case, Hurston's strange tone makes this last moment seem like a resonant disruption. On hearing these words after the performance of a song that evokes suffering men, singing in their struggle to hoist the sails for a global industry that is built on their blood and sweat, it seems that Hurston has turned their song into a kind of carnival act. Her tone implies that she has turned to the machine—like turning to the camera in a sitcom—to talk to an audience, possibly one she imagines in the near or far future. The listener wonders: What is Hurston trying to sell? And to whom? Is it for a white audience? Is it a tongue-in-cheek wink to a Black audience? Why? And, of course, who's to say that is Hurston on the recording at all? In the cataloger's description, she goes unnamed, and the date she gives is different from the historical notes taken by Lomax: the date she gives is off.[38]

* * *

The presence of social and technical distortions in Hurston's recordings resists simplified notions of authority and authenticity on which protocols for preservation, access, and scholarship in academia, anthropology, and government are based. Distortions are a reminder that space, time, and personhood are relative to the tools and people at hand. On the 1935 recordings, Hurston sounds present. I hear her as an active and authoritative voice, but the copresence of sociotechnical distortions on the recordings and associated logs and metadata resist my own practices of subjectivation that would name her and that would have her name her subjects—many of whom also remain unnamed in the recording log and the resulting metadata. The 1935 and 1939 recordings invite scholars to consider how the social and technical distortions in Hurston's fieldwork can amplify lower frequencies that disrupt the cultural record, so that scholars can hear institutional processes for what they are: methods for fixing identity, time, and place to construct a history and culture that serves a particular narrative. She who is recording, recognizing, and naming the Black other goes unrecognized, remains *un*named, and goes unrecorded in authorized representations of these events,[39] but the sociotechnical distortion in the recordings that mark her absence also mark possibilities for resonance, inviting conjecture and opening up the recordings as interrogative texts that inform alternate understandings of Hurston's complex presentations of Black folk. When Mrs. Rolla Southworth, state director of the Professional Service Projects of the WPA in Florida says on one 1939 recording, "My greatest interest is in the Negro Folklore and how justly proud we all are of Zora Hurston, whose fine literary ability and wealth of experience has made our recordings possible today," I consider Hurston's many "off-key" ways of gathering, recording, and preserving the Black folk for which Mrs. Rolla Southworth is claiming such pride.[40] Distorted performances of Black culture by white culture also play out to alternate ends in Hurston's published folklore collections, where there is a wide range of stories about Black slaves and workers who laugh, play, and love. There is, of course, the fast-talking John Henry, who regularly outwits the master and the devil, but there are also the Black women who fight for authority like Big Sweet in *Mules and Men* or like Janie in *Their Eyes Were Watching God* and go on to author their own lives.

I was forced to listen, and in listening I soon became involved to the point of identification.
—Ralph Ellison (1995, 232)

3 Interference: Silence and the Ideal Listener in Ralph Ellison's American Novel

Audio recordings from the 1953 Harvard School Summer Conference on the Contemporary Novel went unheard for over sixty years until they were rediscovered in the basement of a Harvard library in 2014. The 7.5-inch reel-to-reel tapes on which the conference was recorded were cataloged and pristine, housed in a climate-controlled subbasement of Houghton Library. Curator Christina Davis found the recordings when looking for reels to digitize, and years later, she discovered more uncataloged recordings from the conference, which were among thousands of reels with half-inch wide spines and appeared unlabeled until she pulled out the respective reel container (Ireland 2014; email to author, September 19, 2022). Their boxes were marked only faintly with the vague and undated title "Harv. Sum. School Novel Conf." The reel boxes had been disguised like any other book on the shelf next to the spines of works by e. e. cummings, Emily Dickinson, and William Shakespeare.[1] The more recent discovery includes Ralph Ellison's lecture at the 1953 conference, which, because the newly discovered reels still needed to be processed, has been heard by very few scholars at the time of this writing.

His talk and the conversations around it at the Harvard conference are noteworthy because in 1953 Ralph Ellison's novel *Invisible Man* (1952)—about a Black activist born in the South who has migrated to 1930s Harlem and struggles with issues of society, individualism, and identity—had recently won the National Book Award, becoming the first book by an African American author to be given that honor. Summer 1953 was also a significant time for the landmark desegregation case *Brown v. Board of Education*, for which the US Supreme Court had at the time of the conference recently ordered a second round of arguments. The politics of segregation introduced a moment in US history that amplified what was personally and socially at stake within democratic ideals for African Americans—a topic about which Ellison wrote passionately—yet Ellison's Harvard lecture, fittingly titled "Certain Neglected Aspects of the American Novel," would refer only generally to segregation, simply calling it "the great moral problem of American life, centered around discrimination and so forth—the unfreedom which lies within the land of freedom" (Harvard Summer School, August 3–5, 1953).

Ellison's *Invisible Man* seems almost prescient of the lost recordings and Ellison's silences on them. When the unnamed, "invisible" narrator in the novel has just witnessed the killing by police of Tod Clifton, a young Black youth leader in Harlem, the narrator considers how such a man as Clifton or himself will go unrecorded by historians who hold the power of making history:

> All things, it is said, are duly recorded—all things of importance, that is. But not quite, for actually it is only the known, the seen, the heard, and only those events that the recorder regards as important that are put down, those lies his keepers keep their power by.... What did they ever think of us transitory ones?... birds of passage who were too obscure for learned classification, too silent for the most sensitive recorders of sound; of natures too ambiguous for the most ambiguous words, and too distant from the centers of historical decision to sign or even to applaud the signers of historical documents? We who write no novels, histories or other books. What about us, I thought, seeing Clifton again in my mind. (Ellison 1952, 439)

Ellison and his fellow participants at the conference were all well-known men of letters and were readily picked up by Harvard's recording machine, so it is perhaps ironic that the conference during which he discussed his novel was nevertheless lost to history. In this case, a close listening to the recordings reveals a process of cultural silencing that goes deeper than the mislabeling of boxes. Ellison's writings about the role of cultural institutions, moral imagination in the novel, dialogic listeners, and audio technology reframes how I listen to the Harvard recordings. Instead of absence, I perceive silences on the recordings as agential *interferences* that make resonant the unknown, the unseen, and the unheard. Listening to Ellison's lecture within the context of his writings, this chapter considers how what is picked up and put on tape can also include traces of the unclassified in history that are resonant precisely *because* they are too silent for the most sensitive recorders of sound.

The August 1953 Harvard Summer School Conference

The August 1953 Harvard Summer School Conference was proposed to facilitate dialogue and to record it. When panel chairman Professor Carvel Collins begins the conference, he describes how it will proceed: each night in Sanders Theatre in Memorial Hall, two participants will give talks, followed by another participant who will respond to the talks, "and we hope further entangle the two speakers and arguments with each other" (Harvard Summer School, August 3–5, 1953). Each evening would be followed by afternoon sessions with lectures by chosen panelists and questions from a private audience in Harvard's Forum Room. Intended to be "a model of postwar inclusive and participatory architecture" and a "new-world-order," the Forum Room had as its centerpiece a turntable and a state-of-the-art sound system, including microphones, speakers, and recording machines, signifying the essential role that sound technology would play in the conversations taking place there (McCarthy, Alison, and Devlin 2020). Noting that many of the participants may not have been used to being recorded, Collins introduced the room's recording system to the participants by reminding the speakers to each "just rise where he is," clarifying, "The way they are scattered around is such that they will pick up the sound for this particular room. So, instead of spending the afternoon stumbling over each other's feet, just speak from where you are at that point" (Harvard Summer School, August 3–5, 1953).

Speaking from where they were intellectually, the conference speakers and respondents represented a mixed combination of backgrounds and experiences. Beyond esteemed literary critics and professors Carvel Collins and Wilbur Merrill Frohock, there was Hans Egon Holthusen, a lyric poet, a scholar, and a German Nazi; Stanley Edgar Hyman, a staff writer at the *New Yorker*, raised as an Orthodox Jew; Frank O'Connor, an Irish writer and member of the Anti-Treaty Irish Republican Army during the Irish Civil War; Georges Simenon, a Belgian author investigated for being a Nazi sympathizer; and Anthony West, the son of British authors Rebecca West and H. G. Wells and author of *Heritage* (1955), an autobiographical novel about being an affluent child shuffled between England and France and neglected by his famous parents. Andrew Nelson Lytle, a critic and professor at the University of the South who was associated with the Southern Agrarians—a group of scholars who heralded the "old South" and largely ignored histories of slavery and espoused and propagated New Criticism in US academic circles—was also present. From where Ellison stood, he was the only African American on the otherwise white male list of scholars and writers.[2]

Perhaps it is not surprising, given their disparate backgrounds, that the participants did not always agree on what became a central point of debate during the course of the conference: whether or not the novel was "an act of the moral imagination" (Harvard Summer School, August 4–5, 1953).[3] Frohock, Lytle, O'Connor, and others would argue that form, aesthetics, and beauty in the novel could exist without a moral purpose and that the author's work could be "purely aesthetic." On one recording, an audience member identified as "Mr. Humes" calls the moral imagination "a useless tool" in the creation of art since art is inherently without a utilitarian purpose in an industrialized society; if you "inject the notion of moral . . . as a creative factor in the construction of a thing of beauty," Humes says, then adds, "it seems to me that we are no longer talking about art, we are talking about the style of a new Ford" (Harvard Summer School, August 4–5, 1953).[4] In contrast, Ellison explains during a panel session that he believes that "despite our intentions, the novel does perform a moral role and the imagination is moral simply because it creates value" (Harvard Summer School, August 4–5, 1953). He also asserts during his lecture that the novel performs that moral role by being "a familiar experience of a particular people within a particular society," which by "appealing to that which we 'know,' uh, that is our body of common assumptions . . . it can proceed to reveal to us that which we do not know or it can confirm that which we believe to be reality" (Harvard Summer School, August 3–5, 1953).

For Ellison, that familiar reality in the United States necessarily concerned race. A key incident in the particulars of Ellison's personal and social experiences in this essay and other writings was *Brown v. Board of Education*. On July 24, less than two weeks before the conference, Ellison jokes about desegregation and his participation in the conference in a letter to his friend Albert Murray, "I'm to speak thirty minutes about the American novel that are apt to [be] thirty of the damnedest [sic] minutes I ever spent. This doggone integration thing maybe is going too fast" (2019, 333). Further, in his essay "Twentieth-Century Fiction and the Black Mask of Humanity,"[5] which he updated for publication after the conference, he discusses the moral role of the novelist specifically as it relates to segregation.[6] He writes,

> Perhaps the ideal approach to the work of literature would be one allowing for insight into the deepest psychological motives of the writer at the same time that it examined all external sociological factors operating within a given milieu. For while objectively a social reality, the work of art is, in its genesis, a projection of a deeply personal process, and any approach that ignores the personal at the expense of the social is necessarily incomplete. Thus, when we approach contemporary writing from the perspective of segregation, as is commonly done by sociologically minded thinkers, we automatically limit ourselves to one external aspect of a complex whole, which leaves us little to say concerning its personal, internal elements. (Ellison 1995, 84)

In the essay, Ellison calls the moral imagination "the fountainhead of great art," and asserts that it is "atrophied" by the clash of ideals inherent to segregation between "the idealized ethic of the Constitution and the Declaration of the Independence, reserved for the white men" and "the pragmatic ethic designed for Negroes and other minorities, which took the form of discrimination" (1995, 91–92, 83).

In contrast to these writings, Ellison seemingly evades the topic of segregation in his comments at the conference and masks his own experiences with current racial politics. In his lecture, he begins by dealing with the revolutionary origins of the United States and discussing African American life or politics in general terms as "symboli[c] of the confusion of democratic ideals," touching on slavery and Reconstruction in a plural personal "we" pronoun that strategically creates an affinity of nationhood between himself and the majority-white audience.[7] He then emphasizes a collective, national post-Reconstruction moral fatigue:

> But, it was with the twentieth century, after reconstruction, after the war, when we decided that we could no longer sustain the uncertainty of fighting this thing out. We had lost many people on both sides and we had made a shambles of many possibilities. We did, however, create others. Thank God. And we were tired. We were no longer willing to face the tragic implications of American life. (Harvard Summer School, August 3–5, 1953)

Continuing to create affinities with his primarily white audience, he talks about his time as a soldier in World War II, when he joined the US Merchant Marine as a cook, and discusses famous, white American authors like William Faulkner, Ernest Hemingway, Herman Melville, Gertrude Stein, John Steinbeck, and Mark Twain. When Ellison pivots to a singular, first-person "I" during his talk, he almost immediately links that "I" with a more personal direct appeal to each audience member by using "you." In this context, he forms a collective "we" with his audience that is in opposition to "other Americans," and he refers somewhat evasively to current racial politics as a fortunate "change at hand":

> What I'm trying to say is this: We assume that America is a known country. It is not a known country. If you go out to Oklahoma, as I have been recently, you'll find that people are different, that distance makes differences, that the air, the climate, the way of life. It's all a part of America. We all speak the same language, but it's not the same thing, it's different. And part of the task of the novel is that of documenting this unknownness. As Mr. Simenon just pointed out, we are curious or should be curious about other Americans. Fortunately, there is a change coming. In fact, there is a change at hand. We are no longer blaming one section of the country for the faults of the other section. (Harvard Summer School, August 3–5, 1953)

Citing the novelist's responsibility "to make America known to Americans and to help forge the image of the American," he strangely uses the example of Anglo-Saxons and Catholics instead of race as a notable difference between Americans, even as he refers to himself in the example: "We usually assume an American to be represented by an Anglo-Saxon of Protestant background, I suppose," he says. "Maybe in Boston it would be a Catholic, but actually we know that the American is many things, many many things and we are still, at least I am still puzzled to know what he is. I know that I am but just what I am is as much a mystery to me as the mystery of what Boston is or what Harvard is" (Harvard Summer School, August 3–5, 1953). After speaking for forty minutes, Ellison concludes by reflecting on the extent to which a present-day reader turns to nonfiction to seek "answers" he cannot find in fiction. With another vague reference to current politics and seemingly referring to desegregation, Ellison empathizes with his reading audience who "sees change around him" and experiences "a certain degree of uncertainty [come] back into relationships."

His obfuscated references to desegregation are made apparent when at this moment in Ellison's talk he suddenly shares an anecdote different in tenor than the rest of his lecture: he speaks directly from his personal experience of segregation and integration. He says:

> I can remember walking during this spring when I was in North Carolina into a certain room in which a woman became physically ill, not because she had anything against me. She was quite willing to have me there, but I violated something which had given her world stability for years and years and she could not

stand this. Her will could not dominate the physical revulsion which this woman felt. (Harvard Summer School, August 3–5, 1953)

In this description, Ellison's tone of voice marks the silent topics on which he has chosen not to engage with this audience. His tone does not change. Ellison relates this possibly horrific moment with the casual tenor of one who is used to this behavior, who is not surprised. He even, again, grants sympathy to the white woman. The poor woman just couldn't help it, he seems to imply. Mitigating any distancing the story might have engendered with his audience, he depersonalizes her physical reaction from her "will" or her moral sense of right and wrong. Standing on the stage at Harvard in 1953 in front of a large, primarily white audience (a "grand of people"),[8] Ellison would, except for this one small moment, adhere generally and collectively to the topic about which he was invited to speak, African Americans and the American novel. He gestures impersonally to his own feelings and experiences, creates empathy with his audience, and only obliquely addresses the current, political context surrounding the "great social changes" of desegregation (Harvard Summer School, August 3–5, 1953).

The tapes are riddled with resonant silences like these in which traces of personal and political tensions are evident. Some seem like larger omissions, as above, but other silences are smaller moments that are hard to hear and decidedly difficult to interpret. A small incident during one of the panels on August 4 provides an example. Wilbur Merrill Frohock and Anthony West are discussing how they perceive a scene in *Invisible Man* differently, one through the lens of aesthetics and the other as it reflects moral values. The timing is in the afternoon after the first evening of talks, and just before Ellison's evening lecture in Sanders Theatre. Frohock had just given a short but formal response to some of the ideas raised in the previous evening's lectures by Stanley Hyman and Frank O'Connor. In the response, Frohock makes the following remarks about the moral imagination:

> Organization of experience, of course, it is, the novel is, and has to be. But why need the motive of the imagination be moral? There are other motives. Suppose, for instance, that some imaginations are urged on by a drive to reorder experience into something more fair and fit. That drive does not have to be moral any more than our feeling is exclusively moral when we find a pigsty or a slum repulsive. (Harvard Summer School, August 4–5, 1953)

During the discussion, West takes exception with Frohock's comparison between the pigsty and the slum and claims that finding a slum "repulsive" does indeed have moral rather than simply aesthetic implications. Frohock quickly interrupts West's comment, justifying his remarks in his talk with an offended tone: "The word was *exclusively* moral act," Frohock emphasizes and adds, "explicitly moral." Frohock then offers a sardonic apology for interrupting West: "I hate to ruin the question," he says haughtily, and attempting to diminish the thrust of West's critique, Frohock adds dismissively, "I see what's coming." Nonetheless, the somewhat flustered West continues his questioning, referring to a scene in Ellison's *Invisible Man* that Frohock had described in his talk as a "hallucination" and "fantasy," in which a Harlem man brandishes a spear and rides a horse through a riot. West asks:

> Well, the question is whether or not it is more of a moral act to be annoyed or disgusted or want to change a slum, or is it more of another kind of act? It seems to me that when you have an imagination without some kind of morality involved, what you get is Celine and not Mr. Ellison or Richard Wright, a writing of that kind. This is the thing that is lacking in much of literature and that is needed. I think when you abstract—if you want to go away from the formalist critics but you want something new, what it winds up with is an investigation of the technique that Mr. Ellison uses in this section of the novel that you mentioned. (Harvard Summer School, August 4–5, 1953)

Frohock again breaks in and responds defensively by starting to describe the scene in which "old Rass is up on the horse throwing spears wearing God knows what kind of costume," but then Frohock halts the debate by feigning forgetting the scene's details as well as the larger point he is trying to make by remembering them. "Uh," Frohock says and then with a swift, lighthearted voice, he vocally gestures to Ellison to fill in what he has missed: "You must remember the place, Mr. Ellison," he says (as if Ellison would not remember the scene he had written). Again, Frohock provokes laughter from the audience. Ellison responds to Frohock, but the microphones—more sensitive to the louder, nearer sounds—do not pick up his words. Consequently, taking advantage of the upper hand he has established with the audience and disregarding West's question to Ellison, Frohock swiftly ends the discussion. He concludes, "I don't see why it has to be exclusively one or the other as in my most unfortunate metaphor—and I wish to God I hadn't said anything—about the pigsty and the slum. If I had just stopped with the pigsty, I'd have been well off" (Harvard Summer School, August 4–5, 1953). The audience's laughter dampens the potential debate. Frohock has diverted attention away from West's unanswered critique, and Ellison's comment is rendered silent.

Interference

When the unnamed narrator of *Invisible Man* concludes in the last line of the novel, "Who knows but that, on the lower frequencies, I speak for you?" (Ellison 1952, 581), he references the role that meaning making can play on a register that many readers might not perceive. Similarly, the moments in the Harvard recordings I have identified above are a provocation to consider how silences can also be agential and powerful instruments for engendering dialogic listening through interference.

On first listening to the tapes, I was excited at Ellison's presence. When I heard his voice, all the things I knew about his history, his writings, his activism began to take shape in my mind's ear, especially in contrast to what I perceived as the conference goers' haughty tones and stilted, academic language. Of course, having never heard Ellison, I did not recognize his voice until Carvel Collins pointed him out. In one of the first tapes I listened to when I received the recordings in 2019, Frohock is responding to another panelist about the "necessary operations of all criticism." Collins takes advantage of a pause in Frohock's lengthy explanation to ask, "Mr. Ellison would you speak to this subject? I'm not at this moment sure what the subject is but would you speak to it?" When Collins calls on him, Ellison says what I imagined he would say about his lost recordings if he had witnessed their rediscovery in the twenty-first century: "In the very business of selection and ordering, of giving a formal pattern, we perform a moral operation, not necessarily in the religious, ethical sense but it's a matter of choice. It's a matter of accepting and rejecting certain aspects of a given experience . . . through extracting the meaning of what has been, we create values of today" (Harvard Summer School, August 4–5, 1953). Likewise, when Collins reminds the participants, "These microphones are not speaking to the audience, merely putting the proceedings on tape and you will be picked up from wherever you are if you just look at the microphone," I perceive the recording microphone as a kind of boundary object that signals and amplifies individual voices across time but also initiates the process of selecting, ordering, and creating a formal pattern of the awkward, messy, situatedness of each speaker in dialogue with an audience

(Harvard Summer School, August 4–5, 1953).[9] For me, Ellison's history in this context as a Black activist speaking during the ongoing *Brown v. Board of Education* hearings and the onset of the Civil Rights movement turned up the volume and amplified his words. I anticipated that what he would say would resonate for me within a larger context about racial history in the United States then and now. However, I wondered that his published essays and talks demonstrate that he was not averse to talking about how segregation impacted him and his perceptions of American society and literature.[10] Why doesn't he openly discuss segregation at the Harvard School Summer Conference on the Contemporary Novel of 1953?

From another perspective, the moments above that I hear as provocative on the Harvard recordings are resonant because they are *not* silenced voicings or absences. Instead, these moments can be heard as agential interferences. A phenomenon described in acoustical theory, *interference* occurs when two sound waves occur simultaneously. If both sounds are peaking, they are in phase and their wave amplitudes will add together, making the wave peak higher. This kind of interference is considered *constructive* interference and leads to "live spots" in a listening environment. In contrast, *destructive* interference occurs when sound waves are "out of phase," when their superimposition in time includes the trough of one wave and the peak of the other, canceling out both sounds. Instead of an amplification, destructive interference results in "dead spots," where signal blocks out signal, creating perceived silences. It is possible to conclude that Ellison was mindfully silent on the topic of segregation, and that he chose to keep some of his opinions to himself in the moments above because he was concerned with his safety, his career as an academic writer, or he just did not particularly like the audience. Whatever the reason, a perspective informed by destructive interference invites a discussion about cancelled noise in which silence is a signal for agency and choice.[11]

In a 1955 essay published in *High Fidelity* titled "Living with Music," Ellison draws a parallel between his moral work as a writer and the properties of sound and audio technology that helps explain how constructive (amplification) and destructive (silencing) interferences function to engender identification or disaffection in an audience (Ellison 1995, 234). In the piece, Ellison describes his attempts to write in a city apartment surrounded by noise. In the courtyard outside, feral cats and dogs and drunks screech and moan, while his neighbor in the apartment to his left plays his phonograph too loudly, and his upstairs neighbor—a vocalist and the primary subject of his essay—practices her vocal range at a strident level. Ellison can ignore the phonograph and one particularly vociferous drunk ("the king of all world's winos") who shouts "to the whole wide world one concise command 'Shut up!'" and causes Ellison a fair share of his writer's block (228). Yet the vocalist gives Ellison the most pause. She poses a "serious ethical problem," because she is a creative. "Could I," he writes, "an aspiring artist, complain against the hard work and devotion to craft of another aspiring artist?" (229) The vocalist's struggle to create resonates with Ellison because it evokes his own feelings from early days of music making as a "skinny kid" in an "ecstasy of rhythm and memory and brassy affirmation of the goodness of being alive and part of a community" (232). In contrast to the drunk's preachings, Ellison writes, the vocalist required his attention: "I was forced to Listen. In listening, I soon became involved to the point of identification" (232).[12] His emotions were amplified in constructive interference with hers.

Ellison uses audio technology as a metaphor to articulate the important role that identification plays for achieving resonance with an audience.[13] Ellison had constructed a sound system in his home "piece by piece," with "a fine speaker system, a first-rate AM-FM tuner, a transcription turntable and a speaker cabinet," and he had also purchased a tape recorder (the "glory of the house") (1995, 233). He notes the dual role the equipment plays for him in his creative work as a source of pleasure and high fidelity, but also as a practical reminder of his work's difficulty and messiness:

> All this plunge into electronics, mind you, had as its simple end the enjoyment of recorded music as it was intended to be heard. I was obsessed with the idea of reproducing sound with such fidelity that even when using music as a defense behind which I could write, it would reach the unconscious levels of the mind with the least distortion. But it didn't come easily. There were wires and pieces of equipment all over the apartment. (Ellison 1995, 233)

Most importantly, his stereo sound system inspired an unconscious engagement with the music it played. Ellison believed a fidelity to the real was essential for creating a resonant experience, but this fidelity is less a call for exactitude and more an experience of "the real" (what Saidiya Hartman [1997] might call "truth"), an embodied resonance that is largely afforded by affective identification where conflicting values, pleasure, and pain can entangle. Ultimately, Ellison will tell an interviewer in the 1970s, the source of an affective engagement (or identification) in fiction comes from immersing an audience in realistic sense experiences:

> I might conceive of a thing aurally, but to realize it you have to make it vivid. The two things must operate together. What is the old phrase—"the planned dislocation of the senses"? That *is* the condition of fiction, I think. Here is where sound becomes sight and sight becomes sound, and where sign becomes symbol and symbol becomes sign; where fact and idea must just be hanging there but must become a functioning part of the total design, involving itself in the reader as idea as well as drama . . . to allow him to involve himself, to attach himself, and then begin to collaborate in the creation of the fictional spell. (Ellison 1995, 802)

Once the world is amplified or made vivid to the point of a "planned dislocation of the senses," an audience's "involved feelings [are] aroused by a more intimate noise, one that got beneath the skin and worked into the structure of one's consciousness—like the fate 'motif' in Beethoven's Fifth or the knocking-at-the-gates scene in Macbeth" (Ellison 1995, 228).

Ellison also provides an example of how deconstructive interference, or "dead spots," can disrupt this kind of affective identification. In "Living with Music," he describes being at his wits' end with the neighborhood noises until he realizes that he can use sound to cancel sound: "Thus one desperate morning I decided that since I seemed doomed to live within a shrieking chaos I might as well contribute my share; perhaps if I fought noise with noise I'd attain some small peace" (1995, 232). Similarly, when he begins to feel overwhelmed with the identification he had begun to feel for the vocalist, he uses music to dampen those feelings. "If she sang badly I'd hear my own futility in the windy sound," Ellison explains. "I'd stare at my typewriter and despair that I would ever make my prose so sing . . . and as my writing languished I became more and more upset" (232). To cancel out the anguish, Ellison decides to turn on and turn up his radio. When he tunes into English contralto Kathleen Ferrier "giving voice to the aria from Handel's Rhodelinda," Ellison suddenly realizes "that with such music in my own apartment, the chaotic sounds from without and above had sunk, if not into silence, then well below the level where they mattered. Here was a way out" (233). A noise interference that "cancels out" another sound has not silenced or stopped the source of that sound. Instead, the resonant frequency no longer registers. Similarly, when he feels no connection with the courtyard drunk's desire for quiet, Ellison does not identify with him—he feels no sympathy or affective consonance. Ellison writes, "Identification, after all, *involves feelings of guilt and responsibility*, and since I could hardly hear my own typewriter keys, I felt in no way accountable for his condition" (228, emphasis added). For Ellison, a lack of identification interferes with a moralistic response. Disaffected, his feelings are dampened.

Significantly, interpreting silence as interference is dependent on the audience's potential for perceiving its possible resonance. When the panel discussion at Harvard turns to which and how novels hold value, Ellison would explain the significant role the audience plays in what will resonate. He asserts that meaning making is the cocreation of values. It "must be a shared experience in between the process of the novel, the process which is a novel, and the audience which receives it" (Harvard Summer School, August 4–5, 1953). To be a meaningful medium of communication, novels must be "fired by the emotions, ideas, feelings of an audience. Thus we have works which come up, that come into being, they're called into being, through certain needs on the part of the viewer, the reader, the listener, and after that need recedes, after the time changes—and they must exist in time, they can only exist in time—they go into the veil" (Harvard Summer School, August 4–5, 1953).[14]

Central to Ellison's sense of the ideal audience is the "little man" (1995, 493).[15] The "little man" is a fictional listener behind the stove in the waiting room at Chehaw Station, near the Tuskegee Institute in Alabama, introduced to Ellison by an early music teacher. He symbolizes the audience "you don't expect," who "will know the music, and the tradition, and the standards of musicianship required for whatever you set out to perform" (494). Ellison imagines this audience of one to be an American Renaissance man, versed in all the arts and all the experiences that a heterogeneous culture entails, coupled with an understanding of that culture's shortcomings. He is Ellison's ideal because the range of the little man's knowledge and perspicacity means that he senses "American experience is of a whole, and he wants the interconnections revealed. And not out of a penchant for protest, nor out of petulant vanity, but because he sees his own condition as an inseparable part of a larger truth in which the high and the lowly, the known and the unrecognized, the comic and the tragic are woven into the American skein" (503). The larger complex "truth of what happens" (Hartman 1997, 3)[16] resonates with this listener because his personal experience of "diverse bell sounds" includes being knowledgeable about the "higher" traditions of music as well as experiencing them from the seemingly lowly place behind the stove. His experience positions him to understand "his own condition as an inseparable part of a larger truth" about the morally contentious sociopolitical context that influences what he hears and what he—a product of the history which sounds around him—also listens for. As both the subject and the agent of the narrative, he imposes "collaboratively his own vision of American experience upon that of the author" (Ellison 1995, 502). With his own history and experience, he is not everyman. He "assum[es] his Afro-American identity, costume and mask" to "aid the author in achieving the more complex vision of American experience that was implicit in his material" (502). He is a product of "our freewheeling appropriations of culture," because as members of a pluralistic democracy, a "'nation of nations,' we are by definition and by the processes of democratic cultural integration, the inheritors, creators and creations of a culture of cultures" (516). Ellison describes this ideal audience member in terms near what may well have been his own positionality at the Harvard conference: "As a citizen," Ellison writes, "the little man endures with a certain grace the social restrictions that limit his own social mobility, but *as a reader* he demands that the relationship between his own condition and that of those more highly placed be recognized" (503). Receptive and perceptive, the ideal audience is a dialogical listener.

Deconstructive interference is a powerful metaphor for understanding how the ideal audience participates in amplifying silences. In a talk Ellison delivered in 1972 at the Black Perspective Conference about Roscoe Dunjee, editor of the *Black Dispatch* in Oklahoma City (for which there is only a published essay and no recording), Ellison heralds Dunjee and Black newspapers more generally for their capacity "to penetrate and affirm the moral ideals of the country, and to describe the failure and breakdown of a society where easy optimism and equivocation were the mode" (1995, 462). Ellison discusses the impact the American Revolution had on what he is referring to as the "American language," by drawing an affinity with his listeners. In contrast to the Harvard audience, this audience is primarily Black: "When I say 'we,' I am quite conscious that we black people were already here causing all sorts of turbulence in the king's town—in religion, music, science, and so on" (457). Ellison also notes, importantly, that slavery is a topic he will pointedly dampen for this audience: "We were here as slaves; everyone tells us that. We all know it, and I am sick of hearing about it. Yes, we were slaves, but we were living persons. We were chattel, but speaking chattel, chattel with a moral sense, chattel with an artistic sense and with a great capacity for creation" (458). Further, when speaking of Dunjee's courage in establishing the *Black Dispatch* in Oklahoma City in 1915, Ellison describes two visits he made in his youth to the site of the 1921 Tulsa Race Massacre. First, Ellison had traveled to Tulsa just before the massacre "to see an older cousin who had a fine brick home in the prosperous Negro community of Greenwood," and then he returned again after "Greenwood had been devastated and all but destroyed by bomb and fire in that riot of 1921" (455). On mention of the massacre, Ellison again immediately defers to this audience's own experience to fill in the gaps of this painful aspect of US history: "I don't bring this up to bore you with how hard life has been for us in the United States," he says (456). For a Black Perspective Conference audience in 1972, gathered to talk about the Black experience, "we" and "us" includes an audience with experiences potentially similar to Ellison's. The Tulsa Massacre and other painful events are a shared history of ugly violence. At Harvard, perhaps Ellison dampens the topic of segregation to avoid this audience's potential identification. For this audience, Ellison does not have to explain the dissonance of slavery and Greenwood for these topics to amplify and resonate. Deconstructive interference marks silence as an absent presence, as a present energy, perceived as absence.

Invisible Man

It is important to understand how constructive and destructive interference relate to Ellison's writings about American literature and *Invisible Man* in order to recognize how silence resonates in the Harvard recordings. In writing *Invisible Man*, Ellison creates moments of constructive interference that pique moral awareness alongside moments of destructive interference that disrupt white identification. Using both tactics allows him to represent what he considered the moral chaos of a racialized US culture without offering up African Americans as "the occasion for self-reflection," fodder "for an exploration of terror, desire, fear, and longing," or "as surrogate selves for meditation on problems of human freedom, its lure and its elusiveness" (Hartman 1997, 7; Morrison 1992, 64). Ellison argues that it is "almost impossible for many whites to consider questions of sex, women, economic opportunity, the national identity, historic change, social justice without summoning malignant images of black men into consciousness" (1995, 102). The contradictions inherent to this racialized mindset reflect "a symbolic state of civil war" in which US Americans "are bedeviled by measuring our assertions of democratic faith against the undemocratic contents of our attitudes and actions" (469). Because the entanglement of race and moral awareness is necessarily at its height "during periods of national crises," it is the portrayal of such moments in literature when "this moral awareness surges in the white American's conscience like a raging river revealed at his feet like a lightning flash" (85). As Saidiya Hartman (1997) and Toni Morrison (1992) would argue decades later, Ellison claims that this awareness can position an African American character in literature as "a human 'natural' resource . . . elected to undergo a process of institutionalized dehumanization" so that "white men could become more human" (Ellison 1995, 85). In "Twentieth-Century Fiction and the Black Mask of Humanity," the essay he publishes after the Harvard conference, Ellison notes how this clash is reflected in literature: "Fiction it is never so effective and revealing as when both potentials are operating simultaneously, as when it mirrors both good and bad, as when it blows both hot and cold in the same breath" (81). When simultaneous modes of interference are creating amplification and low-frequency signals on different registers, "the veil of anti-Negro myths, symbols, stereotypes and taboos" is "drawn somewhat aside" and the symbolic role of the African American in literature can be "seen operating even when [he] seems most patently the little man who isn't there" (85).

Constructive interference functions in *Invisible Man* when Ellison uses the voice of Oklahoma Blues musician Jimmy Rushing as a model for portraying the central character, Bliss Proteus Rinehart. Memorializing Rushing for the *Saturday Review* in 1958, Ellison describes Rushing's voice as exemplary of the dichotomous reality of two entangled US cultures in the Oklahoma City of Ellison's youth in the 1920s and 1930s—the thriving, exciting, and hopeful Oklahoma Blues and the staid, inherited prestige and wealth of white, institutionalized privilege that had an equal presence. "I could hear Rushing four blocks away in bed, carrying to me as clear as a full-bored riff on 'Hot Lips' Page's horn," Ellison writes of his childhood hero's voice:

> Heard thus, across the dark blocks lined with locust trees, through the night throbbing with the natural aural imagery of the blues, with high-balling trains, departing bells and a great groaning of the wheels along the rails, switch engines made up of trains of freight unceasingly . . . it was easy to imagine the voice as

setting the pattern to which the instruments of the Blue Devils Orchestra and all the random sounds of night arose, affirming, as it were, some ideal native to the time and to the land. (1995, 274)

The duality of violence and hope that sounded in Rushing's voice intermingled with the sounds of nature and industry became Ellison's model for creating art that could record the complex African American personal and social experience, especially in Oklahoma in the 1920s, when racial violence was at a peak:

> [Rushing] expressed a value, an attitude about the world for which our lives afforded no other definition . . . we were pushed off to what seemed to be the least desirable side of the city (but which some years later was found to contain one of the state's richest pools of oil), and our system of justice was based on upon Texas law; yet there was an optimism within the Negro community and a sense of possibility, which despite our limitations (dramatized so brutally in the Tulsa riot of 1921), transcended all of this rock-bottom sense of reality, coupled with our sense of the possibility of rising above it, which sounded in Rushing's voice. (1995, 274)[17]

The blues musicians he knew as a youth had a "technical mastery of their instrument . . . the subtle rhythmical shaping and blending of idea, tone, and imagination demanded of group improvisation" that "expressed their attitude to the world . . . with a fluid style that reduced the chaos of living to form" (Ellison 1995, 229). When Ellison calls the novel an "ethical instrument," he does so by praising "the ambivalence" of the word. The essence of the novel's power and pleasure is its ability to hold, like Rushing's voice, contradicting ideas that amplify each other (99).

In contrast to his written explanation above, in which he takes with utmost seriousness his moral responsibility as an author of literature in the United States, Ellison presents his writing motives with a different tenor at the Harvard conference. When he tells his audience that Rinehart is how this important "call to chaos" was given form in *Invisible Man*, Ellison demonstrates how using humor functions as a destructive interference that attenuates the novel's racial politics for some audiences:

> I had a situation in my novel where I wanted to personalize the creative flux. And somehow a bell rang in my head and I remembered a blues sung by Jimmy Rushing and there was a refrain that went something like this: Rinehart, Rinehart, it's so lonesome up here on Beacon Hill . . . it was exactly the call to chaos. Come out, let's go on a rampage, let's sell our phonograph records, let's riot. And this exactly, it was so fitting. (Harvard Summer School, August 4–5, 1953)[18]

Much like Frohock's description in his talk of the scene in Harlem as a "hallucination" and "fantasy," the reference to blues singer Jimmy Rushing singing about Beacon Hill, a tony Boston neighborhood, as inspiration for Rinehart, who is at times a gambler and a pimp, might have been almost ludicrous to the Harvard crowd. Ellison's audience laughs when he cites the line about Beacon Hill, and Ellison laughs with them, seemingly silencing the amplified contrast by blithely explaining, "I was simply trying to exploit my own folk background. I don't think this blues was the product of any . . . 'mind' but a product of this mixture that we have in this country right now."

Ellison continues to express his development of *Invisible Man* to his Harvard audience in the Forum Room by equivocating and diminishing his intentions to a "simpler motive" that is possibly more appropriate for this crowd:

> Someone asked me the other night why I chose to write in the first person. And they said, 'Well, uh, isn't because you wanted this to be everyman?' And I said, 'Yes,' but there's a much simpler motive behind it and that was to be able to move in on the speech patterns that I find around me. I mean I wanted to be able to exploit the rhetoric, I wanted to exploit the scientific terminology, I wanted to exploit the sermons and the hollers and the slang, because I think finding it in a form of pattern gives the reader a pleasure and it certainly gives me some of the pleasure that Mr. O'Connor has been talking about. The delight that you get from trying to write a novel comes from the delight in putting over a good yarn, a good lie. I'm a professional liar and I can't get away from it. (Harvard Summer School, August 4–5, 1953)

Ellison describes his motivations—exploitative, extractive, equivocating, pleasure-seeking—in contrast to the political tenor of *Invisible Man*. While the narrator of *Invisible Man* laments "those lies his keepers keep their power by," Ellison broadcasts the "pleasure" of the "good yarn" and the "good lie" in order to mitigate any threat that a discussion of his novel might invite for the present crowd (Ellison 1952, 439). Plainly describing him to his Harvard audience, but not actually mentioning him, Ellison explains how the little man might approach the constructive and destructive interferences in meaning making that *Invisible Man* invites, and in so doing, gives sound advice on listening to the Harvard recordings as well: "Not only does speech and does imagery operate here and there drifting back and forth through social layers, through region and so forth," he says somberly, "but the tendency of the human mind to adopt and find significance in the same symbols is very much a part of this kind of unity, this flux and flow, this bobbing, weaving, this fluidity of American life" (Harvard Summer School, August 4–5, 1953).

* * *

Toni Morrison cautions that discovering the African American presence in US literature is an interesting and worthwhile endeavor, but more important, she warns, is a deep regard for its absence in founding literature and a deeper regard for how those silences "may be the insistent fruit of the scholarship rather than the text" (2019, 175). Certainly, all things are not duly recorded, and Ellison reminds his readers, "In some ways we are fortunate that it isn't, for if it were, we might become so chagrined by the discrepancies which exist between our democratic ideals and our social reality that we'd soon lose heart" (Ellison 1995, 598). A final example from Ellison's experiences with scholarly institutions serves to demonstrate some of the discrepancies scholars encounter in trying to address "the known, the seen, the heard," and "those events that the recorder regards as important" (Ellison 1952, 439).

In 1979, Ellison spoke at Brown University at the unveiling of a portrait of Inman Page. Before being a childhood mentor to Ellison, Page was Brown University's first African American student. He began his career in education at Brown, eventually earning an honorary master's and two honorary law degrees and moving to Oklahoma City in 1920 to become "supervisor of education of Negroes" and principal of Douglas High School, where Ellison was a student in the 1930s. Ellison's speech in honor of Page, forty years after Page's death, displays "the very business of selection and ordering" that led to Page's tribute. Ellison alludes to the university's long silence regarding Page's good works and bemoans his mentor's being "overlooked by those who record the history of American education" (Ellison 1995, 597). Ellison refers to the political nature of recovery work at the university as "the intricate relationship which obtains between Brown and American history generally" and calls the discovery of his boyhood relationship to Page an "ironic fact" given the delayed appreciation for Page and his sudden recovery due to Ellison's fame. Ellison notes, "in the two hundred years of our national existence a great deal has been overlooked or forgotten" (598). Glibly suggesting that perhaps "some developments become obscure because of the sheer rush and density of incidents which occur in any given period of time," Ellison concludes in a more serious tone. He argues that some aspects of history "fade through conscious design, either because of an unwillingness to solve national dilemmas or because we possess such a short attention span and are given to a facile waning of our commitments" (598). Ellison recognizes that the scholarly apparatus has simultaneous and dichotomous powers to obscure and herald the memory of his mentor (597). He thanks scholar "Michael Harper and his assistants" and the university's commitment to historiography, but it is clear from the historical context and the tone of Ellison's description of it that Page's sudden historical recovery resonates with Ellison. The complexities of Page's silencing and the politics behind the recovery of his work interfere constructively and destructively to both amplify "the fact that not all of American history is recorded" and to dampen the idea that a truly democratic culture is possible.

I may not be an ideal reader, but in 2022, so near the hundredth anniversary of the 1921 Tulsa Race Massacre and on hearing Ellison's recently discovered speech to a primarily white audience on the eve of the Civil Rights movement, Ellison's only direct reference in *Invisible Man* to the 1921 Tulsa Massacre resonates with me. The reference occurs in a pivotal scene in *Invisible Man* when the narrator, a Black boy from a local high school, has been invited to give a talk in front of a room of high-society white men. The boy is elated and proud, but when he arrives at the venue, he is subjected to unbelievable physical and psychological violence before he is led to the room where he is supposed to give his speech. When he is finally introduced to his white audience, the convenor says, "I'm told that he is the smartest boy we've got there in Greenwood. I'm told that he knows more big words than a pocket-sized dictionary" (Ellison 1952, 29). The scene can be interpreted—has been interpreted—on so many levels, but Ellison's relationship with the Greenwood District goes largely unnoticed by most scholars or readers for whom the Tulsa Race Massacre may well have been, as the first chapter in this book shows, an unknown history.[19] The unmarked scholarly reference to Greenwood during this scene is a silence that also resonates with the interferences I sense when I listen to Ellison speak at Harvard in 1953.

I am in the domain of silence,
the kingdom of the crazy and the sleeper.

—Anne Sexton, "For the Year of the Insane" (1999, 133)

4 Compression: The Entelechy of Records in Anne Sexton's Poem "For the Year of the Insane"

On July 31, 1963, the day after a particularly fraught therapy session with her psychiatrist, Anne Sexton wrote the poem "For the Year of the Insane."[1] She was anxious about her upcoming departure for a long stay in Europe, funded by a grant she had received from the American Academy of Arts and Letters in recognition for her acclaimed poetry collection *All My Pretty Ones* (1962). Her emotions heightened, she went into a trance and spent much of the session huddled on the floor in front of an air conditioner, moaning and crying while her doctor tried to wake her up. Sexton had been meeting with her psychiatrist Dr. Martin Orne two or three times weekly between completing her first book and while working on her Pulitzer-prize winning collection *Live or Die* (1966). For therapeutic reasons, they were recording each session on reel-to-reel tapes and Sexton was listening to the recordings in between sessions, often more than once, and taking notes in a journal on what she heard. The recording made on the day Sexton wrote "For the Year of the Insane" is almost inaudible. Voices are muffled under the roar of the machine, and her journal pages are also all but illegible, scrawled in a flattened script. The poem remains the best record of what happened that day: on a manuscript page for "For the Year of the Insane," Sexton notes, "A poem about madness and the terrible need to communicate" (HRC 1963).[2]

Archival tapes and journals comprise what I call Sexton's therapy text, and in this chapter, I am particularly concerned with how Sexton's compression practices generating the therapy text influenced her poetry writing. In communication and media studies, *compression* has been defined both as a "condensation of thought and language" and as a technical term for data compaction or dynamic range in audio (Sterne 2015, 32).[3] Most importantly for a discussion of Sexton's therapy text, Jonathan Sterne has associated compression practices with a modern anxiety over a loss of meaning based in assumptions about technology and its ability to produce verisimilitude (32).[4] As this chapter demonstrates, Sexton was deeply motivated by the relationship between the compression practices that produced her therapy text and her ability to create meaning through poetry. Her biographer Diane Middlebrook speculates that she wrote very little during the first year of the therapy recordings because listening to the tapes and writing her reflections in her journals occupied so much of her time, but Sexton's daughter Linda Gray Sexton remembers that tape listening and poetry writing were eventually deeply entwined practices for Sexton: "Spending hours listening to the tape recordings of her therapy sessions, and days rewriting her worksheets," Gray Sexton recalls, "she slowly pulled poetry from the dark core of her sickness" (Middlebrook, 1991a, 139; Sexton, Sexton, and Ames, 1977, 29).[5] In this chapter, I consider how Sexton's material-discursive practices using recording media (tape and journal pages) helped Sexton negotiate a gendered pathology and encouraged an expression of identity in the poem "For the Year of the Insane" that evolved from an anxious desire to document a prescribed "true" self to a more empowered sense of the entelechy of recordings as a condition that invites an expression of the potential self.

The Therapy Text

Therapy
Their therapy recording process began with a gendered pathology. "While to some extent each of us is selective in what we remember," Dr. Orne would write in an introduction to Sexton's biography, "Anne's selectivity was extreme in the sense that she literally remembered almost nothing of relevance from one session to the next. . . . In short, it was clear that she had a condition that traditionally was known as hysteria" (Middlebrook 1991a, xv).[6] Sexton's parents and her husband, Alfred Muller Sexton II (Kayo), believed her hysteria was also the reason she shirked marital and maternal duties. Taping the sessions was meant to capture the "talking cure" directly by creating a record of her memories and their discussions of them that would allow her insights that, in turn, would aid in these self-destructive and inappropriate behaviors. At times, Sexton believed in Orne's diagnosis: "If I could find a record," she says explaining why the tapes fascinated her, "I would like to look at it. My own record. You know anything like that, you

know, looking in the nurses' books. I am curious. I want to know" (March 7, 1961, AESL). She saw the recordings as a solution for what Orne and others considered her hysterical forgetting: "Oh I say I can't be objective—I know I say that too—but you're right, there is another mind that we can use, my objective mind, when I'm not in here, I see it. . . . There's no way I could ever remember it like the experience of hearing it" (January 28, 1961, AESL). They agreed that taping would increase her ability to think about her sessions objectively and, later, that sharing the tapes might help others experiencing mental illness.[7]

Yet almost from the start, the process left Sexton feeling disempowered. Early on, when her husband Kayo, who was often spurred to outrage and physical violence, called her out for failing to remember something, Sexton wrote she felt "powerless but angry" (January 13, 1961, Journal, HRC).[8] The potential that she might squander an opportunity to better understand herself thus plagued Sexton, and she complained that the process of remembering via tape could be worsening her condition: "Talked about tape and its effect—I wondered if it would disturb me—(I am so stunned by end of the apt [sic] that it's hard to recall the rest)—agreed it was my decision to tape but still it is an assault, an attack upon my neurosis" (January 26, 1961, Journal, HRC). When she tried to listen, she worried about not being able to recognize significant information as she heard it: "I might miss one little thing but I have to sit there for fifteen or twenty minutes listening to myself and not liking myself without learning anything that's new," she says, "and I'm not so detached that I can listen to it like it were my patient" (March 7, 1961, AESL). Orne believed that the recording method had potential to be "a true collaboration, in which Anne could discover important insights and share them with me," making "the relationship between us far more equal than in the past" and providing Sexton "a major step forward when she was able to show me that I was wrong!" (Middlebrook 1991a, xvi). Despite Orne's ideas about collaboration, Sexton repeatedly acknowledged the unequal nature of their relationship and her feelings of failure at disappointing his expectations about the method. When Orne reminds her in one session that "it started as a collaborative thing," Sexton responds, "Maybe, you see, I didn't know what I was going to—I didn't know what it meant. I mean, I didn't know how I would even feel about it. You know, I went into this blindfolded. I didn't know" (March 7, 1961, AESL). Trying to be objective about herself was an experience that would continue to frustrate Sexton. A full year into the process of relistening to the therapy recordings, Sexton attempted to copy a session verbatim from a tape and then noted in her journal, "I feel like a failure, I know I can't do it . . . every time I listen something happens to me, yr asking me to be my own Dr and I don't know how to be" (January 16, 1962, Journal, HRC).[9]

While the taping process often left Sexton feeling disempowered, it also meant she could witness the gendered power dynamics that shaped the process. One of the main reasons that Orne and Sexton began recording the sessions was Sexton's inability to remember what happened during her "trances." During these half-conscious states, Sexton would consistently perform two female personalities: "Elizabeth," who was often stubborn or unconventional, and "baby girl Anne," who sounded and acted like a recalcitrant little girl. From the first recording on January 24, 1961, Orne responds to Sexton's "baby girl" as an authority figure reacting to unreasonable temper tantrums: "You're not a child that I give a lollipop to for being a good girl," he says in one of the first recorded sessions, "even if it's difficult, you start to make a commitment to yourself to write down what happened because it's your treatment . . . it's easy to pat you on the head and say I love you . . . it's just not going to make you well." "All I wanted you to do was love me," she says to Orne. "I'd rather have you get angry than not love me." Orne responds, "Then maybe you don't need to act out." In a pleading tone, she says, "I can try" (January 24, 1961, AESL).

Before hearing the recordings, Sexton was not aware she took on these identities or how Orne reacted to them. Sexton's revelations about the "trance tapes" typically happen on what she would eventually call "insight tapes," during which Sexton and Orne have lengthy conversations about the therapeutic process. On the insight tapes, they talk more about her current life rather than her past, about her children, her poetry readings, the recordings (especially the trance tapes), and the journal writings. Sexton also makes observations about the Elizabeth and baby-girl Anne personalities and notes that these performed identities are encouraged by the context and that her realization of them is mediated by the mode of recording. When Orne and Sexton discuss her initial reactions to the voices, Sexton describes to Orne how the recording offers her an opportunity to observe that she was "being a little girl. I mean, I was being—beyond the fact that I was just horrible, I mean, I admit it. There's nothing much I can say, except that my, I was relating to you like a little girl, which I had been, you know, in trance." Sexton proclaims, laughing, "I'm the most terrible brat I ever knew! Because I never knew. I can't see myself, but you can't help it when you listen. You know" (January 28, 1961, AESL).

Recording

What emerges out of the process of relistening to the tapes and then reading over old journal entries is Sexton's simultaneous recognition of the relationship between the institutionalized and gendered power dynamics that shaped her sense of self and how those dynamics influenced her experience of the material conditions of the recording process. From the beginning, she is aggravated by the version of herself that the tapes reflect, and she has an increased sense that the tapings are a proxy—a "mechanical" reminder—for Orne's control over how and when she expresses her feelings:

> Hate tapes—every pause thought of it—want to pull it out—Feel very exposed and inhibited—angry—(wow! almost forgot) he said he'd get a tape—a 60 minute tape—this is what made me angry—said that I had thought that how people feel about me has nothing to do with how I act—[crossed out] My action is what reveals how they really feel—he says I feel cheated by remark about 60 min. Tape. I said the tape makes therapy mechanical enough—and they are bad enough without making them a device to get rid of me—I am not a tape. I'm a human being. (January 31, 1961, Journal, HRC)

The tapes become such an essential aspect of Sexton's understanding of her therapeutic process that she quips to Orne during one conversation: "As a matter of fact, if the tape broke, I would have to leave. . . . It would be like we hadn't existed" (March 7, 1961, AESL). Sexton was equally thoughtful about the way the journals mediated her experiences. Years later, having relistened to the tapes, reread her journals, and tried to make new notations, she tells Orne that the journal notes she has so painstakingly written would be indecipherable to him, observing that reading them all together "would take us quite a while," because he wouldn't be able to read her handwriting. Besides, she says, her notes are compressed beyond utility: "It's at a removal. It's written down and it's smaller. And I don't think I could go back and take notes because they'd be, then, I'm not removed enough to really judge it. . . . Probably it's of no use." (March 19, 1963, AESL). Ironically, Sexton explains that her journal entries about the audio recordings are so compressed, she would have to read them out loud to him for them to interpret them together.

Most importantly, the tapings and journaled observations dislocated Sexton from her sense of self and her process of self-expression. It is useful to quote some sessions at length to show her mentally working through how the method Dr. Orne prescribed for remembering, observing, and expressing her objective "true" self through taping and journaling was deeply at odds in her mind with her evolving understanding of how her identity was being constructed in her sessions. From the beginning, she talks about "not the me on the tape, but my superego":

> As a matter of fact, I'm so sick of her! ... The most horrible part of the first tape is after I come out of the trance, and I won't leave. and I listen to it, and I want to shout, for Christ's sake will you get up and leave? ... I mean I'm just awful, I just won't leave. And I wanted to get up and shake the tape and say, 'get out of there.' You know, [laughs] 'Move! Go!' And there she sat there. And I can't, I can't help but be that far away from it. You know, it seems like two actors on the stage even though I know it's me and you and still, there she is, and I can't stand it. (January 28, 1961, AESL)

Sexton recognizes that listening to the tapes is pushing "two problems at me at once": she is simultaneously listening to herself and she is listening in on Orne listening to her, a double consciousness of her own observations on how she resists others' interpretations of her:[10]

> The thing that upsets me is the affect that the tape has on me ... you cannot understand what it does to me. It has nothing to do with us ... you're pushing two problems at me at once ... there is some sort of invisible issue with the tape that I can't even explain to you I don't understand what it does to me but it's changing things ... I'm doing it and I don't know what's happening but I guess maybe it's increasing my resistance in a way and it's kind of making me depressed but not—I'm trying not to be I still think it's a very good idea ... I don't quite know it's too different already without making a thing out of it about when I leave which is already a thing between us but it's between us; it isn't something to do with a tape—I feel—I'll tell you one thing—I don't want to keep talking about the tape or I refuse to do it. I'm wasting too much time talking about it. It's doing too much—I can't. I don't think you even believe me—how strange this tape thing, I mean how it's affecting me. I can't keep talking about it—I mean it's hard enough without if I keep remembering it, I might as well start not coming in here. It's confusing me ... well it's making me uncomfortable ... it's going to make it difficult for me to talk. (Anne Sexton Therapy Tape, R 2867, January 31, 195?)[11]

Sexton's observations are complicated by her increased understanding that Orne might perceive her in ways that she cannot discern listening to herself.

"Something you said wasn't so, at least from listening to it," she tells him at one session. "The problem was, was that I didn't know where I was or who I was or else there's something that's on the tape, there's some way I'm acting or something you can see that I can't hear. As I'm re-experiencing it, I think, 'this girl doesn't know what in the hell is going on'" (April 25, 1961, AESL). The taping process required a feeling of distance that left Sexton feeling alienated from a sense of self, but it also facilitated a multiplied positionality in which she found a potential expressive power:

> It's me and I don't like me! And it isn't just news, it's me! I just can't stand it! But then I feel a little better by the time I get to the new tape because I'm curious, you know, somewhat. Having heard it once I do know more than we have given me credit for. Because it's certainly, it's much more familiar than having written it down and heard it, you know. I still want to know what I've forgotten. However, if I had the ability to study, just to study it, and not to think of it as me, then I could always learn more. But this takes, you don't know what resistance I have, I hate myself so. It's this huge, you know I think I'm never going to go in there again. I don't like this. I'm going to stop. (March 7, 1961, AESL)

On this tape from March 1961, Sexton sounds gleeful, elated, and gushing about her observations—a tone and thoughts to which she would relisten, again and again over time, as she experimented with her evolving ideas about the gendered nature of her pathology, the self and self-expression.

Compression

When they started recording the therapy sessions, Sexton was already a well-established poet, but the compression practices required by journaling what she heard in the audio recordings influenced her ideas about how the self could be represented in writing: "It's different, the writing is very different than hearing it," she tells Orne after hearing her first recorded trance. "I mean it's just a million miles away from it. Because I write. I've already condensed things, changed them. You know that everything is out of scale. Even though I try to quickly write it down, I can't. I mean it's very obvious. I miss the whole. I just remember a couple of details" (January 28, 1961, AESL). The trance tapes brought these conflicting notions of self, disempowerment, and empowerment to the fore more than the others because they were particularly difficult for Sexton to express in writing. Translating the trance tapes into writing was challenging because sometimes her words were almost inaudible. Ambiguous inflections and tone might be perceptible, but these signifiers were not easy for Sexton to express in writing. After listening to that first trance tape, she tells Orne, "And one thing I noticed from these is that the inflection of voice gives the whole thing away, which I can't ever write down the inflection of voice and I can't be conscious of it when it's happening, but here, on this small scale, I can tell from my voice when I'm about to go into trance. And I have such a little voice in trance, you can't hear me, you know, but it seems to me it's distinctly a little girl" (January 28, 1961, AESL).

In trying to make sense of the compression practices required by her therapy text, Sexton recognizes that generating a verisimilitude of the "true" self in writing is impossible. Sexton's representations in writing feel distorted, "out of scale" and missing "the whole." Asserting that she wished "there was some way I could squash it all together," she explains that "in each appointment there might be four major attitudes, let's say, or something that I should notice. If I could only push them into something that would only take ten minutes. I have to listen to for one hour for these things, you know ... I take so long and I'm so irritated with myself" (March 7, 1961, AESL). Eventually, she tells Orne that she has stopped synthesizing what she hears. When she has a trance tape, she just writes "down the whole thing" because "I can't condense it. It's a terrible work because I don't understand it. It's like a dream or something. I don't know what's important and what isn't. I don't ever understand the thing as a whole" (August 19, 1961, AESL). She warns Orne, based on her own experience in listening to the trance tapes, that he won't be able to make sense of them either: "You can't take all that in. I can't because it's me" (March 19, 1963, AESL). Sexton admits in 1963, two years into the recordings and just months before writing "For the Year of the Insane," that her inability to translate the trance tapes made her uneasy: "There was a time when I didn't write down trance because I didn't think that was the right thing to do."

Generating the therapy text gave Sexton a sense that identity was performative and a process of identity construction that is always mediated by institutions and media. This understanding empowered her to recognize that she had some agency in Orne's prescribed therapeutic process. In initial discussions after she has listened to her first trance tape, she is already recognizing the potential power of her ongoing multiplicity in Orne's therapeutic

Compression

process when laughing with Orne she says, "You don't think taping this is going to make me develop another personality, do you?" (January 28, 1961, AESL). Months later, Sexton again references the agency she has to resist Orne and potential institutionalization: Audibly inhaling on a cigarette, Sexton tells Orne, "I was thinking about the time Lowell went crazy. And I withdrew. I would not be drawn into this. When? If I get stuck in an institution I want to get out." Then, Orne asks, "In what sense?" Sexton responds in a self-assured tone, "I don't know. I want to rebel against the thing I went for." She laughs, "I guess. I don't understand it. I don't understand how I switch from one thing to another. I don't even understand, I don't understand these tapes. I don't understand anything. I am confused but I am not, I know who I am" (April 25, 1961, AESL). Sexton realizes that expressing the self within conventional institutions that do not accept her means of expression was maddening, and to produce her own sense of identity, she would have to "rebel" against conventional norms.

Her experience of an authentic self—"who I am"—became a process deeply entangled in the material-discursive nature of therapy and poetry compression practices. After reading all her journals from the first two years, she describes to Orne how she went about making "an object out of chaos," using a compression process she employed as trial and error based on the media (books, paper, tape) she was using:

> If you read it all at once—and the other book, there's this book and this book and then one little book. In the little book I didn't write as much so it's, you can tell quicker. You don't have to read through so much material because I distilled it. Of course, I might have left things out, you know, but, generally if you keep doing this it's pretty distilled, more than I do now, because I have bigger paper or I don't do the work of distilling it. Or I want it all. Or, like today, I started cutting off the last of what we were saying and then I'd gone along for five minutes and suddenly I stopped the tape and I had to write it down because it's important. (March 19, 1963, AESL)

Turning on and off the tape, writing things down and not, using different kinds and sizes of paper, sometimes writing by hand and sometimes typing, Sexton is describing how the material process of expressing the self resonated for her. On February 29, 1964, three years into recording and nearing the last months of this method, Sexton explains to Orne how the intermedial and unconscious nature of the process inspired her to use poetry to buck the conventions in which doctors, parents, and Kayo sought to pathologize her sense of self. "Then I got over it all by myself. . . . Partly by listening to the tape," she tells Orne. "I get more constructive after I listen to it in my other life. I was feeling very rebellious. I wanted to write a poem. I'd like to title a book called Fuck You! Stick my tongue out at the whole world! Anyone who's conventional" (Skorczewski 2012, 144).

Resistance to the recording process becomes an opportunity for Sexton to doubt, dislocate, and, eventually, disregard the idea of an objective "true" self that she is supposed to compress and "remember" in their sessions. It is this resistance against institutional mores that gives her a sense of self. The anxiety and self-realization she experienced is demonstrated six months into the recordings, when Sexton writes a letter to Orne, which she tucks into her journal.[12] "There is no doubt about it," she says in the letter, "my unconscious is not interested in conventions." In the letter, she details her dreams about having sex with her father and Dr. Orne—two men who conventional institutions (including the church, the psychiatric profession, and general society) tell her are sexually forbidden. At peace with her unconventionality and in a newfound mode of acceptance, she pushes back against the tapings in her letter. She signs off with, "I guess I'll have to go listen to yesterday's tape, though I hardly need to. Things are staying in my mind. I am starting to plan on getting well" (July 16, 1961, Journal, HRC). Importantly, in this letter—where "things are staying in her mind"—Sexton is "starting to plan on getting well," and she proclaims self-confidence and defiance against the norms to which Orne and others want her to adhere. It is a letter about dreams in which Orne, her father, and Kayo shape the narrative, but both the dreams and the letter temporarily throw off the power over Sexton's memory that Orne has established through the recordings. Dreams are impossible to record in real time on audio or in print with verisimilar accuracy. Dreams are mediated by the dreamer's perception. As well, the letter, like the poem (but unlike a recording), is a genre in which Sexton controls content, time, tone, and the intended audience. "I would have been to shy to tell you this dream in person," she tells Orne in the letter (July 16, 1961, Journal, HRC). "For the Year of the Insane" places dreams in "the domain of silence, / the kingdom of the crazy and the sleeper," and perhaps more importantly, outside of Sexton's and Orne's control, but this dream's content and the poem "For the Year of the Insane" also places Sexton's acts of self-expression squarely within the institutions against which she is also trying to rebel (1999, 131).

Poetry

Faith

In a draft of "For the Year of the Insane," Sexton refers to her session on July 31, 1963. She writes about the machinations of the therapeutic process, her frustrations with expressing that experience in language, and an institution and a mode of expression in which she still has faith: church and prayer. In contrast to the objective portrayal therapy demanded, a poetic response was more in tune with what Sexton perceived as the unconscious reckoning she achieved in a trance. In listening to a trance, she notes that she becomes "emerged in it . . . this is the same way I teach poetry . . . the same way I write . . . my unscious [sic] is doing the work . . . I can come up with intuitive things like I would in therapy, a discovery . . . but it's never common. . . . But now I realize this is the way I read a novel . . . now actually maybe it is the thing that allows me to write" (January 16, 1962, Journal, HRC). In the draft poem, the narrator has collapsed on the floor of the therapist's office, infantilized "to the air conditioner / the taker and the giver of breath, / . . . like a large mother" and rendered powerless, without any speech beyond the ritualized language of prayer: "i pray, curled on the floor as a child" (HRC, Typescript, 1963). Often ambivalent to Catholicism, Sexton uses its rites and practices of faith in the poem as a metaphor for the many institutions (academic, church, filial, marriage, psychiatric) that influenced her behaviors and the gendered pathology that dictated her means of expression as a white, middle-class woman in the United States in the 1950s and 1960s. Reading "For the Year of the Insane" as both a prayer and as a reference to the therapy text process means to read it as Sexton's complex proclamation of faith in institutional practices, against which she struggled, and in the expressive power of poetry to signal that struggle as a process of identity construction. In "For the Year of the Insane," Sexton uses faith, liturgical language, and time to represent how she negotiated the perceptual and cultural limits institutions prescribed for self-expression.

A prayer in the Catholic church belies a faith in its dogma and its promise of potential salvation. Sexton writes to her friend Brother Dennis Farrell in November 1962 that she believes in God even as she "opposes authority": "How strange we should meet. It is a gift for me, a prayer in sickness that was answered . . . me who opposes all authority, who struggles against misery and belief alike and even as I think of myself as an unbeliever . . .

then why do I love God?" (Sexton, Sexton, and Ames 1977, 148). She lacks the "right" words to pray but sees writing poetry as an indicator of her religious beliefs; "In deep ugly need a few weeks ago," she writes, "I tried to pray without knowing the rt words. . . . I don't know how to pray. I'm waiting and always without praying . . . tho you say that writing a poem was a kind of prayer" (148). For a different audience, Sexton is more unconventional, almost flippant about the entangled feelings she has about her faith in God and poetry. In a letter to her agent, Cindy Degener, on which the subject line is "New Book of Poems. Live or Die," Sexton writes about sending over her book contract. She quips to Degener, "I think I do know the poetry business and as I swore on the typewriter and my Gideon bible and my Holy Bible Revised Standard Version, you know about the other junk. Cindy, you have a problem here. Poetry to me is prayer—the rest of it is leftovers" (287).

In the context of institutions that tell her she's hysterical or her thoughts are wrong-headed, Sexton continues to believe in the struggle to express herself and find peace through poetry. The narrator's consequent place in "the kingdom of the crazy and the sleeper" in "For the Year of the Insane" indicates in the final words of the poem that the root of the narrator's madness is feeling captured in the wrong expression of self by instituted, mediated practices of word and deed meant to cultivate a culturally prescribed self—a singular self against which the self can evolve only in resistance. "For the Year of the Insane" is explicit about the narrator's resistance to the church as an institution, but the poem is also about faith and hope. The nonbeliever worries the rosary beads, engages in communion, stumbles "word for word" through the catechism. Similarly, having "entered the year without words," the narrator writes a poem and engages in the process of prayer that a reading of the poem necessitates.

Liturgy

When Sexton performs "For the Year of the Insane" at a reading in 1965, she tells her audience that the poem was "written from the inside; it's a prayer—for Mary but for someone to reach in and grasp—this place where there are no words; tried to make verbal what is indeed non-verbal."[13] It is her only poem subtitled "a prayer," and it begins with a comment on how the Catholic catechism represents faith born of speech acts and performance.[14] In the first stanza, the narrator beseeches Mary to "hear me now / Although I do not know your words," and concludes the stanza in the process of her attempts at expression: "Word for word, I stumble." Like the crucifix to Christ, the Catholic practitioner's belief and faith are embodied in the words of the catechism, yet the narrator experiences them as empty performances of belief and faith in generalizable, rote language that she experiences with little emotion, half-heartedly: "There are no words here except the half-learned / the *Hail Mary* and the *full of grace*" (Sexton 1999, 132). These prayers are like the Eucharist the narrator experiences without the passion it is intended to evoke, demonstrated by a voice of a disembodied, disengaged observer: "The glass rises in its own toward my mouth / and I notice this and understand this / only because it has happened" (132).

From the therapy recordings, Sexton learned how one could discern emotion beyond the words being used to express it. Listening to the trances, for example, she would intuit what she had been feeling, even if she could not adequately recapture her emotions in words. "It's funny," she once told Orne, "I write down the facts and forget some of the emotions" (March 7, 1961, AESL). Consequently, listening and trying to capture what she remembers feeling, Sexton discerns that emotion does not have a one-to-one relationship with the words spoken or the actions she could overhear. Memory could be elicited in between words, through objects, and alongside actions. After listening to the first trance tape, for example, Sexton notes that unlike her previous doctor, Orne used sounds to elicit her emotions: "Where you say 'uh-huh,' he would be silent and your 'uh-huh' is very reassuring. It means, 'I understand you, yes, go on' or, you know, it's uh, it is a response and without this response, I would feel like I was in a vast, snowy waste, you know, with no one" (January 28, 1961, AESL). Listening to the tapes, she recognizes, "I never was aware that you said 'uh-huh,' I mean, I kid you about it, but I really wasn't aware of the rhythm of the thing" (January 28, 1961, AESL). Nonverbal sounds and actions (including hand holding) were a significant part of how she and Orne would relate to one another, and unless she said what she was feeling out loud, the tape could not record it. "Well, whatever it was that I was looking for is only, only exists when I'm in trance," she tells Orne after listening to the first trance tape. "Listening to it, doesn't really seem, it doesn't sound anything like what it is. What I said before. I don't really verbalize because boy, something really big is going on with me, inside me, even though I don't really seem to say it very well. I mean it has a huge emotional effect" (January 28, 1961, AESL).

In a session a couple of months later, she tells him, "I hate the fact that I'm not expressing the emotion with you. . . . You see, the most remarkable thing is that I never sound like what I mean like. I know I have but I haven't lately. [inaudible]. It makes me mad. I'm mad at my own defenses" (March 7, 1961, AESL).

In the poem, when the narrator is rendered both speechless and prone, "curled like a dog on the carpet," her faith in the ritual process of prayer introduces a potential for selfhood beyond words and actions. The poem proclaims, "Now I have entered the year without words. / I note the queer entrance and the exact voltage. / Without words they exist. / Without words one may touch bread / and be handed bread / and make no sound" (132). In a letter to Brother Farrell written the day after she has drafted "For the Year of the Insane," Sexton gestures to this idea that the ritual of expression can enact potential selves even as the finitudes of writing practices (and institutions) tether her to an inexact method of expressing them: "Words bother me. I think that is why I am a poet," she writes. "I keep trying to force myself to speak of the things that remain mute inside. My poems only come when I have almost lost the ability to utter a word. To speak, in a way, of the unspeakable. To make an object out of the chaos. . . . To Say what? a final cry into the void" (Sexton, Sexton, and Ames, 1977, 171).

Time

One objection that Sexton had to Orne's therapeutic practice was that an "objective" appraisal of self ultimately depended on the memory she supposedly lacked, but the tapes—meant to ameliorate her forgetting—also made time and memories manipulable and unstable. Listening to a trance via tape, Sexton hears a recording of herself at another time inhabiting a little girl of yet another age of her life as well as anticipating a future listening to that self being currently taped. "I was just thinking," she comments to Orne during the first month of recording, "I was switching to really thinking of myself listening to this right now and I would say 'Come on, cry, you jerk, I can tell from your voice that you're going to.' You know, and I think well of course I don't know what the future of the tape is right now. It hasn't been created but I suddenly thought of that person listening. . . . Well maybe I won't analyze it for a while. It's kind of confusing" (January 28, 1961, AESL). In addition, while she could not access exactly what she was feeling while in a trance, she recognizes that the act of listening to the trances brought strong emotions in the present that seem to connect to what she must have been feeling at the time:

> Well because I suppose it's almost like a defense against myself by the time I have to listen. You know, here is something that I know but isn't there. What I know about this appointment isn't there on it. Like last time, somewhere, and I don't know where, because I kind of felt that way when I came in, and you can kind of hear it in my voice, I'm a little bit—I felt like I was going to cry and I wouldn't cry and not that I won't cry but that I don't express this, you know, at least that I feel so terrible. And I was looking when I was listening. Of course, when I come out I have an overall feeling of the appointment that I, colors the whole thing. It may not be there the whole time. (March 7, 1961, AESL)[16]

So, while the tapes could not help her remember exactly what she was feeling in the past, the strong emotions she experienced on reading the journals and listening to the tapes in the present nevertheless felt like an immersion in a memory:

> And I started to cry listening to the tape, and I think those were the first two tapes that I re-experienced instead of listening and doubting and thinking this or that. I was inside them because I had so completely forgotten them. It was happening to me and I'm sitting there crying . . . it seems as though it was just a minute ago, like just a minute ago—there was no distance between us at all. This had just happened, but and I start to cry and I'm sitting there sobbing away, listening to the tape. And I think both of these tapes are the first time that such a thing has happened . . . I was feeling it. It was just like an appointment. I mean somehow because it was news to me. I had forgotten it all. And it wasn't not real because it was happening to me. (March 25, 1961, AESL)

The recordings are not useful to her to aid her memory. Instead, emotion in this description serves as a compressed reaction that evokes the "whole" of a memory.

Listening to the tapes, Sexton blames her sense of time as the reason she cannot write down what she hears. She says testily about one trance tape, "I didn't write down the trance tape. I wrote down yesterday's. I wrote—this happened Tuesday, but it seems like it happened yesterday because that's when I wrote it" (April 25, 1961, AESL). In contrast to her experience writing the therapy text, Sexton believed she had the means (a "gift") to hold temporal slippages in her mind on an unconscious level:

> But if you say I can do this in spots, I can't cuz I can't rem that long . . . therefore I lose it, I have to do it all at once or I can't, I can't rem, I can't retain it (ah) all I can do is be emotional about it, I can't be reasonable about it . . . but I still live thro

> it, only part of personality allows me to do both now, but this is something I do uncsiously, everything I've done in my life, I now realise, I've done uncsiously, its the only gift I can bring to this type of thing . . . I cn't run it, if I try to run it with my so-called conscious intelligence I can't, the uncscious maerial overwhelms me. (January 16, 1962, Journal, HRC)

In March 1963, just months before writing the poem, Sexton reads through all the therapy journals, going back over fifteen months of work, and discovers that condensing what she reads into an objective synthesis is not only impossible, but beside the point. Instead, the journals provide her the means to access the emotions she currently has about what happened over time. She explains to Orne that when she is relistening and rereading, her experience "is almost impossible to pull it into a few words because it's kind of a drama. It's got to happen a few times before you can see it and then I can't really distill it. I become involved" (March 19, 1963, AESL). Triumphantly, she tells Orne, "I don't ever read back. I don't do this. I mean I read a long stretch you see kind of the rhythm" (March 19, 1963, AESL).

Sexton recognizes that a recording is not a record that maps to what happened at a particular session. It is a provocation, like the Catholic liturgy, to feel in the present what Sexton intuits occurred across time. In poetry, Sexton would perform the disorienting temporality of the therapy text and the ways it mediated resonant emotions and memories.[15] In a draft worksheet for "For the Year of the Insane," she uses the figure of the mother whose daughter becomes the mother to express this kind of fluid identity temporality: "Closer and closer comes the hour of my death / as I reseract my mother, grow young, / forget language and hear voices . . . as I move, as through water / through time" (HRC, Typescript, 1963). In the published version, Sexton evokes the slippery nature of time in the moment of communion. A resurrection of Christ's giving of his body and blood in the last supper, communion is when faith becomes an action that enacts the folding of time, the past in the present: "Closer and closer / comes the hour of my death / as I rearrange my face, grow back, / grow undeveloped and straight-haired" (Sexton 1999, 132). In both cases, the narrator's experience of mothering, praying, and the immortal Christ simultaneously move her forward to her death and back through time to her childhood. In the process of creating the therapy text, Sexton tries to be objective and capture a "true" self in words, but she is confused. She feels distant; she forgets. Instead, she uses poetry to immerse her narrator in a compressed, embodied, and wordless experience of an institution in which identity becomes faith in the situated and mediated experience of expressing a potential self.

* * *

The entelechy of the recording and the poem is the self. For Sexton, these records became snapshots of identity as it is experienced beyond the finitudes of those media; they evoked the potential of selves across time. Approximately three weeks after the session for which she writes "For the Year of the Insane," just before she leaves for Europe, and when she is likely still working on the poem's multiple drafts, Sexton discusses a picture she has taken of Orne to ward off the fears she feels in leaving him. She ruminates on how the artificial sense of time captured in the photograph lends to a slippery, more expansive sense of her identity through *her* observation of *him*: "You have become people I haven't met, not just men, but what I will be and what I am. And I don't know if I can write that picture. I want to leave, really" (August 20, 1963, HRC). Sexton tries to explain her intermedial sense of what the photograph evokes—"I don't know if I can write that picture"—that helps frame how she uses her experience of intermedia in poetry to mediate a sense of identity as movement and process across time:

> I know I took your picture because I have it. And some day when therapy is done, I'll explain to you what the picture of the therapist does to the patient. It's a fine thing. I don't know but it's something different. You don't really look. I said to Maxine, she said, oh it's a poem. I said, he knows who you are, but you don't know who he is, really. You know all that time. She says this was some sort of poem. And it's true. You know, I know who you are, but I haven't really looked at you. I didn't know you wore a wedding ring. How many times have I held your hand? . . . I never noticed it. I haven't really looked at you. I don't know who you are. I love you as I love a friend. A real friend. But you're not . . . You're not, uh, I don't know who you're not. You're you. You knew who I was. You could put the picture on the desk and know. But for me, who you are, it's very strange and I would think, I'm making a strange sort of forecast—that it would be interesting towards the end of therapy for a patient to take a picture of a therapist—towards the end of therapy. It might not be the best thing, but it might be required what I'm doing now, I don't know, but I would think towards termination that it would be a big help. Because you don't know who you're leaving. You think you've leaving all of them. You've left them. You love that person but it's something different. (August 20, 1963, HRC).

When looking at the photograph, Sexton has an instantaneous recognition of Orne's whole identity in terms of what he means to her but also recognizes the fact that he has whole parts of himself, his life, that she does not, cannot know. Through the entangled process of listening to the tapes, writing in the journals, and creating poetry, Sexton eventually begins to see her poems as records of her process of self: "Let's put it this way," she says during a session in which they talk about keeping or destroying the tapes, "I don't want them [to disappear] any more than I want poems to disappear" (March 7, 1961, AESL).

The last lines of "For the Year of the Insane" amplify how Sexton associates her sense of identity dislocation with institutional infrastructures (filial, marital, medical, religious, social, and professional) that imposed what must have felt like material constraints or like walls around her sense of who she was: "I am in my own mind," the poem concludes, "I am locked in the wrong house" (Sexton 1999, 133). Finitude is expressed in the poem through a faith in the mind-walls that hem in the narrator, which are represented by a faith in the confined version of self that the church dictates even though the narrator does not believe the message, a faith in words even though they are slippery, and a faith that there is an authentic feeling of self that resonates even if the narrator cannot see it, hear it, or fully express it in words. Sexton's "For the Year of the Insane" is about the limits prescribed for her by institutions such as the church, society, medical professionals, and the poetry profession, as well as those limits dictated by her mental illness and others by the words of her craft. That these experiences of self are mediated by the mind—and a sense of the *wrong* framing of mind to Sexton—mirrors how Sexton's expression of self was mediated by the culturally and technologically negotiated acts of generating the therapy text and her poetry. For Sexton, potential self-realization was made possible by the walls prescribed by society and the process of recording its expression.

This is what I do, this is what I do with my life, I talk to people. I do this . . . It's all about creating meaning.
—Gloria Evangelina Anzaldúa, "Using Meditation and Occult Tools" (Anzaldúa Papers, 2020)

5 Reception: Conocimiento in Gloria Anzaldúa's Spirituality Tapes

Gloria Evangelina Anzaldúa was a Chicana scholar and activist best known for her groundbreaking theories on disability, gender, nationality, sexuality, and identity, and scholars have written extensively about the more than one hundred interviews she taped as part of her writing and revision process.[1] "I like to do one-on-one talks because I discover things about myself," she says in one interview. "I make new connections between ideas just like I do in my writing. . . . When I'm speaking it's kind of like I'm writing in process, orally, so that I have to expose myself" (Anzaldúa 2000, 3). Besides the recorded interviews on which scholars typically focus, there are approximately forty of these other tapes, labeled "spiritual recordings" and archived in her papers at the Nettie Lee Benson Latin American Collection at the University of Texas (Anzaldúa Papers). Anzaldúa participated in palm readings she gave and received, tarot readings she gave and received, meditations she created and were created for and with her, as well as lectures she gave and listened to on palm readings, tarot readings, and meditations. Listening to Anzaldúa's "spiritual recordings" indicates that the taping scenario—the equipment setup, the recording process, the saving, the sharing, the relistening—influenced how Anzaldúa articulated spirituality as a form of knowledge production.[2]

This chapter is a reflection on close listening to these tapes as a process of Anzaldúa's concept of *conocimiento*, which addresses the potentiality of meaning making from a spiritual state of knowing and acting that is at once physical, technological, psychological, material, emotional, political, and spiritual. For Anzaldúa, to be open to conocimiento—that "feeling that there was something out there greater than myself"—is to be receptive. She enacted conocimiento through writing, which allowed her "to cultivate an acute awareness of processes at work in [her] own psyche and to create symbols and patterns of its operations . . . to make the fleeting process known," was to "create a virtual reality of the experience so the reader goes through it" (Anzaldúa 2015, 95). Following suit, in this chapter I create a "virtual reality" of my knowledge production process by using Anzaldúa's description of conocimiento's seven stages of knowing. I reflect on what I perceive and can articulate about what resonates for me while listening. In articulating my process of conocimiento with Anzaldúa's spiritual recordings, I amplify my positionality and modes of world making. I make known how my interpretive practices are (and are not) in tune with what others may (or may not) find dissonant in Anzaldúa's collection of spiritual recordings and how her ideas about human and technological receptivity interfere with institutional, personal, and collective values to co-create the possibilities for what I, in turn, make resonant.

Conocimiento

A function of conscious raising, self-awareness, and self-reflectivity, conocimiento is a dialogic process of knowledge production that goes "beyond the subject/object divide." It is "skeptical of reason and rationality," and "questions conventional knowledge's current categories, classifications, and contents" (Anzaldúa 2015, 119).[3] Anzaldúa describes it as an epistemology that values spirituality over science and rationality, and links "the inner life of the mind and spirit to the outer worlds of action" via creative acts such as "writing, art-making, dancing, healing, teaching, meditation, and spiritual activism" (178, 119). Significantly, conocimiento is an experience of the world that Anzaldúa would liken to tape recording:

> Like when I had too much, it was real painful. I couldn't process it. It was like being bombarded. It was like I would be sitting here and I would be hearing the subway, the birds, the heat, you, what you would be feeling, the people below. Uh-hm. Um. I was like a tape recorder. Like this tape recorder would pick up everything, where as you and I are listening to each other and you're focusing on what I'm saying and the other sounds would fade. Right? With me it was different. Everything came on, came in at the same volume.[4]

Anzaldúa articulates reception as a vulnerable stance, an openness to what Ralph Ellison (1952) and Paul Gilroy (1993) might call a lower-level frequency, where meaning is contingent on what one does not know one perceives.

Step One: Your Foundations Are Shaken

Anzaldúa describes the first stage of conocimiento as *un arrebato* (earthquake) that propels you into receptivity. You are shaken physically, emotionally, intellectually, spiritually, from solid ground and find yourself in "the bridge between the material and immaterial; the point of contact y el lugar between ordinary and spirit realities; the midground in the vertical continuum of spirit/soul that places spirituality at the top end (heaven) and soul at the opposite end (underworld)" (Anzaldúa 2015, 29). Knowledge in process begins in a liminal state of dialogue. While listening to Anzaldúa's tapes, there are preconceptions about Anzaldúa, myself, authority, the nature of intermedia records, the nature of their materiality, the nature of their ephemerality, and their capacity for indicating evidential truths that are shaken. For Anzaldúa, this "liminal, transitional space . . . between before and after" describes *nepantla*, a receptive positionality "where the outer boundaries of the mind's inner life meet the outer world of reality" (122). When you are experiencing nepantla's liminality, you are most receptive to a state of interiority, "a zone of possibility" where "you are exposed, open to other perspectives, more readily able to access knowledge derived from inner feelings" (122).

According to Anzaldúa, a state of nepantla and an attention to spirituality are predicated by "unsafe" behavior: a vulnerable, receptive stance is needed to resist the comfort of the usual paradigms for knowledge production and transform "perceptions of reality and thus the conditions of life" (Anzaldúa 2015, 122). Beyond her biographer AnaLouise Keating, very few scholars have written about the marginalization of spirituality in Anzaldúa scholarship and how that marginalization has shaped and limited what has been written about cultures generally and Anzaldúa in particular (Embry 1996; Henderson-Espinoza 2013; Keating in Anzaldúa 2000, 2015; and Keating 1996, 2005, 2008). Anzaldúa recognized how the conversation about her spiritual writing in academia was muted: "The 'safe' elements in Borderlands are appropriated and used," she says in an interview, "and the 'unsafe' elements are ignored. . . . As long as it's theoretical and about history, about borders, that's fine; borders are a concern that everybody has. But when I start talking about *nepantla*—as a border between the spirit, the psyche, and the mind or as a process—they resist" (Urch, Dorn, and Abraham 1995, 85; quoted in Anzaldúa 2000, 7). Keating argues that avoiding spirituality in Anzaldúa studies stems from a fear (1) of being considered "unprofessional" since no self-respecting scholar would write about tarot card and palm reading sessions, especially not women-of-color concerned for the precarity of their careers; (2) of diminishing the significance of Anzaldúa's writing to the everydayness of common practices or the illogicality of "'New Age' escapist ramblings"; and (3) of encouraging Anzaldúa's romantic view of indigeneity and her seeming desire to "resurrect 'old gods'" and "reclaim an 'authentic' precolonial spirituality or religion, or in other ways nostalgically reinvigorate pseudo-ancient traditions or beliefs" (Keating 2008, 55–56).

Nepantla is a receptive stance that has an element of danger, of precarity in its liminality. Being receptive means I am placing myself in a state of possible "resonance with the other's feelings and situations," willing "to give the other an opportunity to express their needs and points of view. To relate to others by recognizing commonalities" (Anzaldúa 2000, 178). Anzaldúa describes the dialogue inherent in creating meaning. "When I give readings," Anzaldúa says in an interview with Jeffner Allan, "What I do is I dialogue. I read. They ask questions, make comments . . . it's like this exchange."[5] She describes the feelings of vulnerability and power inherent in speaking to an audience that is unreceptive initially but ultimately receptive to her ideas: "The Haight reading was full of white hippies and ordinary people and I felt so at home with them. I couldn't figure out why I felt so at home. Part of the reason was that they were so open to my work" (147). Maria P. Chaves Daza (2015) describes listening to an online recording of Anzaldúa giving a lecture at the University of Arizona and the danger of her being so open:

> On the University of Arizona's recording, I can hear in Anzaldúa's laugh a relish in her ability to take up space, to have before her an audience of more lesbian, gay and queer writers to contribute to her several anthology projects. Her voice is filled with a nervous excitement; after all, there is always a danger in being queer. *Her laugh resonates as a physical instantiation of the risk of her own existence and of the other queers in the room.* [emphasis added]

Is this audience receptive to Anzaldúa's risk? Do they feel the precarity? To listen in on a dialogue as Daza has done is to overhear meaning making in a liminal state: the speaker's, the audience's, the listener's. Daza describes a receptive stance that can be considered threatening, particularly if you are a woman of color, a Chicana, a lesbian. Being receptive is "to find that

Reception

inner authority and give it legitimacy" (Anzaldúa Papers, "Using Meditation"). Listening before writing, listening while writing, is being poised in a liminal state, precariously between trying to understand and knowing. In a talk called "Using Meditation and Occult Tools" that Anzaldúa gave to an Adult Degree Program class in Montpelier, Vermont, in 1984, she tells her audience, "We don't know how to listen":

> Before we get into the writing and stuff, I wanted to give another little spiel about listening, about, we all the time listen to other people, outside authorities, teachers, people with degrees, officials, politicians, and we very rarely listen to ourself, the self we have inside us and around us. Listening is something that comes very hard to Americans because we want to talk. We have a viewpoint to present. We have a stance to present to the world. For us to listen, to receive, is threatening . . . being exposed to these new things will shake us off that, those concepts that we have—so receptivity is a very maligned and put down activity . . . we aren't used to, at least as women. That kind of receptivity is now adays put down because that's too passive.[6]

Listening is a receptive stance that creates meaning by destabilizing authority in a process of "[g]iving feedback, taking frequent reality checks, and clarify[ing] meaning" (Anzaldúa 2000, 178).

Listening to the sounds—picking up on the signals—that are muted in scholarship is a means to articulate my own motivations concerning how intermedia and the scholarship of actors and thinkers like Hurston, Ellison, Sexton, and Anzaldúa (among others) influence what I can know about my approach to listening and writing. And then there are my listeners, my readers. In the process of conocimiento, I lay myself open to what the reader may overhear beyond what I say, what I write. Listening, reading, and writing become entangled practices. What is one without the others? Being receptive invites the possibility for dialogue, for connectivity, and it undermines the notion of an authority, one voice, or of media as singular modes of engagement. Dialogue is the precarious realization of self and other, speaker and listener, writer, and reader. In dialogue, I am receptive to the idea that authority and truth hang suspended in a liminal state.

Step Two: You Start to Rethink What You Thought You Knew

I listen for liminal sounds that signal knowledge in production, the making of meaning rather than meaning made. These sounds evoke conversive, messy, collaborative, nonlinear, and waffling aspects of "truth" and "authority." They sound to me like an invitation to ask questions. On the tapes, liminal sounds can include voicings (sighs, sniffs, whistles, clicks) and everyday sounds "that border on the linguistic" (Dingemanse 2020, 188). Mark Dingemanse explains that these sounds have been marginalized in linguistic scholarship for technological reasons, when "recording and transcription methods were not up to the task"; for theoretical reasons, when a "focus on idealized competence led a generation of linguists to look away from what was seen as the flotsam and jetsam of mere performance"; and for ontological reasons, because these sounds sound like "not-talk" when scholarship is focused on the "talk" aspects of conversations recorded in real time (188). Consequently, these liminal signs are described in linguistics as vague, equivocating, somewhere "between showing and saying, giving off and giving, symptoms and symbols" (191). Liminal sounds represent an invitation, a charge, for scholars to create alternative narratives. "Living in nepantla," Anzaldúa writes, "the overlapping space between different perceptions and belief systems, you are aware of the changeability of racial, gender, sexual, and other categories rendering the conventional labelings obsolete . . . you know that the new paradigm must come from outside as well as within the system" (2015, 119).

I think we are mostly unaware of the liminal sounds we make. Liminal sounds are typically dialogue sounds that mark the in-between space of words. They happen when words take too long, require too much from your tongue, your larynx, your lips, your mental, emotional, psychological state of mind, perhaps. Liminal sounds happen when you still desire to communicate; when you aren't quite sure what words your audience will understand the way you mean them; when you want to locate your meaning between everyday speech and high theory for an audience that is full of people with whom you are unfamiliar, even as their willingness to be receptive, to listen, is evident. When I was a teenager, I had a tonsillectomy. I couldn't speak for almost a week. I got out of the habit of making the sounds of conversation that people make when they are actively listening to one another. Those sounds ("huh," "uh-hum," "uh-huh") took too much energy when it hurt to speak just the words I needed to be fed and cared for. I thought I knew what participating in a conversation entailed until I didn't make those sounds. These liminal voicings evoke meaning by way of an ambiguity that unsettles categorization, analysis, or a sense of intention. I wasn't aware until I didn't make them, that I make liminal sounds when I don't have the precise words, but I still want to signal my desire to be in conversation.

Being receptive to liminal sounds shifts my listening practice to listening for a meaning-making process. Listening to Anzaldúa's liminal sounds, I amplify how laughter, for instance, can mark Anzaldúa's dialogic process of meaning making on her spirituality tapes. Daza calls Anzaldúa's voice "a soothing mechanism; her laugh momentarily takes the edge off of some of her words as it reaches out, touches, and brings together queer people of color" (2015). That is, Anzaldúa's laughter renders her accessible in ways beyond or complementary to her words. Her meditational voice and the way she speaks with her friends is also soothing, relaxing. She speaks quickly, easily. She has, comingled in English, a south Texas, Spanish-speaker rhythm and cadence. She giggles, a lot. Anzaldúa concludes her "spiel" about receptivity and listening, for example, by noting her own resistance to listening. She makes a joke. Being receptive and vulnerable is "pretty hard when you're a woman," she says. "It's pretty hard when you're a woman of color, and it's pretty hard when you're a lesbian, and it's pretty hard when you're short," even when "those can be your very strengths" (Anzaldúa Papers, "Using Meditation"). On the recording, Anzaldúa laughs when she calls herself short. The audience laughs. I think it's funny too, but I laugh somewhat uncomfortably. Anzaldúa *is* a smaller woman, but I know it's likely due to her health issues. Perhaps, that is also why she laughs? It seems evident to me that laughing creates a shared affect—humor, in this case—and increased audience receptivity around something messy, unfamiliar, or difficult to understand. In this way, laughter facilitates dialogue and resonance. I am receptive to Anzaldúa's ideas in part because, laughing together, I feel included in her "we" rather than her "other people." Listening to the tapes, I am not in her audience in Vermont, and I do not identify as a person of color, a lesbian, or particularly short, but I feel included in the list of what's "pretty hard" for her audience when I listen to Anzaldúa speak. When Anzaldúa's interlocutors—her audience—laugh, I smile along. Laughing together, she opens me up for listening, makes me feel that new ideas are safe.

There are other sounds the women make in the course of their conversations on Anzaldúa's spiritual tapes. When she and her friends give tarot readings to each other, they share seeds and nuts, eating audibly. Receiving and sharing foods and moods, they are comfortable, they talk over each other, interrupting and laughing.

In a tarot reading Gloria Anzaldúa conducts for Sally Gearhart in May 1981, Anzaldúa whoops and whistles when Gearhart has a propitious card; she does this multiple times. Anzaldúa also mispronounces the word "propitious" multiple times. Gearhart points out the mispronunciation, and Anzaldúa doesn't seem to care. Anzaldúa just laughs more. She likes the word and Gearhart knows what she means even if it doesn't sound quite right. Anzaldúa seems to like Gearhart and Gearhart's partner Jane, who is not present but is mentioned. Their comfortable tone signals a conversation between friends. They are not required to explain their contexts to each other, the nature of their relationship. As a listener, I have to guess. Before the taping begins, it seems that Anzaldúa has laid out the tarot cards to do a reading for Gearhart. Anzaldúa interprets the presence of the Hierophant card, which is usually a card signifying traditional values and institutions, as an indicator of Gearhart's relationship with Jane. Anzaldúa explains that "the person represented by the Hierophant is very much concerned with family. She has a lot to do with a—male person in her life. Could be her father. When she resolves certain things with that male person, that authority figure, she will own up to her leadership." Gearhart makes a noise that sounds dismissive. Then she says, "Would you say that again, louder. I'll play this tape for Jane," meaning for Jane to hear the advice about the male authority figure. Gearheart guffaws, and quickly adds, "That's important." Awkwardly, Gearhart must explain to Anzaldúa that she is "just teasing." Laughing with her, Anzaldúa responds almost defensively. She either didn't understand Gearhart's intention, or perhaps, Anzaldúa is kidding when she replies about the tape recorder, "I think it's picking up pretty good."[7]

I can hear Anzaldúa mishearing or *mis*-listening to Gearhart. I can only assume I do that too. As a listener, I am sure I fill in spaces with conjecture. I know I do not and will not have an accurate, full understanding of their history, of the nuances between these two women, or the other women, or the other tapes, of the things I am not even aware I do not hear. When did they meet? How often do they speak? How often do they do tarot readings together? The only evidence I have is what I can hear recorded on this tape, this tape that happened to be saved, to which I happen to be listening. This is not happenstance, entirely. Just like this could be the best day of their friendship or the worst or perhaps it is an average, typical day. For the most part, the spiritual recordings are conversations between two people who know each other. These are not performances for me. There is much unsaid that is also recorded, of which I try to perceive traces, but like Anzaldúa, I create a narrative about what I think I hear. I interpret what I hear to resonate with what I think I know.

Even so, listening to the tapes is important. Liminal sounds are not often transcribed in printed transcripts of recordings. They go unheard in print. People are rarely eating, laughing, or uh-huhing on the printed pages of scholarship. Transcribing is a process by which scholars note what they think is important in a transaction. Most often, when people transcribe a recording, they note just the words people say, but if there are the sounds of chickens in the background, the sounds of gunshots, sounds of a car—if the sounds provide proof of important auditory contexts such as evidence of the farm, the war, the urban landscape—transcribers might note these too. Certainly, it is slow work to transcribe all the nuanced voicings, all the "uhs," sighs, sniffs, whistles, and clicks.

Keating, whose relationship as editor and scholar with Anzaldúa began with her first interview with her in 1991 and continued through multiple edited works, has edited many of Anzaldúa's recorded interviews and produced several published versions.[8] An experienced and thoughtful editor, Keating has omitted vocalizations, turns of phrase, or side comments in her transcriptions, purposefully. She is transparent about the complexities of editing: "My goal as an editor is to make the interviews compelling and readable—to make them flow—while remaining true to the spoken word, the oral rhythms, and (of course) to the original meaning . . . also tried to avoid excessive repetition" (Anzaldúa 2000, 13). Besides, for what do these liminal sounds provide proof beyond liminality or ambiguity, vagueness, and circuitousness? Transcribing the messy detritus of speech might not be on par for professional, publishing protocols and could create confusion depending on the goals of providing the transcription in the first place. Trying to be receptive to all the sounds, like a tape recorder, could lead to in-between perceptions, where meaning could go in multiple directions.

To listen to Anzaldúa hedge and ahem and guffaw and laugh and whoop it up, and to perceive these sounds as important, is to place significance on the idea that knowledge is produced and perceived in a place and time in conversation. It is me saying that the guffaw, the whoop, and the holler are meaningful, but they are also ambiguous, subjective sounds. It is me saying that it is okay for meaning to go in multiple directions. On the audio recordings, I can hear what we normally do not record in print. I can hear knowledge production happening as an embodied process then and now, in the liminal sounds of everyday dialogue where authority and truth are suspended.

Step Three: Overwhelmed by the Chaos, You Feel Despair
Being in unstable territory, where categories are in flux and unsituated, can be confusing. It can feel threatening. When I try to share Anzaldúa's comments about situated, dialogic listening and being a woman of color, lesbian, and short with an audience at a conference in Austin, Texas, they don't laugh. I don't have permission from the Gloria Evangelina Anzaldúa Literary Trust to play the recording of her "little spiel about listening," so I am reading it out loud, and I don't set her joke up right. I am white, cisgender, and heterosexual. Telling them she's a smaller woman before saying the line where she calls herself "short" would make its inclusion alongside the more overtly political labels in her list of identity categories ("Chicana" and "lesbian") less humorous. If I tell the audience beforehand that she's small, that detail's inclusion would lack the impact it is given by Anzaldúa's slight shift from serious to silly, her verbal slide from racialized identities to height. Her presentation of forthrightness and vulnerability that is her charm and that makes her words and thoughts so accessible to a diverse audience would be lost. In my delivery of her words, her being short seems like a non sequitur, maybe even a deprecation or a meanness, perhaps. I don't have to tell my audience that I am not a woman of color, a lesbian, or particularly short. Describing her joke instead of telling it seems to create a distance between myself and my audience. I don't tell it in the right order. Or maybe I've left out a detail? They look confused, possibly dismayed by my seemingly insensitive reference to her height. It's not funny.

The experience of listening shakes the foundations of what I think I am supposed to be doing and writing about with these tapes. Being receptive to new ideas can threaten the sense of self you depend on to interpret your experience. At moments, the juxtaposition of Anzaldúa's kind, inviting voice on the tape recorder talking to me and the hard truth of what she says is jarring. What she says can sometimes be difficult to hear. In one guided meditation, she tells her audience to imagine "roots growing out of your cunt."[9] At the slang term, I'm disconcerted, disconnected from what I am hearing. I am thrown back on myself. It is not a word I typically use or expect in a guided meditation, smoothed over into just a "regular" word through Anzaldúa's soothing tone. Why am I thrown off? My reaction immediately makes me feel stuck up, classist, prejudiced. I am an outsider.

Anzaldúa's work can be powerful and uplifting, but also damning and earth-shattering—for me. She writes about white women and four-letter words:

> The privilege of whiteness allows [white women] to evade questions of complicity with those in power; it gives leave to disrespect other people's realities and types of knowledge—"race" and "soul" remain four-letter words. Their socialization does not allow women-of-color consciousness to transform their thinking. Afraid of losing material and psychological privilege, they drown others' voices with white noise. (2015, 145–146)

The difference in feeling between how her writing talks about me and my experience listening to her as if she is speaking with me in dialogue shakes my faith in my own perceptions. I sense my own biases, my own hopes for what I hear. Receptive, trying to be open, I must ask myself as she speaks to me in ways that are both comfortable and uncomfortable: Is she talking to me? Is she talking about me? What is my role in this dialogue as the person listening in on someone else's conversation? In a previous chapter, I note how Saidiya Hartman (1997, 3), Toni Morrison (1992, 37), and Ralph Ellison write about how primarily white authors use events of racial tensions to reduce African Americans to "a human 'natural' resource who, so that white men could become more human, was elected to undergo a process of institutionalized dehumanization" (Ellison 1995, 85). I am reminded that my experience listening to Anzaldúa includes a complex sense of self-making as a process—hers *and* mine in dialogue.

Being receptive to the idea that identity formation, "becoming more human," is a conversation in process is especially unsettling when I listen to Anzaldúa. Anzaldúa makes paralinguistic and liminal vocalizations that bear significance in the context of gendered, abled, and nationalized formations of identity that I do not share. In the chapter "How to Tame a Wild Tongue" in *Borderlands* (2007), Anzaldúa begins with an anecdote about her "wild" tongue getting in the way of a tooth extraction. She likens this experience to having her identity "bridled" by childhood classroom admonitions about speaking "American" rather than Spanish, and she asserts that "ethnic identity is twin skin to linguistic identity—I am my language . . . I will have my voice: Indian, Spanish, white" (81). Anzaldúa asserts that "language is a male discourse" when she writes about first learning that the feminine form of "we"—nosotras—existed and when she first understood that there were words (hocicona, repelona, chismosa) that were derogatory only when applied to women (76). In response to the gendered nature of language, Anzaldúa seeks to "overcome the tradition of silence" with her wild tongue, her "serpent's tongue—my woman's voice, my sexual voice, my poet's voice" (81). In *Borderlands*, she writes that "wailing is the Indian, Mexican and Chicana woman's feeble protest when she has no other recourse . . . a sign of resistance in a society which glorified the warrior and war and for whom the women of the conquered tribes were booty" (55).

Anzaldúa's version of the world is not beyond reproach. There are criticisms levied against how her perception of identity and her theories of the "new mestiza" are shaped by personal biases and "exclusionary logics" (Feghali 2011). There are other arguments that her claims to indigeneity are cultural appropriations and that her ideas about "new tribalism" entrench, in a romantic fiction, "the imaginary Indian at the center of Chicana/o identity" (Perez 2014). Keating also describes the reactions to Anzaldúa of her students, who found Anzaldúa relied on "stereotypes and monolithic categories." Keating addresses their concerns by insisting that the full trajectory of Anzaldúa's work demonstrates that her intentions were inclusionary and that she remained open to academic dialogue until her death and that Anzaldúa's "nakedness" and willingness to be personal, vulnerable, are what generates connection with others (Keating 2009, 11–12, 1). The argument seems to be that because Anzaldúa intends to be receptive, she is listening, but what if she mishears? What if I do?

Keating admits in the introduction to *Interviews* that she feels uncomfortable using her personal voice and talking about personal things. She asserts, "I am the product of the U.S. university system. I have learned to mask my own agenda—my own desires for social justice, spiritual transformation, and cultural change—in academic language" (Anzaldúa 2000, 3). I am a product of the same system, and I am curious how scholars unmask a personal agenda by being personal. Did that work for Keating? For Anzaldúa? Like

Keating, like myself, Anzaldúa likewise stood in the liminal space between trying to listen and writing about what she experienced.

Step Four: You Tap into Your Spirituality

Anzaldúa defines spiritual receptivity as the struggle to get past or within yourself. What is beyond perception is spiritual. "What your eyes, ears, and other physical senses perceive is not the whole picture, but one determined by our core beliefs and prevailing societal assumptions," she writes. "To understand the greater reality that lies behind your personal perceptions, you view these struggles as spiritual undertakings" (119). In her attempt to push beyond her own societal assumptions and biases, Anzaldúa made spirituality a daily practice, because in "the ability to recognize and endow meaning to daily experience (spirituality) furthers the ability to shift and transform" (Anzaldúa 2015, 150). This daily spiritual practice necessarily extends to the dialogic scenarios Anzaldúa created and recorded, and to which she likely relistened. Practicing dialogue with others—what she calls "relatedness"—one remains flexible to the paradigmatic shifts inherent in spiritual receptivity and is open to orienting toward a new belief system. Such dialogic practice means

> you listen with respect, attend to the other as a whole being, not as an object, even when she opposes you. To avoid miscommunication, you frequently check your understanding of the other's meaning, responding with, "Yes, I hear you. Let me repeat your words to make sure I am reading you right." When an experience evokes similar feelings in both, you feel momentarily in sync. Like consciousness, conocimiento is about relatedness—to self, others, world. (Anzaldúa 2015, 151)

Anzaldúa associates dialogic listening with a connection to others as well as her spiritual beliefs because dialogic listening includes opening to the in-betweenness of a perception of self in the process of integrating with another.

The properties of sound provided a model that Anzaldúa would use to signal this liminal space in which—between embodied and othered, between one belief system and another—one is receptive to spirituality. In a 1983 interview with Christine Weiland, Anzaldúa describes her beliefs that sound has spiritually transportive properties. In explaining how she can give herself an orgasm through meditation, she describes her imagined lover as a multigendered goddess and the activity as "making love to the divine, this soul" (Anzaldúa 2000, 108). At the pinnacle of Anzaldúa's orgasm, the goddess loses form and becomes the physical properties of resonant vibrations without sound. It is "a drumbeat or something," Anzaldúa writes, ". . . like a vibration . . . like the wind, listening to the wind, but it's a different rhythm. I put on my earplugs, and I still hear it. But if I put my earplugs on, I can't hear the subway rumble" (110). It is significant that the experience is sonic—it is both physical and perceptible, but also beyond Anzaldúa's ability to describe in words. "What does it sound like?" Weiland asks. Anzaldúa responds,

> It sort of sounds like the ocean . . . it's like a breath. Have you ever been in a forest, when the wind suddenly goes through it? . . . It's like that but it's regular. It's like a machine, like a metronome. But with the feeling, like chimes of the wind and the ocean and the trees. But it's steady, like a metronome or a pulse . . . first you think it's a mechanical thing, like a motor. Then it becomes like a song, like music. That's why I think the stuff about the word is really about vibration. It's like a heartbeat and like your cuntbeat, but it's not. It sounds more like the ocean would sound like if there were trees in the ocean and it was autumn and the wind was blowing. I don't know how to describe it. (2000, 110–111)

At the core of this spiritual experience for Anzaldúa is the property of sound that is inherent to but exceeds audible perception and description in words and images: vibration. The vibration is embodied, a "heartbeat" or "cuntbeat" but also mechanical. It is of nature, made by water or by wind or by both at once, pictured as a sound scenario (autumn trees in water) that is improbable if not impossible. Vibration is a sound sensation to which the body is receptive regardless of will, culture, or identity. You cannot close your eyes or plug your ears against it.

Anzaldúa found sonic vibrations so evocative that she uses them as primary catalysts for the main character's spiritual transformation in the short story "Reading LP" (Anzaldúa 2009). In the story, la Prieta—a semiautobiographical character—reads a book that echoes the life she is leading working on a farm. Anzaldúa's manuscript pages for the story include multiple, expansive draft sections that did not make it into the version that Anzaldúa was revising at the time of her death.[10] Many of these earlier versions include different examples of Anzaldúa using sound vibrations as a device to transform la Prieta's spatiotemporal reality and to prepare her entrance into a dream or spirit world. In her writing notes, Anzaldúa calls la Prieta's experience of conocimiento "a shamanistic event which awakens her" and "a paranormal event where different realities converge." The conocimiento event results in "a radical shift in the way of seeing the world, a coming-to-consciousness result[ing] in changes in her identity" (2009, 250). Another note reads, "Sense—find a

Reception

way to go to other world."[11] The catalyzing, transportive sense in two early versions are the sounds and vibrations that come from the farm life:

> The steady drone of the machine, the vibrations entering her body through her gloved hands, her denim clad buttocks. The sun not yet overhead, she finds herself sitting on an idling tractor listening to a voice reciting whole passages of the book. What she did with the rest of the morning, she can't recall. (Anzaldúa Papers, "Entremados de PQ," notes)

A later moment includes la Prieta being transported by listening to a barbed wire fence, "The whining pitch of its vibration fills her ears . . . she finds herself in the bathroom not knowing how or when she got there" (Anzaldúa Papers, "Entremados de PQ," notes).

When la Prieta realizes she is living the book, that the book is writing her life, la Prieta burns it. After the burning, la Prieta feels intensely how the sounds and vibrations transport her bodily and spiritually:

> In one hour she reads the whole book in her head. Again [she hears] that shrill whine of a wire stretched to the its breaking point. She stretches out her arms toward the wall, her hands disappear. She pulls them back, examines them. They look the same. She hears the voices . . . In the middle of the night they wake her . . . Silence, the voices have vanished. No there's a sound like the whine, a tautly pulled wire. There behind her. The sound gets louder and louder. Sweat breaks out under her armpits and adrenaline [pumps] through her body. [Swiftly] she turns swiftly to where the sound is coming from [and] is [suddenly] caught off balance. Floundering and [S]eeking to right herself she puts the palm of her hand against the sheetrock and [flounders then grabs the bedpost. She] feels her hand go straight in [through] and her whole body falls into a thick wind, a gelatinous current. There is no wall. She is alone, sucking great gulps of air[.] [A]alone[,] in air so thick and blue . . . She's absorbed by vibrations of sounds she cannot hear, by glimpses of murky objects that advance toward her and fall away just as they are about to touch her. She is about to grasp an intimation of an absolute, law that will explain what is happening to her, but that too swims out of sight [is swept away in the silence] just before reaching her and she realizes there are no absolutes . . . Madness is being caught between walls. (Anzaldúa Papers, "Entremados de PQ," notes)

La Prieta is transported into the blue-aired, gelatinous space of the spirit world between the walls of the house by "vibrations of sounds she cannot hear." The published version of the story ends with la Prieta getting a hammer from her tool shed to take down the walls in her house through which she has entered the spiritual world. In multiple, unpublished drafts, la Prieta seeks to end her spiritual journey by cutting off sound, the source of the vibrations. In these versions, Anzaldúa concludes with the line, "She puts a thumb in her ear" or "She puts her thumb in her ear—the ear is an opening to another world."[12] A mindful as well as bodily sensation, sound vibration is for Anzaldúa the experience that best represents the spiritual aspects of liminality, which engages "a more spiritual, psychic, supernatural, and indigenous resonance" and a feeling of relatedness to the world beyond the self (Anzaldúa 2000, 176).[13]

Step Five: You Desire Order
But what is "a more spiritual, psychic, supernatural, and indigenous resonance"? How do I engage with such a comment in a scholarly way that addresses a description of resonance that seems, at best, vague and, at worst, essentialist? In the fifth step of conocimiento, in the desire for order, "You scan your inner landscape, books, movies, philosophies, mythologies, and the modern sciences for bits of lore you can patch together to create a new narrative articulating your personal reality" (Anzaldúa 2015, 123). I search the literature to find discussions about the relationship between sound technology and spirituality. I discover Friedrich Kittler and Jonathan Sterne noting that the telephone's hearing apparatus was designed based on a dead man's ear (Kittler 1999, 75; Sterne 2003, 258). I find Jacob Smith following the history of laugh tracks on television, which are often the guffaws and giggles of people now dead, laughing (Smith 2012, 534). I find a history of the representation of death from Thomas Edison's invention of the phonograph and his desire to hear the dead (Gitelman 2008), which leads to how this desire to hear the dead is tied to the preservation of supposedly dying languages and the dehistorization of marginalized, often indigenous, cultures (Sterne 2003, 17). Also relevant, I discover Alexander Weheliye's treatment of dub reggae and "the haunting at the center of the 'real'" as represented by the printed version of sorrow songs in W. E. B Du Bois's book of essays *Souls of Black Folks* (Du Bois 2007; Weheliye 2005, 103). Here, the uncanny sonority of the "spectral absent present" is created (rather than recreated) by the inclusion of slave songs in Du Bois's essays, where they are performed without sound and without bodies: "the sonorous facets of this spectral ontology" at the limit of empirical knowledge: recorded yet still inaudible, a "dead sound" (Weheliye 2005, 103). I find Erna Brodber's novel *Louisiana* (1994), in which the recording machine is a microphone for spirits, and David Burrows calling sound "the most important

single contributor to our notion of the otherworldly," claiming that "if we are believers, then we can believe that the spirit is moving us in our ritual music" (1980, 191). Gitelman, Kittler, Smith, Sterne, Weheliye, and Brodber would seem to agree with Burrows that sound has historically evoked an otherworldliness as it performs a "haunting" absent presence. For the listener, such an experience—a "haunting"!—is unsettling because where absence is present there must be a liminal state between the two, between death and life.

A liminal, spiritual state is not limbo for Anzaldúa. In her papers, I find references to scholars to whom Anzaldúa may have turned for guidance about liminality and spirituality. One folder in the Anzaldúa Papers, "Pysch/Meta/Health Notes—Life Stages—Mid-Life 1984," has within it some of Anzaldúa's writing notes, including an extensive quote about liminality from Jungian Murray Stein's book *In Midlife*, first published in 1983. She writes in pen his definition at length:

> When the ego is separated from a fixed sense of who it is and has been, where it comes from and its history of where it is going and its future; when the ego floats through a territory of unclear boundaries and uncertain edges; when it is disidentified from the inner images that have formerly sustained it and given it a sense of purpose. Then, the unconscious is disturbed in its archetypal layers, and the self is constellated to send messages: big dreams, vivid and powerful intuitions, fantasies, and synchronistic and symbolic events. The function of these messages is to lead the ego forward, and this guidance helps it to do what it has to do, whether this is to enter liminality further or, later, to emerge out of it. (Stein 1983, 22)[14]

In contrast to the *OED* definition, in which a state of liminality is to have "the lowest amount necessary to produce a particular effect; minimal; insignificant,"[15] Stein's definition of liminality concerns the disturbed ego spurred into action.

Reading these scholars (and reading Anzaldúa reading Stein), I reconsider how the significance of all Anzaldúa's tools—the texts, the tapes, the cards—lies in the practice of shaking things up. Anzaldúa's intermedia "occult tools" provided opportunities for achieving a state of liminality, which spurs the interlocutor to spiritual action, not death.[16] Anzaldúa describes the creative process as an intermedia practice in which "every sensory experience" can include "the rhythm of the words and the flow of images," which "evolve [into] a structure and act as catalysts for combining information in a new way" (2015, 101). For Anzaldúa, these catalysts could include "dreams, meditations, journal entries, films she had seen, scribbled in notebooks and on pieces of paper, article clippings, scholarly books, observations from her interactions with human and nonhuman others, lecture notes, transcripts from previous lectures and interviews," and other "writing notas" (Keating 2015, xii). Tarot cards, palms, and the I Ching (an ancient Chinese divination practice) were also important "spiritual tools to deal with various problems, large and small" (Anzaldúa 2000, 151). Anzaldúa's tarot-reading friend, Sally Gearheart, writes that the tarot represented a means of recording oral traditions via pictures:

> using pictures as a storage device, a highly elaborate filing-and-retrieval system . . . the ideal vehicle for encoding an elaborate and complex cosmological/metaphysical oral tradition. Pictorial encoding was not only safer; in an age when writing was a restricted art, it made messages more accessible. (Gearhart and Rennie 1977, xi)[17]

The cards are a provocation to dialogue, to the in-betweenness of meaning, not its proof. The tarot is not an exact replica of a time or an exact history of a place; it is an invitation to create an accessible space where liminality and the possibility of meaning making occur. Meaning is dependent on what you perceive in the cards in a moment in time, in a context, with a particular audience.

Subliminal persuasion tapes were another tool Anzaldúa found transformative for changing her body and her mind. She explains during a 1998 interview with Keating that she has the power to heal herself with these tapes, which helped her bypass her sense of self and spoke to the belief system beyond her awareness.[18] She tells Keating:

> So I really believe in subliminal tapes where the conscious mind, uh, won't hear, but the subconscious mind—and the reason that we have these belief systems is that someone told us over and over and over "you're a bad boy. You're no good. You'll end up in jail. You always mess up." So that becomes a belief. So one of the ways to change that is to hear over and over again the opposite so you can reprogram your belief system.[19]

Like the sonic vibrations in la Prieta's story, the media environment facilitates a provocation to bypass the reasoning mind and "slip between realities to a neutral perception," where "a decision made . . . becomes a turning point initiating psychological and spiritual transformation, making other kinds of experiences possible" (Anzaldúa 2015, 150–151). Anzaldúa believed her intermedia "occult tools" activated varied modes of seeing and listening, directing her perceptions beyond the "surface" self and toward relatedness and spiritual activism. Order, structure, direction, scholarship—the objects of study here that order my interaction with Anzaldúa's spiritual beliefs are the tapes.

Step Six: You Try and Fail to Persuade the World with Your New Story
I include her recordings because I hear the influences in what she says, but that's also what I want to hear in what she says. I began this chapter saying I would consider my own process of conocimiento by being receptive to spirituality and technology in Anzaldúa's creative process, that I would amplify my modes of world making and expose my interpretive practices with intermedia as cultural records. In the process of conocimiento, I would describe my process of listening to the spiritual tapes and articulate some of the institutional, personal, and collective values that cocreate the possibilities for what I signify, what I make resonant in Anzaldúa's recordings. For Anzaldúa, audio, the body, flora and fauna, images, and texts were all intermedia for stimulating and conveying spiritual transcendence. "You become aware of a supernatural being," she writes.

> It shares with you a language that speaks of what is other; a language shared with the spirits of trees, sea, wind, and birds; a language that you'll spend many of your writing hours trying to translate into words. Walking between realities—one strange, another familiar—you experience the shock of recognition, the pleasure it gives you. A deep sounding from the landscape resonates through your body-mind. You get a hint of the ground of writing and a few tenuous tendrils groping for a trellis. You begin working the soil. (Anzaldúa 2015, 101).

Of course, I am biased toward a narrative in which Anzaldúa's theories are influenced by sound technologies.

This is not to say I'm making all this up. Anzaldúa writes about technology as a tool in her daily spiritual practice that influences the world and how she is situated within it. Above, Anzaldúa explains how the subliminal tapes are a means to "reprogram" a belief system, like rebooting her computer she names Amiguita—her "girlfriend"—the computer where, when she's writing she places an "altar on top of the monitor with the Virgen de Coatlalopeuh candle and copal incense burning" (Anzaldúa 2007, 97). There are other examples where she mixes spirituality and technology. In "Now let us shift...," Anzaldúa describes "relatedness" with people as "interconnectivity," as "a mode of connecting similar to hypertext's multiple links—it includes diverse others and does not depend on traditional categories or sameness" (2015, 151). While I listen to Anzaldúa's recordings for liminal sounds, I also listen for her and her interlocutors' awareness of these material aspects of the recording scenario. I want to use these moments to make my claims about how her experience of liminality and spirituality intersect with her experiences with recording and playback technologies.

Perhaps it is because I am listening for indicators of Anzaldúa spiritual work as a daily practice that includes media and technology that I discover where there are omissions to these references in published versions of the interviews. Above, Anzaldúa likens being receptive to being like a tape recorder. In another interview, Anzaldúa compares a state of receptivity to having an imagination that takes in data like a computer that projects what you perceive. The published version of the interview omits the computer analogy. During the interview on tape, Anzaldúa says, "And you let your imagination act as a brain, a center, like in a computer. There's a center in the computer that connects and sorts through all the data and comes out with what you want? I think the imagination does that. And look at the clouds. And it'll project certain images on those clouds so that you see certain patterns."[20] The published interview reads: "And you let your imagination act as a center that connects and sorts through all the data and comes out with what you want. I think the imagination does that: it will look at the clouds and project certain images in the clouds so you see certain patterns" (2000, 160). In another example, Anzaldúa compares receptivity to hearing radio frequencies. During the interview on tape, Anzaldúa says, "The analogy that people that I read have used is, um, a whistle when you want a dog that humans can't hear or the frequencies in a radio station. Certain species will pick up a wide range of these frequencies and others won't and then the body itself can tune into all these stations, you know? All the radio stations. If we knew how?" (Anzaldúa Papers, Keating interview, 1991). The published interview omits the radio references: "Let's use the analogy of a whistle. Humans can't hear it, but a dog can. Certain species will pick up a wide range of frequencies and others won't. And the body itself tunes in to some of these frequencies but the reception remains subliminal. If only we learned how to retrieve the messages" (Anzaldúa 2000, 162). Omissions about her thinking through technology and receptivity pique my interest because I wonder if scholars omit them because they find them irrelevant to the narrative they are trying to forward. Are the traces of recording technologies like liminal sounds on a recording? Are they insignificant or differently significant to some readers?

Certainly, transcription is a messy process in which editors must winnow what's said to what's most resonant with the goal of the transcription. As noted, Keating has omitted vocalizations "to remain true" to "the original meaning" (Anzaldúa 2000, 13). Transcripts in the archives with Anzaldúa's edits indicate the important role Anzaldúa played in going over the transcripts with Keating and preparing them for publication. The words that Keating and Anzaldúa omit in the transposition for a perceived audience are those they find less significant together; these omitted words might seem repetitive or excessive compared to what they both perceive to be Anzaldúa's intended meaning. Perhaps they omit the computer and the radio analogies to present Anzaldúa's ideas to be more in line with what Anzaldúa calls an "indigenous resonance," because moments later in the interview Anzaldúa contrasts "us" in the United States, who "privilege the mechanical, the objective, the industrial, the scientific," with "the Aborigines in Australia," who pay closer attention to the alternate realities of dreams, rituals, and imagination (2000, 163). In any case, Anzaldúa had a version of her story she wanted published in print no matter what she actually said. Noting the omissions, I again rethink what I thought I knew about authority and evidence in the making of history. How do they function?

I, too, am receptive to certain signifiers—computers, the internet, radio stations, and recording technologies. In the omitted comments, I see that the everydayness of language through and about technology can include a spiritual element to which Keating and Anzaldúa may not have been receptive. There is an exchange between Keating and Anzaldúa that follows the comment above about radio frequencies in which Anzaldúa is explaining why she thinks people's receptivity and expanded awareness are limited. Then, quite suddenly, there is a problem with the tape recorder. The published version of this interview[21] includes Anzaldúa's explanation about limited receptivity almost verbatim, but omits Anzaldúa's following comments after the pause:

[AnaLouise Keating] **ALK:** But nobody's cared and nobody's learned how, really. Right?

[Gloria Anzaldúa] **GA:** No, so that a very large percent of our brain goes unused, a very large percent of the reality that we get to take in through the senses is not used because we have been trained to youth that this is the only way we can see. So that the people who can see like this are either crazy or they're, um, you know, shamans or creative people. [pause]

GA: Do you have an hour?

ALK: I thought it was supposed to be an hour. Man, this is driving me nuts.

GA: You know there's this little thing where you can have it at half speed and so you can get an hour in 30 minutes.

ALK: Is that what it is, but will I be able to hear it as well?

GA: Yeah.

When this moment is over, the recording cuts short and then clicks back on. The next thing I hear is Anzaldúa telling Keating she should repeat what she has just said when the recorder was off. Keating declines. Between the recorded segments, time has leapt forward and the dialogue has continued while the recorder is off. These are small moments in which Anzaldúa is hyperaware of the recording machine. In them I hear traces of how the recording process could influence Anzaldúa's capacious sense of listening and of reception, how what people say at one point in time can be taken in, not or misperceived, and then heard differently later.

Listening to other people's listenings as represented in the published interviews, it is clear to me that I hear what I think I hear, that my reality is what I am receptive to perceiving. In trying to persuade my readers—my listeners—of the reality I experience, I compare what I hear to what others perceive. Which version of Anzaldúa's comments is correct? What she originally said or what she eventually thought she intended to say? Can it be both? Somewhere in between? An authorized account sits in liminal space between fact and opinion, event, and perception. Authority is created in the process of knowledge production.

Step Seven: You Embrace the Inner Conflict, Engage in Daily Practice, and Enact Spiritual Activism

In *Borderlands*, Anzaldúa quotes from the I Ching and notes that "all movements are accomplished in six stages, and the seventh brings return" (2007, 110). Each step, all the steps, can happen within another. A return happens within all seven steps of conocimiento, which are intended to be circular, interconnected, nonsequential, and happening "concurrently, chronologically or not" (Anzaldúa 2007, 124). The inner and intellectual conflicts I embrace in this chapter, I also engage in the other chapters. I question and engage evidence. I question and deploy authority. I transcribe recordings and question the act of transcription. I acknowledge that the practice of scholarship is imperfect, inexact, and as biased as my own representations of Anzaldúa's audio recordings are imperfect, inexact, and biased. I acknowledge that text and print media are easier materials than sound recordings for academic institutions to create, disseminate, and preserve. I admit I'm writing a book about audio recordings in print.

In my attempt to embrace these conflicts, I lay my cards on the table for the reader. I am including a transcription I have made of a tarot reading that Anzaldúa had with Lisa Levin in Brooklyn, New York, on November 30, 1984. In November 1984, Anzaldúa was completing *Borderlands*, published in 1987 (Vivancos Pérez 2021, 21). Many of the themes in *Borderlands* and Anzaldúa's other spiritual writings were developed as part of the "inspirational idea-generation" stage of her writing process; the recordings are a reminder that this process included Anzaldúa's conversations with other women during friendly gatherings over tarot cards, outstretched palms, and charts of the stars all recorded on a simple home recording device (Keating 2007, 544). I am sure there were many other conversations that were never recorded, and this conversation might be far different than or very similar to those. The metadata for the MP3 to which I listen tells me that what I have transcribed below is a recording of 31 minutes and 37 seconds, but reading the words in print could take more or less time depending on the reader's preferred method to skim or read it closely. The conversation I transcribe includes Levin and Anzaldúa discussing embodiment, gender politics, identity construction, oppression, poverty and fame, power imbalances, and the tension between spirit and body that exists in a liminal state of nepantla, all in a context of openness and receptivity while the two women laugh, manipulate the audio recorder, eat from a bag of nuts, and handle the tarot cards.

I learn while listening and transcribing that even with good reception, there is amplification as well as muffling. I have included this transcript with liminal noises I can describe in letters ("uh-huh," and "uh-hm") as well as their interruptions, the crinkling noises of plastic bag, the laughter, when Anzaldúa or Levin tap on the cards to emphasize a point, and when Anzaldúa and Levin's mouths seem full of food. What is not quite right in print is the tenor of the conversation, which is both quick and light-hearted at times and serious as well as contemplative at others. Among other things I cannot record, I can't seem to get in print the in-between cadences of two women who are deeply comfortable with a daily practice of talking about intimate topics, who can easily slip between body, spirit, and mind while laughing. I acknowledge I have no way of knowing how close or far they sit from each other, what they are wearing, what color the light is outside or inside. What room are they in? Do these things matter? Maybe. The indicators of in-betweenness are difficult to record.[22]

Lisa Levin (LL): I'd say this indicates a change in the spiritual order of your life.

Gloria Anzaldúa (GA): The servant of one of, the set, the two of

LL: Crossed by the chariot. It says while you have made somewhat of the gains, your higher conscious self is in some sort of power imbalance or concerned about the loss of balances of power within you.

GA: Mm-hm. That sounds, that sounds real true.

LL: And um, the subconscious, your subconscious is strong, unified, but embattled.

GA: Embattled.

LL: Embattled.

GA: The empress card, ah, no, the queen of swords.

LL: In some sort of, engaged in some sort of struggle, perhaps concerning power.

GA: Oh, that's so true. I wonder why. I wonder why that battle is going on. Because I have been feeling it, especially since I went into my 12th house.

LL: Uh-huh. I'm not sure what, what the imbalance of powers within you represents, what, what the nature of the problem is. But, uh, what it indicates is that you're seeking a spiritual resolution through the goddess's energy but solve it.

GA: Yes, yes I am.

LL: Um. In your past oppression reversed strife and your adjustment to whatever emotional problems these cards represented. I don't know. I haven't been in touch with your life that much so I don't know what, what sort of shit has hit the fan.

GA: So that the placing over there is, what is that, the placing mean?

LL: Oppression. Uh, in the past. And strife. And, uh, it shows that you've been working on adjusting or reconciling the, uh, results of very serious or grave emotional problems.

GA: Health. Yes. My operation in the, the uh teeth and just real heavy-duty child, childhood, like, um, traumas. So those three over there represent the past. Past.

LL: Past, yeah. And it shows you're making an adjustment, which the uh middle column definitely shows that you're working, doing goddess work on yourself to heal and comprehend what's out of balance within you.

GA: Hm-mm.

LL: In the future, debauch, uh, reverse, if you don't, if you follow the voices from the past, from the Akashic Files or the collective unconscious, whatever spirit guides you happen to be in touch with and don't give in to whatever, um, your particular form of self-indulgence is.

GA: Self-pity, it usually is.

LL: Self-pity.

GA: Yeah.

LL: Then, um, the path of, of, uh, the fool, the wanderer, the spiritual innocent is yours.

GA: Right in the I Ching the other day I got 25, which is innocence.

LL: Innocence.

GA: Yeah

LL: So it seems like you're in an embattled position, but you're struggling to overcome it and you're making a good fight doing it, but the outcome wouldn't be so clean because that's one of cleanest highest cards in the whole deck.

GA: What, what do you think is the um, the form of the battle and your nature, I mean the struggle within? Is it, is it?

LL: It's a—in the cards, I'd say, it would be, um, a battle between the worldly side of yourself and the spiritual side of yourself.

GA: Hm. Yeah.

LL: Because it shows that, that your mind is very concerned with the power imbalance. And it shows that there's money there and that you, you, that some part of you is concerned with amassing it.

GA: Yeah, I just. I've been poor for so long.

LL: Yeah. You're tired of it.

GA: I would just like to be able to pay my rent, and

LL: Uh-hm.

GA: I'd like to get a word processor.

LL: I've never even seen one.

GA: Oh, they're great. I fooled around with a couple of them. What I don't understand is, um, okay, this is the conscious and this is the unconscious? And, uh, this is the

LL: The problem.

GA: The problem is the seventh of the seventh chariot.

LL: The chariot that

GA: What I set into motion.

LL: Uh-hm. And, and crossing the position of it says that the change in the order of your spiritual self, there's some change going on within you, and the way you order your spiritual self. The way you—

GA: Yeah. That has been going on ever since I started my midlife crisis.

LL: How long ago was that?

GA: All of '83. But I think it started it started like when I was 37. But it comes to a head, like when you're 41, 42. And I think it's supposed to be over by the time you're 45, but I'm not sure. Maybe it keeps on. [*laughter*] Okay, um, so this is the troublemaker.

LL: It's not necessarily a troublemaker. It's just that you're, you're—it's change, a change in the order of your spiritual self. You're breaking it. Let's, maybe you're shedding—

GA: Oh, then this is very positive—

LL: Possibly a shedding of skin.

GA: Like, you know?

GA: Yes. Yeah. Then this is very positive.

LL: Yeah

GA: Because numerologically, uh, I have my total self is a double 7 and my inner self is a double 7. So I have 4 sevens. And then the Queen, the Empress. What, what is her relationship? The relationship with the Empress to the Queen of swords.

LL: I'd say that the relationship is—this would be your subconscious identity, perhaps concerning your—it seems like the relationship is struggling to preserve your own worth. I'd say that's your identity card. And this placement here is at the bottom of your identity of struggling to maintain and preserve it. In the face of what spiritual changes are happening to you at this time of your life, at this particular junction.

GA: Because I can, I identify more with her. I even wrote a poem about her once.

LL: The queen of swords? Yeah.

GA: She's the mask, she uh, cuts through the bullshit. She unmasks. She, uh um, discerns. She distinguishes. She's very quick. She's sort of like, uh, Uranus energy.

LL: Yeah.

GA: What, I was trying to understand the, the way that you place the cards, I just, well, you know, because you use kind of like a Celtic Cross, but I was wanting to know.

LL: It's a little different. Yeah.

GA: Yeah. So that, this is the unconscious and this is sort of like my identity and this is how I am struggling with it. And this is my conscious.

LL: Yeah. Super conscious.

Reception

GA: My super conscious is the disc's gain under—

LL: Well, the gain—

GA: in the ninth.

LL: And power reverse means your higher self is in a power struggle and balance in spiritual power, struggle and balance.

GA: So the struggle is between, uh—

LL: I, I think.

GA: Within myself.

LL: It's between the need to go out in the world and make a fortune and the need to, uh, preserve the spiritual innocence, the fool.

GA: Uh-hm. And this is the nine of disc's gain is, um, Venus and Virgo, card.

LL: Sounds uh, in detriment when this is in Virgo.

GA: Can you talk some more about this?

LL: Hm-hm.

GA: The future?

LL: Well, I always think this is the spiritual messengers from the past, coming through either your work or your dream life. And if you listen to them and don't let whatever emotional indulgence, let's say, because I don't think you're indulgent on a physical level but emotional indulgence—

GA: No. It's emotional.

LL: indulgence

GA: It makes me ill.

LL: Get in your way and either corrupt or halt the messages. That, uh,

GA: right

LL: your spiritual innocence will be preserved through your work and through the voices that, uh, speak to you from the past. I think you've got a good chance [*voice softens; tone: smile*].

GA: This is the final outcome card.

LL: That's the final outcome card. Uh, hm. That's beautiful.

GA: I think a part of it. I have a couple that are favored. One is resistance, stubbornness, the other one is self-pity.

LL: Uh-hm.

GA: I used to go into martyrdom a lot, but I quit that.

LL: [*Laughter*] Wow. I don't know how accurate it is because I have to do—

GA: Oh, I think it's very accurate. It's very accurate. And, and what about this is, uh, the—

LL: The goddess energy.

GA: The significator is the

LL: goddess

GA: the priestess.

LL: Yeah.

GA: This is the significator.

LL: She's the one running the whole show. And, uh, the significator being the priestess and the outcome being the fool, I think those are the strongest cards in the reading, and um, definitely very positive. I don't think anything could fuck with your head or get you down for long. Either head or body.

GA: [*Moves away from the microphone*] Well, I want to write down the spread.

LL: Sure.

GA: So I can,

LL: lay it out

GA: so I can later listen to the tape and look at the script.

[*Tape cuts*]

GA: What does reverse mean to you?

LL: Uh, it can mean the, uh, intensification of whatever the card contains. Intensification, magnification, um, corruption, of what the, uh, whatever card, the symbolism the card contains.

GA: That's what it means to me too. Yeah.

LL: Not that I remember it as well as I should. [*nut bag crinkles*]. The Potential? Um. [*Mouth full*] But you could—

GA: What I lack?

LL: What you lack.

GA: My ideal? No. What was it?

LL: What you lack and what, what, um. I'm not sure.

GA: What I hope for—[*bag crinkling*]

LL: What you hope for, yeah.

GA: What I hope for [*mouth full*]. [00:12:30] And this was, um, [*nut eating*]

LL: What you feared, [*eating*]

GA: What I feared [*nut eating*] and then this were my lovers. [*laughter, bag crinkling, eating*]

LL: You fear your spiritual master? [*eating nuts*]. That's interesting.

GA: I fear my spiritual master?

LL: Uh-hm.

GA: You mean like my, my spiritual teacher?

LL: Uh.hm.

GA: I do. [*eating*]

LL: Oh yeah?

GA: Is it a teacher within?

LL: I don't know. It's probably a combination of within and without [*mouth full*]. Yeah, true, with or within.

GA: It's what?

LL: I suppose within and without.

GA: Oh. So I fear my spiritual teacher within and my spiritual teacher without, outer. Why do you think?

LL: I don't know. You're writing this script, honey.

GA: My writing?

LL: I said, you're writing this script.

Reception

GA: Oh, maybe I. Maybe I fear it's going to interfere with my writing, too [*laughter*].

LL: Oh. Right.

GA: Look at all those thorns, nails, up above.

LL: Yeah [*eating, bag*]

GA: Maybe if you're, you're going to be crucified. It has to do with a little child within, huh? [*crunching nuts*] The woman

LL: holding a scepter or a sword. Is that a sword?

GA: This is Osiris. This is Isis. And that's Horus. But what does she mean? [*mouth full*] The feminine me? God. Well, at least I'm not afraid of, um, things like, uh, flesh and blood people.

LL: It's only the biggies, Gloria [*laughter*]. You know. All right. The teacher.

GA: Hmm. Well, that makes sense [*bag crackles*]. We're eating nuts. That's for the tape recorder [*laughter*].

LL: No, we're nuts eating.

GA: We're nuts eating. She's a bigger nut than I am [*laughter*]. I refuse to take—she, I, I'm a pecan and she's a, what is the big one?

LL: Brazil nut [*mouth full*].

GA: She's a Brazil nut [*laughter*]. I don't mind being an almond. I like being an almond.

LL: Uh-hm.

GA: Okay. [*bag crinkling*] This is what I fear.

LL: What you fear, what you hope for, your potential. [nuts eating]

GA: What about my potential? [*mouth full*] The emperor. [*bag crinkling*]

LL: Well, He's got the makings of war. He has the shield and the makings of peace in equal balance.

GA: Hmm. A lot of energy, huh?

LL: Uh-huh. His position is defensive, his legs are crossed, and he's holding the scepter against his chest.

GA: Mm-hm.

LL: He's holding the orb in his left hand though, and that's probably what he's trying to defend.

GA: But doesn't this represent traditionally, like, patriarchal authority?

LL: Mm-hm.

GA: Oh, God, I want to be in control, huh? Is that my potential? To be in control?

LL: Yeah

GA: I don't want to be in control [*bag crackling*].

LL: Maybe you've wanted to be for so much for your life that it shows up in the reading [*bag crackling*]

GA: But the thing is, I have been in control so much of my life that I no longer want to be in control [*laughter*].

LL: [*Tapping*] That's why you need a spiritual master [*nuts in mouth*]. To surrender to, my dear.

GA: Hm.

LL: I'm not saying a man or a woman.

GA: I know [*nut cracking, bag crackling*]. The Hierophant is like the male high priestess.

LL: You've got both of them going together in one reading. That's incredible.

GA: Uh-hm.

LL: I don't see anything of the material universe in this reading except for the Emperor.

GA: Ok.

LL: It seems to have it made.

GA: Swords? Hm?

LL: Uh-hm. Very much struggle. Oh, there's the—

GA: No. They're all, none of them have to do with—

LL: hmm.

GA: Except the discs. What about?

LL: Don't take them seriously too much because these four cards are mainly—

GA: I know.

LL: What it's about.

GA: I know.

LL: It looks like you should start really heavy duty tending your spiritual garden.

GA: I know. I have, ever, ever since the soul disappeared and went away, I stopped my meditations. I just do a little prayer-like meditation every night. And, uh, I used to do [*mouth full*] two, three, four hour meditations every day.

LL: [*Whistle*] What kind of meditations?

GA: All kinds: creative, silent, mindlessness, mindfulness, whatever. Um. And now I just do the ones I do with my writing, which are more like dialogues. Um.

LL: And how do they go? [*mouth full*]

GA: [*bag crinkling*]

uh, sort of getting reactions from the subconscious.

LL: Hm. How do you do that? [*mouth full*]

GA: Well, [*tongue sucking*] you say, uh, to yourself, uh, hm, "Lisa deserves to be happily married." And then you wait for the voices. Say that: "Lisa deserves to be—"

LL: Mm-hm. Ok. [*mouth full*] What voices?

GA: Say it again. Repeat it again.

LL: Lisa deserves to be happily married [*murmurs*].

GA: Say it again.

LL: [*Bag crinkling, mouth full*] Lisa deserves to be happily married [*bag crinkling, eating*]

Reception

GA: Okay. Are you getting any reaction anywhere?

LL: Yeah, a lot of question marks. [bag crinkling]

GA: What, what is a question mark?

LL: [Bag crinkling] Say what? [bag crinkling] Uh.

GA: Say it again.

LL: I don't seem to be getting much back from it. [mouth full]

GA: Well, it's hard in the beginning. You have to sort of like cultivate it. And then you hear these voices that say, um, 'What? Aren't you forgetting your art?' Or 'What? You don't deserve that.' [mouth full] You get all these kinds of things from your subconscious.

LL: Hm. Well, [bag crinkling] I almost got married last summer.

GA: Mm-hm. And?

LL: It didn't work out because Marie died. I went into a period of mourning during which I couldn't get married.

GA: Why did you want to get married?

LL: [Nut cracking] Um, it wasn't that I wanted to get married, but I felt that this was right man for me then.

GA: Was it, John?

LL: Uh-hm. He asked me to marry him on my mother's death bed so it was a pretty heavy scene.

GA: Well, say, 'I will marry John' and see what the voices say. I will marry John.

LL: Well, I'd probably just get a wild peal of laughter.

GA: [Laughter]

LL: [Cough] Yeah

GA: Well, I do these, I do ten of them, I do like, I'll say this and I'll wait for the reaction and write it down. And then I'll write it, I usually do it, it's better if you do it right in that moment. Then I write the statement again and then, um, pretty soon you really get at what in yourself is blocking you from it.

LL: Hm.

GA: Sometimes it does some good and sometimes it doesn't do any good. So [coughing] what about what I lack? [coughing]

LL: Vibrant, vital life force.

GA: Yup.

LL: Happiness. Contentment and pleasure.

GA: Yep. That's it. And what I really want?

LL: Is spiritual premise supremacy and, um, transcendence.

GA: [Coughing] Connection with myself?

LL: Mm-hm.

GA: Balance?

LL: Yeah, and when you attain that, that level of, uh, spirituality, of course it's balanced.

GA: But basically she means what to you?

LL: [*Bag crinkle*] The grower of all things.

GA: The grower of all things?

LL: Mm-hm

GA: She's also the Virgin. The woman, the woman complete unto herself.

LL: [*Crinkle*] Yep.

LL: What you fear is the spiritual master. [*pace slows down*] Perhaps because of this strong goddess card, there's a struggle between that, these two cards with you.

GA: Uh-huh. I think they're probably the same. I think she's the—

LL: You think so?

GA: I think she's a female manifestation and he's the male. But.

LL: It seems like you're really—

GA: I think the struggle is more between her, her and him, the emperor. This is like real Martian energy, and that's the kind of struggle that I've been having lately.

LL: You're in Aries.

GA: It's like she is content to being, being, to being, and he wants to be doing and organizing and taking care of business.

LL: Who's running the show?

GA: So it's about becoming and being or like a, huh?

LL: Who's running the show, who wants to?

GA: But.

LL: Manipulation, authority, governance, responsibility, benevolence—possibly.

GA: See, I'm still fighting the ghosts.

LL: Uh-hm.

GA: Look at this. My lover is the Prince of Swords. And she has got her hand on that, uh, very grounded, even though she's up in the clouds. She's grounded and then with a sword, she's fighting all this confusion.

LL: Hm.

GA: An Amazon, huh?

LL: Yeah.

GA: The other lover, the ace of Disks. A lot of Wings, huh? [*coughing*] Spiritual.

GA: Maybe I have a spiritual lover. And this is—

LL: A missionary.

GA: This is a missionary? The peace? [*bag crinkling*]

LL: No. Which one? [*bag crinkling*] It's a combination of these and sets means and [*nuts eating*].

GA: Crystal? Coin?

LL: No. Nata?

GA: Oh, you mean the words?

Reception

LL: Omega. That's not the omega? Oh, round the circ-order. That's the omega?

GA: O-Me-ga. Let's see. Oh. O-h-p-i-o-n. Ohpion?

LL: It's probably Greek.

GA: Ohpion and there's me— Meca. Meca-ohpion? I wonder what that means. Huh. Mecca.

LL: It's Greek.

GA: Huh. Well, I'll look at Crowley's uh, Crowley's—you know Crowley's book?

LL: Hm-huh. I don't have it.

GA: He probably has what it means. And then I have the peace card, two of swords.

LL: That's what you want. You want peace for a lover, Gloria.

GA: With the swords piercing the rose,

LL: Uh-huh.

GA: the flower.

LL: Strange symbolism for peace, I think.

GA: It's a Libra card, mourning Libra.

LL: Hm. [nut eating].

GA: Well, that's great. Okay. Now, I only want to do a couple more for where I'm supposed to, about my living situation.

LL: That's why you're still in New York? I don't see what that has to do with specific location, but. What was this one?

GA: You better repeat everything you said [*laughter*] because I don't think it was recording. [*laughter*]

LL: No, like hell.

GA: [*Laughter*] Okay, I.

LL: You'll just have to make do [*bag crinkling loudly*].

GA: I'm in New York because I'm adjusting to things that showed up in the reading before. Strife and oppression.

LL: Strife and oppression.

GA: Oppression and, um, so that I can recover my spiritual practices. Start back on that track. Because I've lost touch with it.

LL: Right.

GA: Or it's not as strong with me. And what else did you say? With the body?

LL: Uh, also adjustment to the physical and spiritual aspects of yourself that seem to be more in combat than, in combat than in harmony.

GA: Yep.

LL: That was from the first reading.

GA: Yep. That's me. That's me. I also, the India, the Indian and the white man in me are like always at each other's throats. [*laughter*] That's a Mestiza for you. Phew!

LL: Supposed to represent.

GA: This is the task or what it is, I, what I need to complete before I can move on to another environment, to another city.

LL: That card has always represented to me stasis. Not motion.

GA: Uh-huh.

LL: And, uh, it's possible that you feel yourself in stasis and you wish to break free that you're using the, uh—

GA: I sometimes feel that when—

LL: The energies [*tapping*], the energies of fire within you to do that.

GA: She's a funny lady. This queen of discs. Look at her horns. She's really receiving a lot of spiritual energy.

LL: Uh-hm.

GA: But I think she's with vegetation.

LL: Uh-hm. Vegetation or vegetating, I'm not quite sure which.

GA: [*Laughter*]

LL: It certainly doesn't seem an active card. It's one of complacency, and, uh, a kind of a certain amount of hauteur and, um, authority. But her very posture indicates boredom rather than activity.

GA: Uh-huh

LL: Perhaps bored with the control of power, and

GA: Uh-hm.

LL: But you're seeking the, uh,

GA: This is my next place, where I'm gonna live next?

LL: Forces of fire to burn you out of it. Yet you feel yourself to be in.

GA: Mm-hm.

GA: Emotional warmth. Emotional [00:30:30] heat. And this card's— He's got the tiger by the tail.

GA: It's a symbolis.

GA: [*Laughter*] Yeah.

LL: Yeah

GA: Look at her antenna.

LL: Right

GA: And here's a sunflower.

LL: Uh-hm. And these flowers are burning, perhaps as a sacrifice to a, to solar energy, I don't know.

GA: So, anyway, these two ladies are real cool.

LL: Mm-hm. This, this is the adjustment.

GA: Cool and collected. And I want some fire.

LL: Cool and static. [*tapping*] And you want some fire.

GA: Cool and static. [*laughter*] And I want some heat.

LL: Uh-huh

GA: Maybe I should move to Mexico. [*laughter*]

LL: Mexico. [*laughter*]

GA: Further south. Thank you, Lisa.

LL: Thank you, Gloria.

I will not interpret this transcription with a close listen or a close reading. I leave that to future scholarship, letting it sit here on the page in all its ambiguities and imperfections, but I will say what resonates with me about the process of close listening to this conversation. First, it's an intermedial dialogue. On tape, the two women are reading cards, interpreting, and making meaning together. I can hear them tapping the cards they are reading for emphasis, a physical index to indicate a connection between what is illustrated on the card and a personal discovery. Second, I enjoyed this recording between friends. I relate to how they relate to each other. I recognize the tenor of the friendship between two women who respect each other, enjoy each other. What they discuss and how they discuss it resonates with my goal for this book, because there is so much said and so much that is silent. I can't see the women or the cards, but I can hear their embodiment and their sense of embodiment, the materiality of the moment in the space between that finger, the lightly tapped cards, the words they use to describe and understand them, and the words I use to describe and understand *them*. To be sure, mine is a partial reading, a cursory listen in which historical background, smell, sight, and taste are largely out of scope. These are all things missing that transcripts and scholarship rarely include. After concluding the seven steps of conocimiento, Anzaldúa writes near the conclusion to "Now let us shift . . ." that "change requires more than words on a page: It takes perseverance, creative ingenuity, and acts of love" (2015, 156).

After: Acts of Love

During Anzaldúa's session reading Sally Gearhart's tarot cards, a bell rings multiple times. At first listen, I think perhaps it is windchimes. Maybe they are sitting next to a window. It is a light sound, not faint, but airy, and somewhat irregular, as though the bell ringer—the wind? a hand?—is moving the bell haphazardly, languidly—not insistently, as one might an alarm. I hear the bell's tinkle during their conversation because I'm listening for liminal sounds, and I note it down. I don't pay much attention to the ring's purpose until Gearhart says, "Can you turn that off?" She hears it too. It is irregular but insistent, and she seems irritable about the bell, so I rewind and listen again. I listen attentively for the bell this time. I listen for what is being said around its chime. I might not have thought to do so if Gearhart weren't so miffed. On the second and subsequent listens, I notice it sounds nothing like a windchime's tinkle. It is brief and fades away quickly. It sounds more like a call bell that you might find on a lobby reception desk, a bell that someone can tap to call someone else to attention. I also notice that the first time it happens Anzaldúa is telling Gearhart about the Hierophant card she has just laid down:

GA: Five years ago, something unique happened in your relationship. The Hierophant is ruled by Taurus so there might be a lot of—

SG: Laughter [*ring*].

GA: What's funny?

SG: Well, that's actually, that's actually when we met was five years ago on May 1, which is Taurus, right? Well, not when we met but when we, you know, first really got together in a sexual way.

GA: Well then, that's a high energy time for you and that's usually the best time for learning teaching situations—and the learning teaching situations don't have to be just about the occult—they can be sexual or personal or emotional or intellectual.

GA: [*ring*] but this is the energy of bringing to you those things that teach, and you usually teach what you want to learn. (Anzaldúa Papers, "Gloria Tarot for Sally Gearhart")

I learn from researching tarot that if Anzaldúa is indeed ringing the bell, then its ringing is supposed to signal that the bell represents the energy of teaching-learning situations or "those things that teach." Searching for more information on bells and tarot, I find that bells have also been used to vibrate the air around the deck and clear stagnant energy. I learn, which I share above, that the Hierophant card is usually identified with convention and tradition. The last time Anzaldúa rings the bell on the recording, when Gearhart asks her to stop, she is explaining to Gearhart how the Princess of Disks and the Queen of Discs represent "lesson" cards that show "where you're off when you're off your path." When Gearhart says, "Can you turn that off?," the bell is worried for a moment longer as its being put away. The women soon say goodbye. I have no idea what's happening emotionally in this moment. Gearhart has, after all, written a book on tarot. Maybe she is humoring Anzaldúa by participating, feels vulnerable letting go of control over her narrative, or does not feel receptive to learning at this moment about herself and her relationship with Jane. Maybe that's how I would feel. I'm struck with the realization that Anzaldúa's recordings are a bell of sorts, a call to attention to pay attention to my intentions. It is difficult work, "staying with the trouble" of breaking down dominant discursive practices (Haraway 2016, 2). Being receptive to the bell and not stilling its dissonant clapper can be an act of resistance.

In a 1996 interview, when Andrea Lunsford asks Anzaldúa about "claiming authority," Anzaldúa responds by asking a question and answering it. She dialogues with herself in her conversation with her interlocutor:

> How does an internal postcolonial writer rewrite the dominant ideology from within to produce a different conocimiento of different versions of reality? She can't. But I'd like to think that a community of writers can. A single author is doing pretty good just to resist reinscribing dominant discourse. Yet, I don't want to be a production of somebody else's legal, political, or aesthetic text. I'd like to think that my cultural productions—reading, writing, speaking, dreaming—are acts of resistance to that production. (Anzaldúa 2000, 273)

Anzaldúa's tapes play authority as dialogic, as process, as "somebody else's text," that a scholar can listen to differently if she is receptive to it and can put it into conversations against the grain of dominant discourse. Against the scholarly grain, Anzaldúa's piece "Now let us shift . . . conocimiento . . . inner work, public acts" (Anzaldúa 2015) ends with a public act, a ritual, prayer, a blessing "for transformation," in which Anzaldúa addresses the reader: "May the words and the spirit of this book, our 'giveaway' to the world, / take root in our bodies, grow, sprout ears that listen/ may it harm no one, exclude none / . . . sending energy out into the universe / where it might best be of service / may the love we share inspire others to act" (2015, 158). This book is my small act.

* * *

This chapter seeks to better understand how giving voice to Anzaldúa's lesser-known spiritual recordings can offer new insights into her theories of conocimiento and receptivity and, in consequence, one scholar's mediated listening to historical audio recordings. It is part of the larger objective of *Dissonant Records* to encourage scholars to listen and to model listening, being receptive, trying to engage in dialogue even with its failings, when it fails. How we retrieve recordings like Anzaldúa's from the archive represents a process of intermedial engagement that resonates with an ontological perspective shaped by liminality—a perspective in between the embodied, sighing, sniffling, whistling, clicking person, event, or object and an institutionalized, standardized ontology that is oblivious, sometimes, to what these sounds signal. For most readers, this kind of inquiry in literary study might be new, so its introduction—a bringing of awareness, an increase in receptivity—is my objective. I could say this chapter could be a voice-over for any chapter in this book: it is an indicator of a general process of knowledge production but saying so would not be quite right. It's personal what I hear, but it's also technical and particular to what's on the tapes. Each recording and listening scenario, each author and their writing and their time in history necessarily entails dissonant records and resonant frequencies.

Coda: Distant Listening and Resonance

> Way back there when Hell was no bigger than Maitland, man found out something about the laws of sound. He had found out that sound could be assembled and manipulated and that such a collection of sound forms could become so definite and concrete as a war-ax or a food tool.
> —Zora Neale Hurston (1999, 70–71)

I have described *distant listening* to literary texts as using computing to "distill the many-layered four-dimensional space of the text in performance (i.e., embodied within the performance network of interpretations with the listener in time and space) into a two-dimensional script called 'code'" (Clement 2013). My definition strikes me as remarkably similar to Zora Neale Hurston's description of folklore as "the boiled down juice of human living" (1999, 69). My definition is not as poetic or as entertaining as Hurston's, of course, and when I wrote this definition, I was "listen[ing] in print" and referring to "the audio relationship between reader and text" (Furlonge 2011), but I believe the definition still holds when applied to audio files. In the definition, I think I could just as easily have used the word "data" and "algorithms" rather than "code." Melanie Feinberg helpfully describes data as "just a description of a thing's qualities"—it's not the thing; it describes the thing—and algorithms as both mathematical operations and, humorously, mediation via "arcane spells" (2022, 3, 230, 3). To distill the many varied experiences of sound as described in this book into data operated on by algorithms, then, would be to filter the experience of human living down into a purified list (or matrix) of the signifying qualities of that sound and to deploy those via a mathematical operation intended to produce resonance or meaning. An updated definition might be that *distant listening* is at root a technically complex matter of fitting a mathematical abstraction to collections of sounds at scale and trying to determine their resonances computationally as data.[1]

When this book was first reviewed for publication, one of the reviewers was dismayed to find out that the book did not make mention of distant listening. Why, the reviewer wondered, when I had spent so many years on big-team, funded grants studying the possibilities for distant listening and the use of cultural-analytic tools to develop knowledge about large caches of recorded audio, would I turn away from that prior work? In the past decade, I have been involved in multiple computational projects with archival audio collections through a project I lead called High Performance Sound Technologies for Access and Scholarship (HiPSTAS).[2] Some of the early HiPSTAS work was focused on using text-to-speech software to "listen" to literature (Clement et al. 2013), but much of the HiPSTAS research focused on using Adaptive Recognition with Layered Optimization (ARLO), a machine-learning application developed by my collaborator David Tcheng for analyzing large sound collections by extracting basic prosodic features such as pitch, rhythm, and timbre for clustering and classification (Clement et al., 2016). In May 2013 and May 2014, with funding from the National Endowment for the Humanities (NEH), HiPSTAS brought together twenty humanities junior and senior faculty and advanced graduate students as well as librarians and archivists from across the United States interested in developing and using ARLO to access and analyze spoken word audio collections.[3] The HiPSTAS Institute had two primary outcomes: (1) participants would produce new scholarship using audio collections with advanced technologies, such as classification, clustering, and visualizations; and (2) participants would engage in the scholarly work of digital infrastructure development by contributing to recommendations for the implementation of a suite of tools for cultural heritage institutions interested in supporting advanced digital scholarship in sound. Because (as the previous chapters show) access and scholarship with sound are entangled practices, we worked to develop ARLO in a second round of funding in 2014 to help users automate metadata description for undescribed sound collections (Clement 2018; Clement et al. 2018). Later, I led two more HiPSTAS projects through a project at the University of Texas at Austin called Good Systems, which concerned the ethics of artificial intelligence. The first project was focused on using machine learning to automatically generate metadata (Xu et al.

2020) and the second was concerned with training librarians and humanists on the ethics of data operations in the archives and libraries (Clement et al. 2022). It seems, the reviewer challenged, that given my experience, the book would provide a chance to comment productively on the debates around cultural analytics that are raging in literary studies right now.[4]

Perhaps. In my experience, machines cannot access or analyze the features of the recordings (silences, distortions, interferences, compressions, modes of reception) in the ways I found resonant for this book. That said, creating a computational model of sounds with the explicitness and consistency that computation requires can be generative. Computational models "force us to confront the radical difference between what we know and what we can specify computationally, leading to the epistemological question *of how we know what we know*" (McCarty 2004), and in this sense, my own distant listening projects have yielded productive inquiries into the cultural registry or the processes of archives, culture, data structures, information infrastructures, institutions, sound, culture, computation and other knowledge production systems.[5]

This coda is not a comment on *what* data to compute or *which* algorithms to use—instead, I have become more interested in the *so what?* of computational analysis with historical spoken word texts in the archives.[6] To the reviewer's query, then, *Dissonant Records* as a whole is my response: interpretive practices with audio are difficult and subjective and always already entangled with the personal, cultural, sociopolitical, and technological context of listening as an agential process. Karen Barad writes that "Mattering is simultaneously a matter of substance and significance," explaining that this is "why contemporary physics makes the inescapable entanglement of matters of being, knowing, and doing, of ontology, epistemology, and ethics, of fact and value, so tangible, so poignant" (2007, 3). Likewise, I find myself interested in distant listening in so far as its pursuit has resonances with larger questions about epistemologies, ontologies, and other areas of study concerned with better understanding dissonances in the cultural registry and imaginary. Distant listening is interesting to me to the extent that its processes hold traces of these entanglements. Thus, while I do not believe computers can do what I do in this book, I do believe it is essential for humanities scholars to better understand the limits and potentials of computational sound analysis for interpretive analysis, because these methods point to the limits and potentials of scholarly research with audio more generally. Consequently, in this coda, I invite scholars to consider possible research questions about distant listening using the same principles I used to introduce resonance at the beginning of this book.

The Material Particularities of the Apparatus Matter

What, exactly, is the matter of audio data? What gets filtered in the process of digitizing sound? Modeling sound for computational methods is an algorithmic process of discretization. Sound is air pressure variation over time. Ears and hands can turn the pressure differences into neural activations while microphones create digital sound by translating these variances into voltage differences. An audio signal is a sequence of mathematical abstractions that map voltage (or pressure) over time in a wave, and frequency is the number of times per second that a sound pressure wave repeats itself (McFee 2020a). To make things more complicated, audio signal processing methods do not work with continuous signals. Instead, before being processed by a computer, sound engineers and computational analysts discretize the sound pressure wave through sampling and quantization, using a mathematical representation of the continuous signal through samples that indicate the whole sound without capturing it fully (McFee 2020b). The sampling process is considered more or less precise when more or fewer discrete samples are used to represent a signal across a period of time, but all the information (all the qualities) is never represented at once. Imagine a sound event as a pebble dropped in a still lake. Digitization would be concerned with the rings that fan around the pebble, in a mathematical matrix of variables that represents the physical dimension of the plop, including information about the water depth, the air temperature, and whatever else impacts the shape, size, and speed of expansion of the rings. Indeed, reconstructing a sound event from a Fourier transform, which describes a sound's frequency mathematically,[7] is entirely possible. In reality, however, while the digitized transformation of the plop has a large enough matrix of its qualities to replay the plop, it is not the plop.

Sampling and quantization imply absence: I can imagine adding *sampling* as a cultural keyword to my list of sound technologies. As *Dissonant Records* has indicated, technical operations such as amplification, distortion, interference, compression, and reception reveal absences, historical absences based on media type and genre, information infrastructures, professional protocols, institutional values and social mores, and personal experience. The process of sampling is, by definition, similarly lossy. I get the sense that when Hurston refers to the "boiled down juice of human living," that juice comprises the traces of life that resonate throughout this book: the violences and offenses, but also the reconciliations, the passion, and the love. Adding water to these qualities of life might make a muddy mess. Likewise, sound can be reconstructed from its frequency samples by computational algorithms, but something is gone. Something new is generated. A scholar might ask: What present absences does sampling reveal?

Meaning Making Is Dialogic

Distant listening research requires a dialogue between humanities scholars, information professionals, signal processing engineers, and machine learning scientists who are all interested in making matter and making meaning with audio differently. On HiPSTAS, I have worked with anthropologists, archivists, data analysts, historians, librarians, literary scholars, machine-learning scientists, musicologists, ornithologists, and poets, among others. When humanists listen, they abstract from sonic event features to consider how events like speech or music influence an understanding of cultural phenomena (Bernstein 2011; Clement and McLaughlin 2016; Francis et al. 2016, 354; MacArthur, Zellou, and Miller 2018; Mustazza 2014, 2016, 2018). When signal processing scientists listen, they consider damping ratios, gain, frequencies, spectra, and pitch energy, and talk about how these features influence sound fidelity. Machine-learning scientists are listening for feature selection, models, clustering and classification, correlation and probability, validation, and optimization (Clement et al. 2014). Librarians and archivists want to consider how large datasets of sound features could potentially be used for basic tasks that facilitate discovery with audio collections, including creating transcriptions, metadata generation (event detection, keyword extraction, speaker disambiguation or diarization, and speaker recognition), and quality analysis (Dunn et al. 2018; Gref, Köhler, and Leh 2018; Harrington 2019; Oard 2012).

Digital humanities projects like HiPSTAS and the Digging into Data Challenge (2009–2019) provide a sample of collections, methods, and outcomes in distant listening research with historical audio collections. Funded by agencies across the Western Hemisphere,[8] most of the projects in the Digging into Data Challenge analyzed image and text; a few provided new methods for discovery with audio files, such as the Structural Analysis of Large Amounts of Music (SALAMI), which included approximately 50,000 hours of a wide variety of music genres from different venues, including live concert recordings, folk, jazz, orchestral, and twentieth-century avant-garde music from across the world. The SALAMI researchers attempted to use machine-learning algorithms to discern musical genres, musical similarity (to mark repeated themes), function (e.g., interlude) and lead instrument (e.g., vocal or guitar) (Bay et al. 2009). Analyzing natural language usage, the Mining a Year of Speech project used approximately 9,000 hours of recorded American and British speech, including the British National Corpus22 and holdings of Penn Linguistic Data Consortium, together with transcriptions. The goal of the project was to assess the challenges of working with large-scale digital audio collections of spoken word. To this end, the researchers decided that a first important step in addressing these challenges was to develop a technology for forced alignment between the audio and the transcripts that would yield a phonemic transcription with detailed timing information, including the start and end of every vowel, consonant, and word. They used this data to consider sex differences in conversational speaking rates, the differences in phrasal speaking rates across genres, dialects, and languages (Coleman et al. 2011). The Harvesting Speech Datasets for Linguistic Research on the Web project comprised hundreds of 25-second snippets from podcasts, news broadcasts, and public and educational lectures gathered across the web. The researchers collected the datasets "to evaluate hypothesized correlations between acoustic form and grammatical and contextual features, and to identify the particular acoustic features (such as pitch, duration, intensity, or vowel quality) that are significant in marking prosodic distinctions."[9]

This same literature indicates that the accuracy and efficacy of these methods remains inconclusive and that scholars are in the early days of epistemological questions surrounding accuracy and efficacy, especially with historical speech recordings (Joudrey, Taylor, and Wisser. 2018; Maringanti 2017; Mascaro 2011; Svenonius and McGarry 1993; Xu et al. 2020). No matter how scientists manipulate damping ratios, gain, frequencies, spectra, and pitch energy, transcription accuracy is influenced by recording quality, accents, and the presence of background noise (among other signals). Data gathering, cleaning, structuring, and feature selection are other roadblocks that Williford and Henry (2012) identify in the SALAMI, Mining a Year of

Speech, and Harvesting Speech Datasets for Linguistic Research on the Web projects. In addition, recent work in the broader field of acoustics, speech, and signal processing relies on features generated or learned as a byproduct of training large-scale deep networks for some general tasks like acoustic scene classification or source identification (Baevski et al. 2020; Cramer et al. 2019), but inductive bias—assumptions about the data that are encoded in the model to learn the target function and to generalize beyond training data—persist, obfuscated in black-box methods that can often resist critical intervention. Indeed, in the textbook *Speech and Audio Signal Processing: Processing and Perception of Speech and Music* (2011), Ben Gold, Nelson Morgan, and Dan Ellis describe the history of speech transmission in terms of a balance between meaning and matter in which infrastructural resources are also a significant variable: "Speech," they write, "conveys emphasis, emotion, personality, etc., and we still don't know how much bandwidth is needed to transmit these kinds of information" (21). In addition, the analysis of such large datasets requires computing resources to which very few scholars have access (Clement et al. 2016).[10]

This sample of distant listening research marks promising inquiries that could potentially alter scholarship with audio, but in their points of interference across scholarly disciplines, these projects also expose how much scholars need to learn together to do this work effectively. Scholars must not only reflect on scientific practices from humanistic perspectives or on the nature of objective versus subjective reasoning. We should also understand these perspectives diffractively as constructive and destructive interferences: superimposed patterns of thinking at the same point in time that, like interfering sound waves, amplify or silence ideas as they dissolve or smooth into one another. Scientists and humanities scholars approaching the distant listening problem space from different epistemological paradigms are concerned with intellectual bandwidths too. What is possible to know? What questions are productive or interesting to ask? Is this work worth the effort and resources needed?

Entelechic and Agential Meaning Making Is Premised by a Co-constructed Field of Possible Meanings

Paradigm shifts across instantiated protocols and practices can be daunting, especially when large-scale concerns impacting institutions of scholarly practice (universities, funding agencies, scholarly societies, and publishing) are always evolving. Christa Williford and Charles Henry (2012) evaluated projects from the first two cohorts of Digging into Data projects for the Council on Library and Information Resources and determined that distant reading and distant listening required changes in how stakeholders (researchers, administrators, scholarly societies, academic publishers, research libraries, and funding agencies) understood research practices. Their recommendations include expanding concepts of research and research data, embracing interdisciplinarity and collaboration, increasing training, adopting new models for sharing credit among collaborators, and sharing resources among institutions, reenvisioning scholarly publication, and generally making greater, sustained institutional investments in human infrastructure and cyberinfrastructure (Williford and Henry 2012, 5–6). These recommendations are premised on large financial investments and the idea that distant listening is a methodology that will produce results of interest. This is one path forward.

From my experience, I sense another path. What I would suggest for humanities scholars interested in knowing more about the potentials and pitfalls of distant listening is to learn more about the process of distant listening and knowledge production in the following key areas.

Audio Data Curation
What is included in audio data? Knowledge about the technologies of audio, of computational methods, and of humanist inquiry to do new kinds of research in this area is essential. As audio-based "virtual assistant technologies" become more prevalent in our phones, computers, cars, homes, and places of work, leisure, and culture, humanists must have a better understanding of audio and machine learning to address how the data these technologies collect do and do not represent the complexities of people and culture. Scholars and academics must do research and design curriculum topics of interest to the humanities to attract other humanities scholars to this work and to address these and other areas of study and practice in the humanities.[11]

Analysis Tools
Interfaces and tools that facilitate audio analysis can be highly technical in nature, asking users to toggle damping ratios, gain, frequencies, spectra,

energy, and pitch energy for a diverse range of sounds from music to speech to bird calls. Some of the most powerful tools for audio analysis are proprietary and owned by large companies such as IBM or Amazon, but free tools are powerful too, such as Audacity, Praat, and SonicVisualizer. These tools offer what could be called "learning interfaces," in which practitioners are able to play with sonic parameters on a single audio file to learn how different features change sound and how it is visualized. In order to take advantage of the methods these tools deploy, however, scholars require technical knowledge of how tools visualize sound amplitude and frequencies as waves and as spectrograms and how these measurements map on to what resonates in the humanities.[12]

Accuracy Thresholds

When is good enough good enough? Audio is always mediated in some format in real time through some mechanism. Historical recordings can be difficult to hear due to poor recording quality or noise in the sonic environment. In addition, underresourced and overworked information professionals without time to listen to every audio file in their collections produce descriptive metadata, which is used for indexing as well as many of the machine-learning projects listed above. When is "good enough" metadata good enough for discovery? While libraries and archives must adhere to professional guidelines that dictate precision and accuracy (often for very good reasons around privacy and copyright),[13] scholars, students, and the public can play with developing transcripts and annotations for audio recordings by creating their own projects, editions, and playlists. Tools and methodologies for engaging the public in describing audio visual collections can both ameliorate the backlog of undescribed audio collections and complicate what "fidelity" to an originary sound recording means.

Scalability

Scalability is also a factor in accuracy. The more data that informs a machine-learning model, the more accurate the model. Institutions with more data, storage, and processing power are best suited to conduct local and large-scale audiovisual (AV) analyses. What scale is enough and how much does it cost? For HiPSTAS projects, which included processing approximately 6,000 hours of poetry performances from PennSound, among other collections, I had access to the supercomputing cluster Stampede at the Texas Advanced

Computing Center at the University of Texas (Clement and McLaughlin 2016). The size of the cluster used to be described in Texas parlance on the website as "Each Stampede node is like a beefy desktop computer" (Texas Advanced Computing Center). At the time, a desktop computer typically had two or four processing cores; Stampede had 522,080.[14] In 2017, Google released AudioSet, which is likely the largest dataset of audio samples available for generating models (Gemmeke et al. 2017).[15] Currently, AudioSet includes 2,084,320 human-labeled 10-second sound clips drawn from YouTube videos and 632 audio event classes (e.g., "music," "speech," "vehicle," "creak," and "gargling"). Google also has the advanced processing power to run analyses across these clips, having recently announced at its March 2023 annual Google I/O developer conference an AI supercomputer with 26,000 graphics processing units (GPUs). For reference, most motherboards on a typical computer allow up to four GPUs, and the world's fastest public supercomputer has 37,000 GPUs. The cost of this work is not limited to the financial cost of the machinery. Studies show there is also an environmental price to running large data centers that needs further exploration (Hogan 2015).

Sustainability
What are local, national, and global scale issues for sustaining literacy, usability, and accuracy? How does this work fit back into the preservation and discovery infrastructures already in place in archives, libraries, classrooms? Standards such as the newest International Image Interoperability Framework (IIIF) guidelines for audiovisual materials can open the closed circle of authority around institutionally driven descriptive practices.[16] IIIF uses the WC3 Web Annotation Data Model standard (W3C 2017) for browsers to facilitate sharing digital image and AV data across technology systems. Third-party software gives users new kinds of access to images and AV, allowing for viewing, zooming, comparing, manipulating, and working with annotations.[17] With IIIF, users can reference audiovisual artifacts linked from Libraries, Archives, and Museums (LAMs) into software that allows them to annotate AV in new ways without impacting the institution's presentation of the item. In these cases, researchers can discover, compare, refer, sample, illustrate, and represent their interpretations of these cultural heritage objects, which in turn encourages their broader use.

Coda

Done thoughtfully, distant listening research around data curation, analysis tools, accuracy, scalability, and sustainability can expose knowledge production as a messy sociotechnical process of interferences that are amplified in moments when meaning making and world building resonate because of or despite personal histories, institutional sociopolitics, and the materials and technologies (modalities, media, and devices) that produce, reproduce, store, and play archival records.

These days I prefer close listening as a research methodology. Since 2018, I have been leading a new HiPSTAS project, called AVAnnotate.[18] Since monks included commentary on medieval manuscripts, annotations have been an essential humanities method for adding context and meaning to cultural objects for use in research, teaching, and publication (Clement and Fischer 2021). The goal of AVAnnotate is to facilitate sharing annotations on AV archives through a sustainable workflow that leverages IIIF standard for AV materials and simplifies the production of standards-based, user-generated, online projects that provide sustainable and much-needed commentary and context around underused and culturally sensitive AV collections.[19] These projects—which resemble AV-centered "editions" or "exhibits"—are a series of web pages, hosted on GitHub, that feature an audio or video recording linked from a library or archive that can be played in the context of user-generated, time-stamped annotations, alongside introductory material and an index of concepts and terms, all of which provide content for searching, browsing, and organizing recordings. Existing projects include curricula for recorded interviews with jailed student protestors during the Civil Rights movement, a bilingual edition of Radio Venceremos programs (the rebel radio station that broadcast during the Salvadoran Civil War, 1981–1992), a documentary of decades of events at the Furious Flower Poetry Center (the nation's first academic center for Black poetry), as well as a set of oral histories from the Syilx Okanagan Peoples.[20] I have also used AVAnnotate to create a compendium of recordings with annotations for this book, including those on Hurston's recordings at the Library of Congress, Ellison's recordings at Harvard, Sexton's recordings at the Harry Ransom Center and the Schlesinger Library, and Anzaldúa's tarot readings at the Nettie Lee Benson Latin American Collection.[21]

The AVAnnotate project helps me put into action some of the goals with which I began *Dissonant Records*. Reflecting standards for simplicity and sustainability that encourage easy-to-use and lightweight technical infrastructures, the AVAnnotate workflow is based on a minimalist computing approach to development: it does not require a heavy investment in a deep software stack. We define success in AVAnnotate in terms of increasing development, elevating awareness, and promoting sustainability around issues of access to AV in libraries and archives; scholarly, pedagogical, and public use of AV collections; standards for AV access and engagement; and the social and political contexts surrounding AV access and engagement. Our primary goal for a new kind of AV ecosystem for public knowledge is to open paths for responsible and sustainable collaborations between LAMs and the public by providing a free and easy way to collaboratively create and share annotations that help describe collections and make them more accessible for interpretation.

I believe that supporting close listening practices accelerates the continued use of AV and encourages information professionals, scholars, students, and the public to produce and discuss knowledge about the remarkable and varied AV artifacts archives hold. Hurston's tale about the laws of sound remains relevant: if a collection of sound forms can become so definite and concrete as a tool, the biggest questions are not how, but to what end? A war-ax or a food tool?

Notes

Preface

1. These numbers for the Internet Archive do not include the 735 billion web pages or the 890,000 software programs also included in the archive.

2. For an example, see Laura Wagner's (2017) work with Radio Haïti-Inter at Duke University Libraries.

3. Jeremy Morris (2012) argues that the move from music on CDs to music as digital files in the 1990s included stripping contextualizing information (e.g., album art, identifying information, packaging, etc.), which information professionals attempt to replace with metadata. Calling metadata a "keystone technology," Morris asserts that metadata "mediate listeners' experiences with music" and "contribute to the rise of what could be called a digital music commodity" (851).

4. Alexandra Vazquez's approach to listening to Cuban musicians in *Listening in Detail* (2013) similarly relies on "retell[ing] the story from the perspective of the detail" (29). She includes breaths, grunts, inflections, nonlexical noises, and pauses, and refrains in her descriptions from applying theory within musical scholarship.

5. Anne Sexton regularly modifies her adverbs differently than I do. When I heard her say "got," I would automatically translate it to "have" and had to correct myself. Sexton places words like "just," "really," "you know," and "kind of" before or after adjectives and verbs in ways I would not naturally, and I had to correct myself, repeatedly, to force myself to write down what she said rather than what I thought I heard.

6. There are many scholars whose amazing work on listening is threaded throughout *Dissonant Records*, but the texts that have perhaps been most influential in shaping my thoughts about listening are the following. Jennifer Lynn Stoever's *The Sonic Color Line* (2016) articulates the relationship between sound, race, and American life with two concepts: *the sonic color line* (describing the process of racializing sound) and *the listening ear* (a figure for how dominant listening practices accrue). Ana

María Ochoa Gautier's *Aurality* (2014) explores how different listening and inscription practices led to "an enlightened cultivation of hearing" that was crucial to the development of concepts about "local culture" and "local nature" in Colombia (3). Jonathan Sterne's *The Audible Past* (2003) considers technologies in acoustics, physiology, and otology to produce a genealogy of constructs of sound, hearing, and listening. Charles Bernstein's *Close Listening* (1998) pays attention to "sound as material, where sound is neither arbitrary nor secondary but constitutive" of meaning (4). Key concepts and methods in Jason Camlot's approach in *Phonopoetics* (2019) include (1) sound signal as an object of critical analysis, (2) the idea of "literary" recording as a discernible category of recorded sound, (3) definitions of audiotextual forms and genres, and (4) the material history that has mediated and continues to mediate our engagement with these cultural artifacts. All these scholars are also aligned with Nicole Brittingham Furlonge's project in *Race Sounds* (2018) to use "listening" to engage with media artifacts, technologies, and literature and interpret prevailing cultural narratives that engage aurality.

Introduction

1. Until this point in the recording, the person is unidentified, so I have chosen to describe them with a plural gender pronoun.

2. Ann Laura Stoler's *Along the Archival Grain* (2009) is a meditation on studying colonial archives as subject rather than just as a scholarly source. To understand the archive along the grain rather than against it is to consider how the archive functions as a social, political, and technological apparatus for cultural meaning making.

3. My metaphors and turns of phrase will invariably bely my own prejudices, but it interests me that terms like "echo," "resonate," "amplify," or "sound off" will sound heavy-handed in a book on sound and audio but terms like "show," "reflect," or "illuminate" are more commonly used verbs.

4. Donna Haraway (1988) talks about how hard it is to completely steer away from "God's eye" objectivism.

5. In "The Poetics of Signal Processing" (2011), Jonathon Sterne and Tara Rodgers use this framing device to talk about "common metaphors of signal processing," such as culinary operations like "raw" and "cooked," as well as travel and voyage metaphors, including "ear canal" and "inner space."

6. Archivy scholars include Carter (2006), Caswell (2014), and Robinson-Sweet (2018). Rodney Carter (2006) examines the manifestation of silences in archives as a function of media well as how silence can be used by marginalized groups to resist state power. Sara White (2012) discusses how a nuanced understanding of the complex embodiment of disabled persons must extend beyond simple paper artifacts. Dominique Daniel (2010) considers how multimedia archives are essential

Notes to Introduction

for better understanding "underdocumented" communities of immigrants. Marisa Elena Duarte and Miranda Belarde-Lewis discuss the "Western European orientation to texts, reading, and the categorical particularization of knowledge" as a practice of "misnaming, particularization, periodization, [and] efficiency" that consistently misrepresents indigenous epistemologies and local needs (2015, 683). In *Aurality*, Ana María Ochoa Gautier argues that Colombian oral cultures from the nineteenth century, "historically inscribed, in bodies, on stone, on skin, and on paper, through rituals and through writing, are, to be sure, marked by highly unequal power in the constitution of the public sphere" (2014, 4). Cait McKinney asserts that information activism in the lesbian community also requires a more capacious definition of documents that must encompass many media and genres such as "newsletters, meeting minutes, telephone call logs, internal memos, letters and other correspondence, online archival interfaces, photographs, catalog records, log books, subject thesauruses, instruction manuals, handbooks, bibliographies, and actual index cards" (2020, 8). Important recent reexaminations of oral history from a feminist and queer lens are included in *Bodies of Evidence* (2012), edited by Nan Alamilla Boyd and Horacio N. Roque Ramírez.

7. Alessandro Portelli (2016) discusses the idea that the "impartiality" of a scientific approach is impossible with oral history since oral histories are always already "unfinished" (they can tell history only from the narrator's point of view): "oral history can never be told without taking sides, since the 'sides' exist inside the telling" (57).

8. An excellent example of this phenomenon is Tom McEnaney's article (2020) on the biography *Me llamo Rigoberta Menchú*, which was based on recorded testimonies. He asks, "Why were so many of the tapes used to write *testimonios* never made available to researchers or the listening public?," noting that in the case of Menchú, "One does not listen for accuracy, authenticity, or evidence"; rather, it is productive to listen to the role of the listener and aurality (394).

9. Scholars include Daphne Brooks (2021), Lisa Gitelman (1999, 2008, 2014), Brian Hochman (2014), Mara Mills (2010, 2011), Jonathan Sterne (2003, 2012, 2015), and Alexander Weheliye (2005).

10. In the words of Portelli, "Written and oral sources are not mutually exclusive. They have common as well as autonomous characteristics, and specific functions which only either one can fill (or which one set of sources fills better than the other)" (2016, 50).

11. Instead, Gitelman encourages "a local and contrastive logics for media," and suggests that the reader "look for meanings that arise, shift, and persist according to media uses" (2014, 9).

12. A *modality* refers to a specific way in which information is encoded, such as graphics, written or spoken language, or music. *Media* is a type of information or representation format in which information is stored, such as printed or manuscript

paper, photographic film, sequences of video frame, audio data, and so on. Media devices include recording machines, movie cameras, editing software, and so on. A synthetic fusion of paper and computational media in electronic literature is discussed by Hayles (2007) as a feedforward, feedback loop, where paper histories and computational infrastructures are tied together in a dynamic heterarchy to shape the multilevel complexity of multimedia works by electronic literature authors. Responsive electronic pieces by these authors, Hayles argues, are intermedia, because networked and programmable media facilitate feedback loops that run in both directions, from the computer's representation of the text to the reader and back from the reader to the text, which changes based on reader reactions.

13. Jens Schröter (2011) delineates five primary theories of *inter*media in scholarship that are useful for thinking about the nature of intermedia in the archives: formal, transformational, synthetic, ontological, and political. Often intermedia theory points to *formal* structures that occur across media (e.g., fictionality, rhythmicity, seriality) and *transformational* features or the representation of one medium by another, as in the *re*mediation of paper-like features in a word-processing application (Bolter and Grusin 2000).

14. Theories of intermedia are what motivated Friedrich Kittler to assert that the gramophone—a register of the "spectrum of noise" and the "unarticulated"—"subverts both literature and music (because it reproduces the unimaginable real they are both based on)" (1999, 22) and Lisa Gitelman (2008) to situate the phonograph within a history of writing and reading inscription devices. Weheliye (2005) places the phonograph and Sony Walkman within a sound recording and reproduction continuum that shapes a reconsideration of Afro-diaspora cultural production, and Hochman (2014) argues that US ethnography (as an example of a cultural paradigm, a profession, and a set of institutions and sanctioned practices) was (and is) deeply entangled in the use of media, including recorded sound, color photography, and documentary film. Other significant studies of intermedia are entangled in histories of aurality (Mills 2010; Moten 2003; Smith 2001, 2006), soundscapes (LaBelle 2010; Thompson 2002; Toop 1999), and ethnographic modernities and acoustemologies (Hirschkind 2006; Ochoa Gautier 2006, 2014). More generally, Sterne's *Audible Past* (2003) establishes sociotechnical cultural critiques of telephony, phonography, and radio while *MP3* (2012) calls for a general "format studies" to study digital audio.

15. As an example of intermedial politics, Schröter cites Lev Manovich's assertion that various technologies and practices in the late twentieth century have rendered notions of monomedia (just text, just audio, just film) untenable even as institutions have insisted on distinct medium typologies that separate cultural heritage collections into works on paper, sculpture, film, video, and so on (Manovich 2001; Schröter 2010, 109).

16. *Oxford English Dictionary*, s.v. "register, v.," September 2023, https://www.oed.com/dictionary/register_v.

Notes to Introduction

17. Benjamin Steege (2012) has a description of the ear in "discourses about acoustical and musical phenomena" in which "we often do not know precisely whether the 'ear' we are describing is a physical, mechanical, organic, physiological, psychological, or cognitive sort of thing. Indeed, the multiplicity of the ear's potential qualities and functions gives the lie to any singular notion of 'the' ear" (2012, 50–51). Katherine McKittrick calls Black music, a "bundling of narrative, praxis, and corporeal feeling," a "resistance, critique, method-making, praxis, and a site of neurological and physiological experience" (2021, 51). In Clement (2014), I include a discussion of the embodied nature of resonance in information theory in which the boundary between embodied matter and meaning is permeable.

18. Citing Judith Butler's theories on performativity (1993, 2004) and Foucault's theories on discourse (1977, 1978), Karen Barad (2007) seeks to account for the relationship between discursive practices and material phenomena by exploring Niels Bohr's insights into the embodied nature of concepts (1958). As a physicist, she draws on "political theory, cultural geography, political economy, critical race theory, postcolonial theory, and feminist theory," and describes contemporary physics as an "inescapable entanglement of matters of being, knowing, and doing, of ontology, epistemology, and ethics, of fact and value" (2007, 35, 3).

19. Objects usually respond to more than one frequency, but they will vibrate easily and at a maximum amplitude at frequencies that map to their resonant frequency. For instance, a cochlear hair cell responds by filtering for its resonant frequency from a complex wave. Most people do not perceive a high dog whistle or the low hum of the electronic grid, because these frequencies do not occur in the resonant frequency range for the hair cell. Further, not all the cochlear hair cells are equally responsive, due to age or other factors.

20. Deaf studies scholars make clear that sound is "multimodal" (Helmreich 2015; Mills 2010, 52).

21. Weheliye describes media materiality as porous, vaporizing around the edges, a research interest that in his work becomes the "interplay between the ephemerality of music (and/or the apparatus) and the materiality of the audio technologies/practices (and/or music)" (2005, 11).

22. *Oxford English Dictionary*, s.v. "audio, n.," July 2023, https://www.oed.com/dictionary/audio_n.

23. *Oxford English Dictionary*, s.v. "resonance, n.," July 2023, https://www.oed.com/dictionary/resonance_n; s.v. "resonate, v.," July 2023, https://www.oed.com/dictionary/resonate_v.

24. Ochoa Gautier (2014, 22) points out this relationality in Western expressions such as "to have a voice," to "listen to one another," to feel a "resonance" or "vibrations" as "expressions used to invoke the idea of participation, the recognition of the

'other,' and alternative forms of the collective." She identifies in these expressions a need that *Dissonant Records* seeks to address: "the need to explore the richness of a multiplicity of variables among what different peoples consider the given and what they consider the made that come together in the acoustic."

25. Sponsored by the Josiah Macy Jr. Foundation, the Macy Conferences where Mead made this comment were a series of meetings that took place between 1946 to 1953 to support scholars from various disciplines, including computer science, neurophysiology, and "a vague 'humanistic' combination of psychiatry, anthropology, and sociology," to develop a science of the human mind. For the Macy scholars, resonance presented a "difficulty" (Pias 2016, 11, 128).

26. Barad writes, it "is only through specific agential intra-actions that the boundaries and properties of 'components' of phenomena become determinate and that particular articulations become meaningful" (2007, 148).

27. Similarly, Brian Hochman (2014) describes cultures as looking more "like moving targets—flexible webs of affiliation and difference that respond, resist, and adapt in the context of broader social pressures . . . what we tend to identify as culture today is neither fixed nor monolithic" (xiv).

28. Ochoa Gautier (2014, 22–23) describes a similar field of meaning making that is generated specifically through sound/listening as "acoustic assemblages." These assemblages include "a listening entity that theorizes about the process of hearing producing notions of the listening entity or entities that hear, notions of the sonorous producing entities, and notions of the type of relationship between them."

29. Beyond the physiognomy of the ear and the throat, scholars find resonance *between* matter and meaning in other systems, such as electrical circuits (Erlmann 2010, 10); the "mosaic" interplay of author, audience, and poem in the compositional works of Charles Baudelaire, T. S. Eliot, and Edgar Allan Poe (McLuhan and McLuhan 1992, 48); and, in the words of novelist Ralph Ellison, "in the shared experience in between the process of the novel, the process which is a novel, and the audience which receives it" (Harvard Summer School Conference on the Contemporary Novel, August 4–5, 1953; see below, note 37).

30. Barad calls this dynamic field of entelechic meaning making "agency": "Agency is not an attribute but the ongoing reconfigurings of the world," she writes. "The universe is agential intra-activity in its becoming" (2007, 141).

31. Cannon and Rubery (2020) use the term *aurality* to refer to all the ways that hearing and speaking are reflected in the production of writing.

32. I do not go at length "to harp" (play the same string repeatedly) on the idea of intermedia as a central focus of study. I take this advice from Fluxus artist Dick Higgins who coined the term *intermedia* in 1965 to discuss the avant-garde in art. He

Notes to Introduction

revisits the term's usefulness in 1981, stating that intermedia "allows for an ingress to a work which otherwise seems opaque and impenetrable, but once that ingress has been made it is no longer useful to harp upon the intermediality of a work . . . it is more useful at the outset of a critical process than at the later stages of it" (2001, 53).

33. I am grateful to Jonathan Sterne for this analogy.

34. Many scholars seek justice for individuals, communities, and cultures by naming the way they have been misrepresented or not represented in the archival process (Caswell and Mallick 2014; Harris 2002; Harris and Hatang 2001). Other scholars actively consider the technical and social precarity of audio archives. Radio broadcasting scholars, in particular, have called attention to the ephemerality and inaccessibility of the broadcast medium and its resistance to dominant forms of critical analysis and archival recovery (Douglas 2004; Hilmes 2014, 2018; Shepperd 2018; Weisbard 2014), while Carolyn Birdsall (2016), another radio scholar, asserts that sound recordings from the German National Socialist era have been preserved, archived, and made accessible through processes of remediation and recycling. Daphne Brooks's *Liner Notes for the Revolution* (2021) contends that the intellectual history of African American women in music goes "unmarked and unheralded" by music archives and archivists because "these Black women artists have operated through their music as the repositories of the past. . . . They have often engaged in active projects to archive their own creative practices, to document the intellectual and creative processes tied to their music" (4).

35. These include the Oklahoma State University Library, the American Folklife Center at the Library of Congress, Harvard University's Woodberry Poetry Room and Schlesinger Library, and the Benson Latin American Collection at the University of Texas at Austin.

36. Cyrus Stevens Avery is often called the "Father of Route 66." The Oklahoma State University–Tulsa Special Collections and Archives acquired Ruth Sigler Avery's collection in 2004 from Joy Avery, Ruth Avery's daughter, as part of the Cyrus Stevens Avery Collection.

37. Harvard Summer School Conference on the Contemporary Novel (hereafter Harvard Summer School), Woodberry Poetry Room, Houghton Library, Harvard University: August 4–5, 1953, PN3319.H37x 1953, tapes 1–8; August 3–5, 1953, PN3319.H37y 1953, tapes 1–7.

38. Joyce Sexton and Linda Gray Sexton, Sexton's daughters, gave the reel-to-reel audiotapes to the Schlesinger Library at Harvard University in 2002 (CD copies were made in 2003), and Sexton's papers, including her journals, to the Harry Ransom Center, where they were processed in 1998 and digitized in 2006 and 2010. Listening to the tapes on an old CD player now at the Schlesinger Library at the Radcliff Institute, where Sexton taught one summer, still requires her daughter Linda Gray Sexton's permission.

39. *Brown v. Board of Education of Topeka*, 347 U.S.483 (1954) (USSC+); Opinion, May 17, 1954; Records of the Supreme Court of the United States, Record Group 267, National Archives, Washington, DC.

40. Community activism is an important component of current work uncovering silences in the archives, especially in the context of silenced race massacres. See Earhart and Taylor (2016).

41. This includes over 700 "tracks" or recorded performances in the 1935 recordings. Most of these are not available online.

42. The Works Progress Administration was changed to Work Projects Administration in April 1939.

43. There are six books based on Zora Neale Hurston's ethnographic field work in Alabama, the Bahamas, Florida, Georgia, Haiti, Jamaica, and New Orleans from the 1930s through the 1950s: *Mules and Men* (1935), *Tell My Horse* (1938), *The Sanctified Church* (1981), *Go Gator and Muddy the Water* (1999), *Every Tongue Got to Confess* (2001), and *Barracoon* (2018).

44. According to Jerome McGann's theory of text, a text's rationale is a consideration for this social condition, made apparent through "the dynamic structure of a document as it is realized in determinate (artisanal) and determinable (reflective) ways" (2001, 137).

45. This disregard for the audio recordings in Anzaldúa's archive is evidenced by their going largely unnoticed in the recent critical edition of *Borderlands / La Frontera: The New Mestiza* (Anzaldúa 2021).

Chapter 1

1. The grand jury found that "the recent race riot was the direct result of an effort on the part of a certain group of colored men who appeared at the courthouse on the night of May 31, 1921. . . . There was no mob spirit among the whites, no talk of lynching and no arms. The assembly was quiet until the arrival of armed Negroes, which precipitated and was the direct cause of the entire affair. . . . We further find that there existed indirect cause more vital to the public interest than the direct cause. Among them were agitation among the Negroes of social equality, and the laxity of law enforcement . . . of the city and country." (Gill 1946, 90–91 [originally published in the *Tulsa Daily World*, June 26, 1921]).

2. Scott Ellsworth interviewed William D. Williams at his home, 2233 N. Denver Blvd., Tulsa, part 2, June 7 1978; Tulsa Race Massacre of 1921 Archive, item 1989.004.1.5.

3. "Fear, The Fifth Horseman: An Anthology: A Documentary of the Tulsa Race War," Avery Collection, boxes 13–15.

4. Basing his argument on a hole cut out of the Tulsa public library's copy of the paper where the editorial would have been, Tulsa lawyer and former member of the Tulsa Race Riot Commission Jim Sawyer sued the heirs of the late editor of the *Tulsa Tribune* in 2003 for inciting the riot (Archaeological Institute of America 2003).

5. See Martinez-Keel (2021) as an example of the discourse in more recent news media.

6. To contrast "truth borne by the vessel of authenticity or experience" (2005, 83), Brown wonders, "What if speech and silence aren't really opposites? . . . What if a certain modality of silence about one's suffering—and we might consider modalities of silence to be as varied as modalities of speech—articulates a variety of possibilities not otherwise available to the sufferer?" (92–93).

7. Alessandro Portelli's article "What Makes Oral History Different" was originally published in 1979 and exhorts historians to pay attention to the orality (e.g., intonation, pauses), narrative form (e.g., velocity of speech), subjectivity, and the relationship between the interviewer and interviewee. It remains a foundational piece and was republished in 2016 in *The Oral History Reader* (Portelli 2016). Alexander Freund (2016) discusses "off the record" silences in his attempt to articulate an "ethics of silence." Such silences are sociotechnical and include actually turning off the recorder or passing a piece of paper with a message that the interviewee does not wish to be recorded audibly: "literally everything that happens in an oral history relationship between interviewer and interviewee that is not recorded may be considered off-the-record . . . they are deferments of voice, relocations from 'on' to 'off,' from speaking to writing and gesturing" (254).

8. Saidiya Hartman (1997, 3), Toni Morrison (1992, 37), and Ralph Ellison (1995) write about how authors use events of racial tensions to reduce African Americans to "a human 'natural' resource who, so that white men could become more human, was elected to undergo a process of institutionalized dehumanization" (Ellison 1995, 85).

9. African American journalist Mary Elizabeth Jones Parrish called the local press "malicious" for its use of the moniker "Little Africa" to describe Greenwood (Parrish [1922] 2021, 7).

10. Parrish collected newspaper accounts in *Events of the Tulsa Disaster*, which remained unpublished until 1989. Martin Brown also reportedly published a booklet titled "Is Tulsa Sane?," issued by the Black Dispatch Press of Oklahoma City in July 1921, but no copies remain (Oklahoma Commission 2001).

11. The gradual absence is noted by the Race Riot Commission report published in 2001 in which historian Scott Ellsworth and Greenwood survivor and historian John Hope Franklin write that the *Tulsa Tribune* systematically ignored the event in its regular feature "Fifteen Years Ago" on the event's anniversary in 1936, as well

as in its "Twenty-five Years Ago" column in 1946. One notable exception is the Black-owned *Oklahoma Eagle*, which began publishing in 1922. Malea Walker (2021) reports that the owners salvaged the *Star*'s printing press to produce annual features about the massacre.

12. Avery has also alternatively titled the project "Fear, the Fifth Horseman: A Race War Documentary" and "Fear, the Fifth Horseman: An Anthology: A Documentary of the Tulsa Race War," Avery Collection, boxes 13–15.

13. Avery's experience was similar to that of Ed Wheeler, a white reporter who relayed in a letter to Avery in August 1976 how his own research had been hampered by the fact that "files which would normally supply ready and competent information had been pilfered of all references to the riot . . . stories and articles concerning the riot had been cut out of newspapers before they were microfilmed for preservation and prosperity" (Tulsa County Historical Society 1976). The missing pages are corroborated by a *Tulsa World* article published in May 2020, titled "1921 Race Riot: Tribune Mystery Unsolved" (Krehbiel 2020).

14. Typed and signed letter from Ed Wheeler, Board of Directors Member, to Ruth Sigler Avery, August 24, 1976; Avery Collection.

15. At the beginning of this project, there were only three survivors left for interviews—Viola Fletcher (aged 109), Lessie Benningfield Randle (109), and Hughes Van Ellis (102). Sadly, Van Ellis died on October 9, 2023.

16. The account remained unpublished until 1989, when Parrish's nephew distributed it through a small boutique press. In 1972, R. Halliburton Jr., a white professor, published the first academic piece titled "The Tulsa Race War of 1921" in the *Journal of Black Studies*, where he primarily references contemporary news articles, but he followed it in 1975 with a documentary compilation of the same title in which he included a large portion of Parrish's previously unpublished work. Besides including Parrish's interviews, almost as an appendix, Halliburton's work relies heavily on newspaper and government records, which later scholars came to consider unfaithful and biased.

17. Community activism is an important component of current work uncovering silences in the archives, especially in the context of silenced race massacres (Earhart and Taylor 2016). Ellsworth heralds Henry Whitlow for "his excellent 'A History of the Greenwood Era in Tulsa,' a paper presented to the Tulsa County Historical Society, March 29, 1973" (1982, 141).

18. Wheeler, a white author, notes that he was harassed and threatened to silence, and his report was rejected by multiple newspapers and magazines.

19. There is also Williams and Williams (2008) and Johnson (2007). These works are not relevant to this study in part because the treatment of the riot itself is only a

small part of the book. These texts, however, use the same resources as those previously mentioned.

20. Avery's interviews were archived as part of the Cyrus Stevens Avery Collection at the Oklahoma State University–Tulsa Special Collections and Archives, which acquired the collection in 2004 as part of the Cyrus Stevens Avery Collection from Joy Avery, Ruth Avery's daughter. Ellsworth, who earned a PhD from the University of Tulsa, would keep his interviews at that university's McFarlin Library (Tulsa Race Massacre of 1921 Archive).

21. The HBO series won twenty-six nominations and eleven Emmys from the Academy of Television Arts and Sciences. Media and published reviews reported that the 1921 event was largely unknown to many of the viewers when the show aired. Critical reviews of the series consistently call the history of the massacre "buried" (Nussbaum 2019). It is perhaps ironic that *The Atlantic* review (Gilbert 2019) references a previous story, published eight years earlier in the *New York Times* (Sulzberger 2011) that details how "Blacks and whites alike grew into middle age unaware of what had taken place." Apparently, the African American actors from *Watchmen* were also new to mainstream audiences. When *Watchmen*'s leading actor Regina King did her opening act on *Saturday Night Live* on February 6, 2021—as only the thirteenth Black woman to host in *SNL*'s 880 episodes—she quipped that while the audience might not know her work in Black film, they might know her from *Watchmen*.

22. There are gendered politics in this historiography. Ellsworth notes simply in an essay on sources in *Death in a Promised Land* that Ruth Sigler Avery was "another scholar of the riot" in her role at the Tulsa Historical Society (1982, 139), but he reports in his 1976 undergraduate thesis ("The Tulsa Race Riot of 1921," photocopy in Avery Collection, box 5) that he avidly sought Avery's advice and used her recording equipment in the 1970s while interviewing some of the same survivors (1976, xvii). Later, as a graduate student doing his own interviews in 1978, he admitted to William D. Williams that he was in direct competition with Avery and trying to avoid her around town (interview, Tulsa Race Massacre of 1921 Archive, item 1989.004.1.5).

23. In contrast, Jewell Parker Rhodes acknowledges that "history lies, obscures, and twists the truth, particularly about women and African Americans," and asserts that her "role as a novelist is to tell better lies which I hope will convey an emotional truth to counterbalance inaccurate history" (Rhodes 2017).

24. Scott Ellsworth interviewed Seymour Williams at his home, 1812 N. Rockford, Tulsa, part 1, June 2, 1978; Tulsa Race Massacre of 1921 Archive, item 1989.004.1.1.

25. A misguided sense of resolution can be coupled with complacency, as Madigan's 'Author's note' to *The Burning* (2001) reflects: "I will never be able to look at a Black person the same way again. I think I'm beginning to understand" (xv).

26. Kathryn Roulston (2019) examines oral histories from the Former Slave Project (FSP), a 1930s work-relief initiative that was part of the Federal Writers' Project (FWP) and employed white-collar workers as fieldworkers, writers, and editors to solicit stories of more than 4,000 former slaves. She found similarly biased perspectives in the conduct of the FWP interviews. The existing context of racial segregation of the 1930s impacted the interactions that took place within the interviews and created "interactional complexities produced by particular interviewer-interviewee relationships" (6). Roulston found that the interviewers and editors represented the oral histories in widely different manners, in varying degrees adhering (or not) to the FWP guidelines about not including racist language, forwarding "a White paternal view of plantation life," and mitigating descriptions of violence or cruel punishment (7). The reliability and factuality of the interviews—which were assessed by the Writer's Unit at the Library of Congress by appraisers "for accuracy, detail, and scope of the content of each narrative, in addition to the ways in which fieldworkers had represented the life stories"—were found to be unverifiable (8). Today, many researchers still find the slave interviews to be less than credible witnesses of slave life (Kane 2014; Musher 2014; Schwartz 2014, Woodward 1985). Interestingly, the appraisers' critiques of the conduct of interviews are removed from the recordings and "must be read in light of the fact that authors were commenting on the *narratives produced from the interviews*, since the FWP interviews were not audio-recorded" (Roulston 2019, 6, emphasis original).

27. Interview of Verna "Vernie" Prince, March 8, 1971, Avery Collection, box 3, TRR-4, track 2.

28. The author was unable to identify the article.

29. Burger, Warren Earl, and Supreme Court of the United States, U.S. Reports: Swann et al. v. Charlotte-Mecklenburg Board of Education et al., 402 U.S. 1, 1970, Periodical; https://www.loc.gov/item/usrep402001/.

30. Interview of William R. Holway, September 9, 1974, Avery Collection, box 3, TRR-6, side 2.

31. Interview of Walton Clinton, September 12, 1975, Avery Collection box 8, TRR-2, 3.

32. Different emotional truths are evident in Parrish's own testimony, in which she recalls riding back into Tulsa on a Red Cross truck on their way to McNulty Park after fleeing from the fires: "We did not enter there through our section of town, but they brought us through the white section, all sitting flat down on the truck looking like immigrants, only that we had no bundles. Dear reader, can you imagine the humiliation of coming in like that, with many doors thrown open watching you pass, some with pity and others with a smile?" (Parrish [1922] 2021, 13).

33. Avery Collection, "Research Materials," box 5. Eddie Faye Gates, a local Tulsa high school teacher and administrator includes a thorough description of retellings during the Tulsa Race Riot Commission research period (1997–2001) from varied

institutions (business, cultural, educational, faith, literary, historical) in interviews with 200 survivors and 300 of their descendants in *Riot on Greenwood: The Total Destruction of Black Wall Street* (Gates 2003). She also surveys a diverse range of media and genres, including books, maps, pamphlets, and photographs in artistic, dramatic, literary, musical, and museum performances and exhibitions (170–181).

34. The typed manuscript notes that there were two readings. The first was from Robert McAfee Brown's *Unexpected News: Reading the Bible with Third World Eyes* (1984). The second was Ellison's (1995). Johnson's typed transcript is in the Avery Collection, box 3.

35. It was likely not lost on Wolf, who presumably chose the reading, that these remarks about media and identity were part of a longer tribute Ellison gave at the unveiling of a portrait of Dr. Inman Page, Brown University's first African American student and a childhood mentor to Ellison, who had grown up in Oklahoma City. In the speech, which I describe in greater detail in chapter 3, Ellison takes issue with Brown's long-overdue homage to Dr. Page and expresses amazement that they uncovered his boyhood connection.

36. Avery also writes a short poem titled "America's Biggest Race War" to conclude the introduction to her manuscript. In the poem, "black bones" play a part in the media of silenced histories, which become "empty tomes". She also includes voicing subjectivity ("we lift our pens" and "now some speak again"), and US government complacency and complicity (the "vacuum" and "idleness" of the Civil Rights movement) as central themes (Avery Collection, "Fear").

37. Askew, an Oklahoman of Cherokee and Choctaw descent who grew up in the 1960s near Tulsa, had also never heard of the 1921 massacre.

38. Brown suggests that speaking about the past in "an attempt to expurgate guilt about what one did not do to prevent the suffering" may be "doomed insofar as the speaking actually perpetuates the guilt by disavowing it" (2005, 94).

39. Interestingly, Askew uses similar nationalist discourse in her introduction to the events in *Fire in Beulah* as "perpetrated by Americans, on Americans, in this promised land," but she does so from the perspective of Indigenous and Black Tulsans who overcame the perpetrators in part due to the "strength and self-sufficiency of the Freedmen, who arrived here as slaves of mixed-blood Indians" and post-Reconstruction African Americans who "came in hopes of freedom and economic opportunity" (2001, 41).

40. Hartman articulates how "the terrible spectacle" of stories depicting violence against Black bodies are dramatizations of "the origin of the subject," in which "to be a slave is to be under the brutal power and authority of another," by performing close readings of the WPA slavery narratives in "Born in Slavery: Slave Narratives from the Federal Writers' Project, 1936–1938," a Library of Congress collection of more than 2,300 first-person accounts of slavery in which Hurston and Ralph Ellison both participated (Hartman 1997, 3).

41. While Lindelof admits that his retelling in the television series *Watchmen* (2019) relies heavily on stories collected in Madigan's *The Burning* (2001), Ellsworth's accounts are the "facts of the riot" from which novelist Rilla Askew would draw while writing the novel *Fire in Beulah* and, evidence indicates, upon which Jewell Parker Rhodes relied to write the novel *Magic City* (Askew 2001, "Acknowledgments"; Rhodes 2017).

42. This work is aligned with Nicole Brittingham Furlonge's project to "listen in print" in *Race Sounds: The Art of Listening in African American Literature* (Furlonge 2018) to examine engaging aurality in African American literature.

43. Rhodes writes that she first saw mention in a *Parade Magazine* piece from 1983 after which she conducted research. Likely, the piece was a syndicated article by Wallace, Wallechinsky, and Wallace titled "U.S. City Bombed During a Race Riot" (1983, 60–61).

44. Similarly, Jenny Sharpe (2020) considers spirituality in the archive through Erna Brodber's novel Louisiana (Brodber 1994), which depicts a Hurston-inspired character working for the WPA to record ex-slaves and discovers the recording machine is an instrument through which spirits enter the modern world.

45. The twelve-part DC Comics series was published from 1986 to 1987 by writer Alan Moore, artist Dave Gibbons, and colorist John Higgins, which became the collected trade paperback and graphic novel in 1987.

46. An "Easter egg" is used in film discussions to indicate subtle references to other media.

47. *Oxford English Dictionary*, s.v. "amplify, v.," September 2023, https://www.oed.com/dictionary/amplify_v.

48. Helmreich talks about a "transductive anthropology," in which "transduction should remind auditors of the physical, infrastructural conditions that support the texture and temper of sounds we take to be meaningful" (2015, 225).

49. Oral historians use the term "deep listening"—"whereby the researcher seeks to engage not only with the words being uttered, but also with the deeper meaning inherent in the narrative as a whole" (Jessee 2016, 678)—but Charles Bernstein's (1998) intervention in close listening is closer in methodology to what I use here, and is rooted in larger conversations about "close reading" in literary study. Close reading has been described by Stephen Best and Sharon Marcus (2009) to include "symptomatic reading," which "describes textual surfaces as superfluous, and seeks to unmask hidden meanings" and "surface reading" as a means "to accurately depict the truth to which a text bears witness . . . surfaces that have been rendered invisible by symptomatic reading" (2, 1). All these definitions are useful in thinking about how to scholars consider spoken text recordings in interpretive practices.

Chapter 2

1. The reference numbers included here are the AFS or "shelf list" number and come from the "Traditional Music and Spoken Word Catalog," a physical card catalog in the American Folklife Center at the Library of Congress (AFC 1935/001). In this chapter, I have shortened the AFS numbers by not including "AFS" and leading numbers. For example, the AFS number for this song, "See Day Dawning," is "AFS 00336 B." I have shortened it to "336 B." Most of the 1935 recordings are currently not available online.

2. Hurston's works include the novels *Jonah's Gourd Vine* (1934), *Mules and Men* (1935), *Their Eyes Were Watching God* (1937), and *Tell My Horse* (1938). The plays *The Great Day* (1932), *From Sun to Sun* (1933), and *Singing Steel* (1934) were all published in Hurston 2008. Her ethnographic writings from this period that were published posthumously include *The Sanctified Church* (1981), *Go Gator and Muddy the Water* (1999), *Every Tongue Got to Confess: Negro Folk-tales from the Gulf States* (2001), and *Barracoon* (2018).

3. Alice Walker first wrote the essay "In Search of Zora Neale Hurston" for *Ms. Magazine* in 1975 and later titled it "Looking for Zora" in 1979. The piece details how Walker explored Hurston's hometown of Eatonville, Florida, and came to understand that it was immensely influential on her works.

4. Hurston was heralded as a feminist icon for her creative work in *Their Eyes Were Watching God* ([1937] 2006) and in her anthropological writings as an avid proponent for the authentic portrayal and the significance of Black culture in the United States. She is labeled a creative genius (Hemenway 1977; Hurston 1979), a feminist (Visweswaran 1994), a critical race theorist (Furlonge 2018), and a dramatist (Hill 1996). While lauded by many, Hurston has also been accused of inauthenticity (Huggins 1971) and encouraging racist Black stereotypes (Brown 1936; Locke 1938; Wright 1937); labeled a conservative (Carpio and Sollors 2011), a segregationist (Delbanco 1997), and a sycophant of wealthy white patrons (Wright 1937); and portrayed as a plagiarizer (Hemenway 1977, 96–102; Hill 1996, 61–76; and Plant 2018) and a child molester (Hemenway 1977, 318–322).

5. Hurston's letters are scattered across archives, such as the John A. Lomax and Alan Lomax Papers in the American Folklife Center at the Library of Congress, the Alain Locke papers at Howard University, William Duncan Strong's papers at the National Anthropological Archives, the Zora Neale Hurston Papers at the University of Florida, the Federal Writers' Project collection at the University of South Florida, and items that were originally given as part of the James Weldon Johnson Memorial Collection at the Beinecke Library at Yale, to name a few. This list does not include the countless contemporaries whose collections also contain Hurston's prolific correspondence (Hurston 2002, 836–837), the archival letters found recently (Cappetti 2010), or the origins of her more recently discovered short stories found in old

newspapers (Carpio and Sollors 2011) and a Howard University sorority yearbook. As of this writing, only one final draft of field notes that Hurston collected as part of her WPA work in Florida, titled "Negro Folk-Tales from the Gulf States" (Hurston 2001), has been discovered in the papers of William Duncan Strong (Strong Papers). Much like the pages for *Barracoon* (Hurston 2018), which was long debunked as plagiarism and only recently published in 2018, the field notes for "Negro Folk-Tales" were more polished drafts ready for publication, not working versions with potential clues to Hurston's methods, intentions, or creative process.

6. WPA field recordings in Jacksonville and Ybor City, S1576, T86-244, June 18, 1939. Herbert Halpert created twelve 12-inch acetate records in Florida from the 1939 recording expedition. In 1986, the Florida Folklife Archives copied the disks onto reel-to-reel tapes, which were digitized by the Library of Congress in 2007. Series S1576 is a collection of tapes that were included in the Florida Folklife program (audio recordings of Florida Folk Festival) and are now available online at https://www.floridamemory.com/. "T86-244" refers to the tape number within that series. In this chapter, footnotes refer to the tape numbers to provide more information about the origins of quotations from these 1939 recordings.

7. As of this writing, scholars have written about Hurston's performances only on the 1939 recordings (Bordelon 1999; Brooks 2021; Furlonge 2018; Hemenway 1977). One exception is Abramowitz (2020), who writes about the 1935 recordings. There are also mistaken listenings. Furlonge (2018, 21–23) quotes Hurston from one of the 1939 recordings, but she does not cite the recording and she mistakenly hears and describes the recording as an interview with Alan Lomax. Perhaps the error stems from Hemenway's own mistake (1977, 168), where he attributes the same quote to an interview with Lomax. Hemenway includes a citation to the recording but the citation points to the 1939 recordings by Halpert. Lomax is not cited in the metadata as present on the day of recording.

8. As evidenced by an exchange with Walter White, July 23, 1934 (Hurston 2002, 307). White was an African American civil rights activist who led the National Association for the Advancement of Colored People from 1929 to 1955.

9. Hartman (1997) is concerned with scenes of subjection that are portrayed in WPA performances, including slaves singing, playing games, telling stories, and dancing, often at or near the auction blocks. These "fun-loving" slaves are performing forced labor or are otherwise in a state of physical deprivation from lack of food, warmth, or kind treatment. Understanding these dramatizations of "the spectacular character of black suffering" as tropes that "inure us to pain by virtue of their familiarity," Hartman argues that the theatrical language used to describe these events creates a distance between these incidents and their white audience (1997, 3). See Hurston, Lomax, and Barnicle (1935) and Winick (2017) for more information about Hurston's and Ellison's participation in the WPA slave narratives.

10. Lynda Marion Hill assigns to Hurston's work what she believes is the only generic typology that can adequately reflect this multigeneric, multimedia oeuvre: "All of Hurston's work can be read as dramatic literature" (1996, xxiv). Daniel Harney sees in Hurston's diverse repertoire a good fit for anthropology's "literary turn" as her work attempts "to define culture and address the problems of its authenticity and representation," but he recognizes that this work is also a resistance that "bear[s] the traces of, and thus cannot be read in isolation from, the simultaneous rise of professional institutional society in America" (2015, 489). Visweswaran notes that even "experimental ethnography has been strangely reluctant to embrace other forms of writing, such as the novel, short story, diary, or autobiography" (1994, 32–33).

11. While the meaning of media-specific materials may seem tethered to its material form, within a repertoire like Hurston's, "even though the embodiment changes, the meaning might very well remain the same" (Taylor 2003, 20).

12. Stetson Kennedy also remembers Lomax telling him this story (National Public Radio 2005).

13. Mary Elizabeth Barnicle, May 15, 1935, Correspondence, Lomax Collection.

14. Many scholars have discussed the role of equivocating in ethnographies. Kamala Visweswaran writes in *Fictions of Feminist Ethnography* that "lies, secrets, and silence" can be some of the most frequent strategies of resistance against authority (1994, 60). Ochoa Gautier (2014) describes the work of a "comparative anthropology" as an opportunity to consider equivocations as "a field of comparative mutual constitution of notions of alterity" rather than an opportunity to "translate the concepts of the other into its Western equivalents in order to adequately 'explain' who the other is, to represent him or her divested of colonial history" (23).

15. WPA field recordings in Jacksonville and Ybor City, S1576, T86-243, June 18, 1939.

16. *Oxford English Dictionary*, s.v. "distortion, n.," July 2023, https://www.oed.com/dictionary/distortion_n.

17. In terms of sound and media technologies, "the normally invisible quality of working infrastructure becomes visible when it breaks" (Star 1999, 382).

18. Gilroy acknowledges that "words, even words stretched by melisma and supplemented or mutated by the screams which still index the conspicuous power of the slave sublime, will never be enough to communicate its unsayable claims to truth" (1993, 37).

19. Most of these are not available online, except for the WPA field recordings in Calhoun County and Raiford (the 1935, and the 1936–1937 recording expeditions), "Wallace Interview" (Hurston, Lomax, and Barnicle 1935), "Bella Mina" (Hurston, "Dust Tracks"), and "John Henry" (Hurston, Lomax, and Barnicle, Expedition

Collection). There are also two tracks available through the American Folklife Center (National Sampler).

20. There are three other recordings in the American Folklife Center's Traditional Music and Spoken Word Catalog: "Bama, Bama" (29 A02), "Bluebird" (1879 A01), and "There Stands a Bluebird" (29 A03), which are listed as "sung by Zora Hurston" and "Petionville, Hait, Alan Lomax, December 1936."

21. Todd Harvey, a reference archivist, curator of the Alan Lomax Collection, and acquisitions coordinator for the American Folklife Center, supplied me with the old, typed inventory via email with the note, "Can't say who made it or when. Alan often typed these by 1937 but not sure about this one." Numerous notations include the phrase "Alan Lomax reviewed the technical quality of this recording in 1980 and commented" (Todd Harvey, email to the author, September 17, 2020).

22. Being a "participant observer" was not an uncommon practice at the time (Lomax often sang with the people he recorded).

23. By April 1935, the Lomaxes were also purchasing discs from Thompson (John A. Lomax and Alan Lomax Papers, images 7 and 17).

24. The fact that listeners cannot rely on the authenticity of Hurston's published versions of the story or her voice invites a "shift from judicial (or indicative) history to subjunctive or conjectural history" that parallels a shift from, what Kamala Visweswaran calls, "declarative (or realist) to interrogative texts" (1994, 72). "[L]ike an unreliable narrator," Visweswaran writes, "the fidelity of the conjectural historian, confronted with the choices if __, then? and if not __, then? cannot be assumed" (72).

25. This is verified by notes in those works as well as in the Library of Congress recording log (possibly added by an archivist after John Lomax's initial notes). "John and Old Mistis' Nightgown" (347 A01; Hurston 1935, 77–79, 111–113), "John and his Rival" (347 A02), John and the Bear (348 a02 and 348 B01; Hurston 1935, 72–73; Hurston 2001, 83–84 [same as *Mules*], 95–97 [more like recording]), and "John and the Coon" (348 B02; Hurston 1935, 80–82; Hurston 2001, 85–86).

26. Some of the titles and the storytellers vary. John Davis is the teller noted in Lomax's log on the recordings, but Hurston credits "John and his Rival" (renamed "Big Talk" but copied verbatim) to Joe Wiley (Hurston 1935, 77–79) and Clifford Ulmer (Hurston 2001, 111–113) in her published books.

27. The FWP included the Folklore section, which was created to gather songs, stories, and traditions for the American Guide Series, as well as for preservation.

28. The title is a play on words on Hurston's autobiography title *Dust Tracks on a Road* (1942). The playlist also includes a twenty-first track titled "Bella Mina" (377 B01), which is the only track from the 1935 trip.

29. Recent scholars in political economy and sociological theory call the work that mostly Black men did in these camps "unfree labor." Nicola Pizzolato (2018) notes that "definitions of unfree labour clarify that, irrespective of the means of recruitment, the payment of wages, or temporality of the situation, the performance of low-paid, dangerous work, the lack of right to protest and penalties for exiting the relation amount to a situation of unfreedom" (2018, 476).

30. Many of the first kind of stories are found in a section of *Every Tongue Got to Confess: Negro Folk-Tales from the Gulf States* titled "Massa and White Folk Tales" (2001, 105–115); the latter are found in a section called "John and Massa Tales" (83–102). Meisenhelder (1996) writes extensively about the subversive nature of the folklore that Hurston collects.

31. Hurston cites the importance of what she called "between-story conversation and business," or the dialogue around the stories and songs she wanted to include in *Mules and Men* (1935), in a letter to her mentor Franz Boas in 1934: "It so happens that the conversations and incidents are true," she writes to her mentor, also calling the dialogic sections "unscientific matter" and claiming, "of course I never would have set them down for scientists to read" (Hurston 2002, 308).

32. WPA field recordings in Jacksonville and Ybor City, S1576, T86-243, June 18, 1939.

33. WPA field recordings in Jacksonville and Ybor City, S1576, T86-245, June 18, 1939.

34. WPA field recordings in Jacksonville and Ybor City, S1576, T86-244, June 18, 1939.

35. WPA field recordings in Jacksonville and Ybor City, S1576, T86-244, June 18, 1939.

36. WPA field recordings in Jacksonville and Ybor City, S1576, T86-244, June 18, 1939. The subject of enunciation as a concept articulated in Lacan (2008, 36) is used by Visweswaran (1994) to differentiate from the "subject in process" as described in Belsey (1980, 106).

37. WPA field recordings in Jacksonville and Ybor City, S1576, T86-244, June 18, 1939.

38. Hurston's declared date May 11, 1935, is likely wrong since there is a record of letters that place her as well as Barnicle in New York in mid-May 1935 (Hurston 2002, 350–352).

39. "Subjecthood," Visweswaran writes, "requires a category or name" (1994, 60). Visweswaran writes about the process of subjectivation and naming in ethnographic history making as one that "suggests a juridical or inquisitorial model of history, one that interrogates the subject beginning with the first question, 'What is your

name?'" and then asks about the broader epistemological paradigm that is foregrounded when the subject resists answering the question: "What is the relationship between naming and identity, between not naming and subjectivation, between speaking 'as' and not speaking at all? How should I name this woman who wishes to be anonymous? And what identity do I construct for her?" (60).

40. WPA field recordings in Jacksonville and Ybor City, S1576, T86-245, June 18, 1939.

Chapter 3

1. Discovering misplaced or unprocessed items in library stacks is not an uncommon occurrence. Processes and standards for cataloguing have changed remarkably in the last seventy-five years. Davis explains in an email to the author that in terms of the 10-inch reels she identified in 2022, "I think it's understandable that librarians thought they were copies. All copies went into a particular duplicate section that we have almost worked our way through. And, let's face it, the live event recordings themselves were usually made by campus technicians or students in that period: so the markings on the reels were not those of an archivist" (Christina Davis, email to the author, September 19, 2022).

2. Curator Christina Davis asserts that even by 1960 only nine out of 1,200 freshmen were Black (McCarthy, Alison, and Devlin 2020). Photographs from the Forum Room events feature Ellison sitting next to an African American woman, whom Davis and I have identified from other photographs as his wife, Fanny Ellison. There is one white female participant named Ms. Hilda Livingston, who attended the third night of talks, which featured publishers, and Katherine Anne Porter was meant to attend, but she was sick and declined at the last minute.

3. Edmund Burke introduced the term "moral imagination" in *Reflections on the Revolution in France* ([1790] 1987) as a consideration for situated cultural elements that influence how people think and act, including how people think and act in the moral sphere of values.

4. This could be Harold L. Humes, who was a professor at Harvard at this time.

5. The introduction to this essay as it was published in *Confluence*, December 1953, mentions that this is an updated version of an essay Ellison originally wrote in 1946 (1995, 81). Listening to Ellison's lecture on August 4, 1953, I have noted sections of "Twentieth-Century Fiction and the Black Mask of Humanity" that are verbatim from the lecture. However, the repeated themes from the conference conversations, as well as research in Ellison's papers at the Library of Congress, lead me to believe that both this essay as it was published in 1953 and Ellison's essay "Society, Morality and the Novel," which he wrote in 1957, were greatly influenced by the Harvard conference conversations.

6. In a letter on August 11, 1953, Henry Kissinger invites Ellison to submit something for a multi-issue topic in *Confluence* magazine, a journal that Henry Kissinger, then a graduate student at Harvard, had started to "build a network of influential acquaintances" (Isaacson 1992, 73). The topic is titled "The Problem of Minorities" and, writes Kissinger, "I am particularly interested in the race problem on literary consciousness and artistic creativity." He implies that this invitation is the result of a conversation he had with Ellison at Harvard (Ellison Papers).

7. Later, in his "Address to the Harvard College Alumni, Class Of 1949," Ellison mentions that it was only after he gave his talk in 1953 that he realized Memorial Hall had been built in honor of Union soldiers who had died in the Civil War (Ellison 1995).

8. Ellison describes his time during the Harvard conference to his friend Albert Murray in a letter on August 6, 1953 (2019, 337).

9. As Nicole Brittingham Furlonge (2018) has noted about using the microphone as an analogy in her reading of *Invisible Man*, the microphone "becomes a site through which the speaker and the group work toward some accord, since *Invisible Man* is only successful and only has a reason to speak if the crowd remains willing both to talk back—or provide feedback—and to listen" (54).

10. Besides "Twentieth Century Fiction" and "Society, Morality, and the Novel," Ellison would also publish "Beating that Boy" in the *New Republic* (October 1945) and "On Being the Target of Discrimination" in the *New York Times Magazine* (1989) on the discriminatory practices inherent to segregation. Both are reprinted in Ellison (1995).

11. Excellent work on agential silences in African American writings and history are Higginbotham (1992), Hine (1986), and Sharpe (2020).

12. In a 1961 interview, Ellison further describes identification as "certain emotions" that he "could only associate with classical music. . . . You got glimpses, very vague glimpses, of a far different world than that assigned by segregation laws, and I was taken very early on with a passion to link together all I love within the Negro community and all those things I felt in the world which lay beyond" (1995, 70).

13. Scholars have written about Ellison's personal interests in electronic radios, cameras, and computers (Blair 2005; Bradley 2010; Wright 2003), and on the impact of electricity, sound technology, and technological progressivism on constructions of race in his writing (Furlonge 2011; Lieberman 2015; Wilcox 2007). Nicole Brittingham Furlonge and Alexander Weheliye have considered Ellison's use of audio as means to "renew" concepts of Black identity as a "reconstitution of a fractured racial self" (Furlonge 2011) and as means "to augment an inferior black subjectivity—a subjectivity created by racist ideologies and practices in the field of vision—establishing venues for the constitution of new modes of existence" (Weheliye 2005,

50). Similarly, Wilcox (2007, 988) writes that electricity, "By virtue of its abilities to carry information and to flow through the very (conductive) materials of which organisms and machines are made," serves as transducer or "an interface between organism and machine" in Ellison's writing, "to couple entities which inhabit disparate ontological orders."

14. Saidiya Hartman (1997, 3) calls "the spectacular character of black sufferings" an opportunity to consider the nature of the audience: "Are we witnesses who confirm the truth of what happened in the face of the world-destroying capacities of pain, the distortions of torture, the sheer unrepresentability of terror, and the repression of the dominant accounts? Or are we voyeurs fascinated with and repelled by exhibitions of terror and sufferance?"

15. The idea of the "little man" was originally created by Miss Harrison, Ellison's piano teacher at Tuskegee Unversity (Ellison 1995, 494).

16. When Hartman (1997) discusses a perceived "truth of what happened," "truth" is an acknowledgment of wrongdoing evidenced by the affect (pain, terror, fascination) that the spectacle of Black trauma inspires.

17. Ellison was an Oklahoman, so the 1921 Tulsa Race Massacre represented a personal point in history and a tension for him that served as a key symbol of the clash that he experienced as a Black man in the United States, where his perceived possibilities based on democratic ideals conflicted with his realities of racial violence.

18. The song that Ellison references, "Harvard Blues," was written by Harvard graduate Charles Frazier in 1941 and recorded by Count Basie, with Jimmy Rushing as the vocalist. The song is brief. It is only eighteen lines, with twelve unique lines, not including the repeated verses. It is about Rinehart, a Harvard student who wears "Brooks clothes and white shoes all the time" (Primus 2002). The song primarily describes upscale private clubs and schools that Rinehart, his parents, and his love interest attend, except for two lines about Rinehart: "Now at Harvard and follow an indiff'rent way / Do my drinking down in the cool Ritz Bar."

19. Ellison's biographer Arnold Rampersad points out that "Greenwood refers both to an actual area of Tuskegee and to the black Tulsa section of the same name destroyed in the 1921 riots" (2007, 226).

Chapter 4

1. The poem was published in *Harper's* (1965) before it would appear in Sexton's *Live or Die* (1966).

2. Two archives are referenced in this chapter. The Harry Ransom Center at the University of Texas at Austin (HRC) houses the Anne Sexton Papers and the Ransom Center Sound Recording Collection. From the Anne Sexton Papers: journals,

1961–1963, series IV, Formerly Closed Materials, 1948, 1954–1974, box 44; typescript for "The Year of the Insane," August 1963, series I, box 5, folder 3. From the Ransom Center Sound Recording Collection: Anne Sexton Therapy Tape, R 2867, January 31, 195?; Anne Sexton Therapy Tape, R 2869, August 20, 1963.

The Arthur and Elizabeth Schlesinger Library on the History of Women in America at the Radcliffe Institute for Advanced Study, Harvard University, Cambridge, MA (AESL), houses Audiotapes and Papers of Anne Sexton, 1956–1988. Cited here: Continuation of session, January 24, 1961, trance, poor sound quality, 49 minutes, MC 645, CD-3, reel 1, box 01; [Sexton] describes listening to and reviewing tapes and being in trance, January 28, 1961, music in background, 49 minutes, MC 645, CD-3, reel 2, box 01; [Sexton] discusses tapes in regard to therapy and work, March 7, 1961, radio in background, 61 minutes, MC 645, CD-3, reel 9, box 01; series II, Therapy Tapes, CD-3, reels 1–101, 1961–1964; Sexton read through therapy notebooks during last week, March 19, 1963, 56 minutes, MC 645 CD-3, reel 83, box 03. There are almost three hundred reel-to-reel recordings of her personal therapy sessions in her papers at the AESL. At the HRC, there are four handwritten and typed journals in which Sexton wrote responses after or while listening to the taped sessions and six recordings of therapy sessions, among other recordings of discussions, interviews, and performances.

3. Perhaps, Sterne argues, a history of verisimilitude, in which scholars define media "in terms of their possibility to transcend the problems of representation and achieve a full identity between original and copy (and the inevitable failure of that transcendence)," serves those scholars less well in their pursuit of understanding mediations of cultural conditions than of the general history of compression, which "instead asks how media manage and enact relations shaped by one or more conditions of finitude" (2015, 39).

4. Given that these anxieties are constructed by what Sterne calls the "technical, perceptual, juridical, cultural" limits or conditions of finitude that are "negotiated in a given assemblage of practices, technologies, institutions, and representations," he suggests a dialogue between media scholars and artists to consider how "we understand aesthetics and experience beginning from an assumption of finitude, rather than comparing it with an imaginary standard of transcendence" (Sterne 2015, 39).

5. I would like to note a special thank you to Linda Gray Sexton for her generosity in allowing me to work with her mother's therapy tapes. Anne Sexton, who eventually committed suicide in 1974, writes boldly in her poetry about her mental health issues. Listening to Sexton's therapy tapes and witnessing how Sexton's attempted to work through her mental health issues is a complex endeavor.

6. "Hysteria," a broad prognosis historically given by male doctors in the eighteenth and nineteenth centuries to label outspoken white women as ill, required professional (often male and institutionalized) help. See Showalter (1993) for a discussion of hysteria as both a medical and a literary phenomenon.

7. Dr. Orne shared the tapes with Diane Middlebrook for her controversial *Anne Sexton: A Biography* (1991a), and in response to a slew of *New York Times* editorials critiquing his actions. Dr. Orne notes that when he tried to give the tapes back to Sexton in 1964, she exhorted him to keep them to "help others" (Orne 1991). Sexton expresses the same sentiment in the recordings multiple times.

8. Sexton makes this comment in a marginal note with an arrow to this point in the text of the journal, where she observes that Kayo would have mocked her for misremembering their discussions, but Orne, in contrast, had been kind in reminding her about something they had discussed previously that she could not recall. It "amazed me," she reflects on this simple kindness, that Orne does "not keeping me wriggling on the hook. I had a similar fight with Kayo Wed. night about not remembering an incident he had to retell me."

9. Sexton's journals are rife with spelling errors, nonstandard abbreviations, and ellipses. In this quotation and others I have tried to just copy verbatim what she writes and how she spells it. For clarity and readability, however, I have taken the liberty to replace lowercase "i" with "I" when she is referring to the singular first-person and the "8" she uses instead of apostrophes (e.g., "can8t") with an apostrophe across all the journal entries I include here. On old typewriters the apostrophe is the numeral 8 with the shift key pressed. It is a replacement comparable with i/I.

10. Middlebrook discusses a similar phenomenon during Sexton's poetry readings, calling Orne one of Sexton's many "male auditors" (1991a, 142).

11. The tape is labeled "Therapy Tape (January 31, 195?)" at the HRC. Based on a comparison of the tape and Sexton's journal from January 31, 1961, however, I believe the latter is the correct date.

12. It is not clear whether Orne ever received this letter.

13. The recording is archived at the HRC with no metadata. I have surmised it was read in 1965 because Sexton mentions that her poem "Little Girl, My Stringbean, My Lovely Woman" (published August 7, 1965 in the *New Yorker*) is coming out "this summer." Wherever she is, it is hot and probably in a city. They open the windows at one point to let in air and the traffic noise outside is considerable.

14. In *Live or Die* (1966), Sexton gives shorthand subtitles to only four of the poems. These serve as explanatory framings for reading. In "Sylvia's Death" (1999, 126–128) and "A Little Uncomplicated Hymn" (1999, 148–152), she indicates that the poems are written for an intended second-person audience, "for Sylvia Plath," and "for Joy," her daughter. "Protestant Easter" (1999, 128–131), which appears just before "For the Year of the Insane," includes the subtitle "eight years old" to explain how to read the narrator's perspective as that of a child. Sexton includes an "author's note" at the beginning of *Live or Die* that explains that the poems "Sylvia's Death," "Protestant Easter," and "A Little Uncomplicated Hymn" were printed and dated in order of their

creation, each within months of when Sexton wrote "For the Year of the Insane" (1999, 94).

15. In Clement (2020) I have written extensively on Sexton's "Flee on Your Donkey," in which clocks run backward as the narrator changes ages during a trance: "In trance I could be any age, / voice, gesture," the narrator says, "—all turned backward / like a drugstore clock" (Sexton 1999, 101).

16. "Looking" in this quote is likely in reference to Sexton reading her journal entries while listening. In the early months, she would write down her feelings right after an appointment.

Chapter 5

1. AnaLouise Keating, editor of three volumes of Gloria Anzaldúa's works as well as a trustee of the Gloria Anzaldúa Literary Trust, argues that orality and aurality were part of her intellectual, creative, emotional, and spiritual practice and informed an "epistemological, intuitive, and communal" writing and revision process with a focus on "cadence, musicality, nuanced meaning, and metaphoric complexity" (Anzaldúa 2015, xii).

2. The spiritual recordings in Anzaldúa's archive also go largely unnoticed in the recent critical edition of *Borderlands / La Frontera: The New Mestiza* (2021).

3. Conocimiento is an overarching theory for Anzaldúa. See Keating (2022, 108–117).

4. Anzaldúa Papers, interview with Linda Smuckler, November 5, 1983, box 153, item 17–18.

5. Anzaldúa Papers, "Dialogue with Jeffner Allan," August 18, 1990, box 152, item 3 (mp3 #36). This quote also appears in *Interviews / Entrevistas* (2000, 48), but it is slightly different in the published interview. AnaLouise Keating has indicated in the introduction to *Interviews / Entrevistas* (2000) that Anzaldúa had an active role in editing her interviews for publication. Where possible, I try to quote from the recordings, to which I had access, and I also include page numbers to the published versions based on my research.

6. Anzaldúa Papers, ADP, Montpelier, October 30, 1984, box 154, item 24 (mp3 #32).

7. Anzaldúa Papers, "Gloria Tarot for Sally Gearhart," May 14, 1981, box 157, folder 30 (mp3 #62).

8. Anzaldúa (2000, 2009, and 2015); Anzaldúa and Keating (2002).

9. Anzaldúa Papers, "Guided Meditation, 3 Persons in Depths," March 1, 1984; "Staircase and Lying on Boat, Meadows," April 26, 1984, box 154, item 21 (mp3 #087).

10. While the published version is a succinct tale, the unpublished manuscript— which Anzaldúa worked on intermittently from the 1970s until her death in 2004

and which she alternately titled "Dreaming La Prieta" and "Los Entremados de PQ"—is sprawling (Anzaldúa 2009, 250).

11. Anzaldúa Papers, "Entremados de PQ," notes, undated, box 71, folder 5.

12. Anzaldúa Papers, "Entremados de PQ," manuscript drafts, 1992, box 71, Folder 1, pp. 22, 25.

13. Perez (2014) argues that Anzaldúa is ascribing an essentialist spirituality to indigeneity that presents a singular way of being that does not represent the multiple ways of being indigenous in the world.

14. Quoted in Anzaldúa Papers, "Pysch/Meta/Health Notes—Life Stages—Mid-Life 1984," undated [1984], box 166, folder 19.

15. *Oxford English Dictionary*, s.v. "liminal, adj.," September 2023, https://www.oed.com/dictionary/liminal_adj.

16. In Anne Sexton's "author's note" to her collection of poems *Live or Die* (1966) she indicates a similar liminal state, to live or die; she chooses "Live" as the last poem of the collection.

17. Four years before the 1981 Tarot reading described above, Gearhart had cowritten *A Feminist Tarot* (1977) with Susan Rennie. Gearhart's book was first self-published in 1977 at Persephone Press, a publishing company founded by a lesbian-feminist collective in Watertown, Massachusetts. Persephone Press also published Anzaldúa's first book, *This Bridge Called My Back: Writings by Radical Women of Color*, edited with Cherríe Moraga (Moraga and Anzaldúa 1981).

18. In a folder in the Anzaldúa Papers titled "Find Deep Meaning—Occult Tools, undated" (box 166, folder 16) is the cardboard backing for a cassette tape titled "Subliminal Persuasion Self-Hypnosis" put out by a company called Potentials Unlimited. On the back of the cardboard, it explains that the listener will hear only music, but "below your level of awareness, yet at a point where it reaches effectively into your subconscious mind, we have recorded a series of carefully researched and tested words and phrases designed to encourage the behavioral change you desire."

19. Anzaldúa Papers, Interview with AnaLouise Keating, December 31, 1998, box 152, item 30–31 (mp3 #8–9); Anzaldúa (2000, 152).

20. Anzaldúa Papers, Interview with AnaLouise Keating, University of Arizona, October 25, 1991, box 152, item 29 (mp3 #8–9).

21. Anzaldúa 2000, 162.

22. Anzaldúa Papers, "Tarot reading for Gloria by Lisa Levin," November 30, 1984, box 157, item 35 (mp3 #63).

Notes to Coda

Coda

1. Using computation to analyze many texts at once in big datasets has been called *distant reading* by digital humanities scholars. See Underwood (2017) for a complete history.

2. http://hipstas.org.

3. The collections that HiPSTAS researchers have investigated include 30,000 hours of poetry performances from the Center for Programs in Contemporary Writing, PennSound, at the University of Pennsylvania (https://writing.upenn.edu/pennsound); 57 shelf feet of tapes (reels and audiocassettes) of folklore recordings at the UT Folklore Center Archives at the Dolph Briscoe Center for American History at the University of Texas at Austin (https://txarchives.org/utcah/finding_aids/00385.xml); Ojibwe storytelling traditions at the Native American Projects (NAP) at the American Philosophical Society in Philadelphia, in over 3,000 hours from fifty tribes; 200,000 field recordings from the American Folklife Center at the Library of Congress (https://memory.loc.gov/diglib/ihas/html/afccards/afccards-home.html); 30,000 hours of oral histories from StoryCorps (https://storycorps.org); hundreds of hours of speeches from leaders of the Southern Christian Leadership Conference recordings at Emory University in Atlanta (https://findingaids.library.emory.edu/documents/sclc1083/); 700 recordings in the Elliston Poetry Collection at the University of Cincinnati (https://www.artsci.uc.edu/departments/english/creative-writing/elliston-collection.html); and thirty-six interviews in the Dust, Drought and Dreams Gone Dry: Oklahoma Women and the Dust Bowl Oral History Project out of the Oklahoma State Libraries (https://library.okstate.edu/search-and-find/collections/digital-collections/dustbowl/).

4. Very likely the "raging" debates to which the reviewer was referring were catalyzed by Nan Z. Da's 2019 piece "The Computational Case against Computational Literary Studies." Responses appear in Jagoda (2019).

5. See Clement and McLaughlin (2016) and Clement (forthcoming) for an analysis of using computational analysis with audio that focuses more on the process rather than the product of computational analysis.

6. I see my work as part of a larger conversation about human biases and epistemologies embedded in data structures (D'Ignazio and Klein 2020; Feinberg 2022; Wernimont 2019) and algorithms (Benjamin 2019; Chun 2021; Noble 2018).

7. The Fourier transform (FT) is a transform in physics and mathematics that converts a function into a form that describes the frequencies present in the original function. The output is a complex-valued function of frequency.

8. Participating nations and funding organizations include: Argentina (MINCyT), Brazil (FAPESP), Canada (SSHRC, NSERC, FRQ), Finland (AKA), France (ANR),

Germany (DFG), Mexico (CONACYT), Netherlands (NWO), Portugal (FCT), United Kingdom (AHRC, ESRC), and the United States (NEH, NSF, IMLS).

9. A more complete description of these projects and their methods can be found in Burgoyne, Fujinaga, and Downie (2016) and Rooth, Howell, and Wagner (2013).

10. Another inherent problem to this work is its focus on the English language. While HiPSTAS scholars were interested in indigenous languages and Spanish data, the datasets were still primarily in English.

11. The "Always Already Computational: Collections as Data and Collections as Data: Part to Whole" projects encompass resources, proof of concept projects, and reports submitted by LAM (libraries, archives, and museums) professionals that focus on using computational methods to process cultural heritage digital data in consideration with the values that characterize LAM professional practices and services (https://collectionsasdata.github.io/). The project leaders have produced studies that address the many ways in which artificial intelligence (often in the form of machine learning, ML) in cultural heritage institutions can be in opposition to LAM values. LAMs, these authors assert, value data heterogeneity, transparency, and shared fluency (in terms of data and computational analysis skills); sustainability and maintenance (and care); and nonscalability over standardized and "clean" homogeneous data, the divisions inherent to ML teams, where fluency is relegated to the ML scientist, the prioritization of efficiency and accuracy, and a focus on scalability as a driving influence that dictates essential project goals (Padilla 2019, 2021).

12. In "Playback is a Bitch: A Feminist Rationale for Inter-Media Textuality in Digital Humanities" (Clement 2023), I detail a use case in which I use an algorithm to listen to pause patterns in recordings by Anne Sexton and discuss the importance of giving scholars the ability to play around with data parameters.

13. See Society of American Archivists (2013).

14. This information pertains to the first Stampede cluster. Stampede3 is projected to be ready for use in December 2023. Its node configuration will include Intel Skylake nodes with 48 cores/node, Intel Ice Lake nodes with 80 cores/node, and Intel Sapphire Rapids High Bandwidth Memory (HBM) nodes with 56 cores/node. In this configuration, fewer more efficient cores mean more powerful processing: https://news.utexas.edu/2023/07/24/new-stampede3-advances-supercomputing-ecosystem/.

15. http://research.google.com/audioset/.

16. Comprising over sixty global members, including major research universities, national libraries, and world-renowned museums, archives, software companies, and other organizations, the IIIF Consortium (https://iiif.io/community/consortium/) has worked together since fall 2011 to create, test, refine, implement, and promote the IIIF specifications for interoperable functionality and collaboration across repositories.

17. Examples of software programs that have been created for use with IIIF are listed at https://iiif.io/demos/.

18. This project began with funding from the American Council of Learned Societies and has subsequently been funded by the Mellon Foundation. See more at http://av-annotate.org. The AudiAnnotate Audiovisual Extensible Workflow (AWE) project was the precursor to AVAnnotate (Clement, Brumfield, and Brumfield 2022).

19. Risam and Gil (2022) define minimal computing as "digital humanities work undertaken in the context of some set of constraints. This could include lack of access to hardware or software, network capacity, technical education, or even a reliable power grid. . . . Minimal computing is an approach that, first and foremost, advocates for using only the technologies that are necessary and sufficient for developing digital humanities scholarship in such constrained environments." Clement, Brumfield, and Brumfield (2022), published in the same special issue of *Digital Humanities Quarterly*, discusses how the AudiAnnotate platform leverages GitHub, which is free for users, to help people build projects around AV.

20. Scholarships, workshops, and presentations and example projects, and more are linked from the AVAnnotate project page at https://av-annotate.org/example-projects/.

21. I have created online editions of recordings from each chapter of *Dissonant Records* linked from my website at http://tanyaclement.org/dissonant_records.

References

Abramowitz, Sophie. 2020. "'Trained and Taught This Song by Zora Hurston': Dramatic Ethnography and Zora Neale Hurston's *The Great Day*." *American Quarterly* 72 (4): 881–908.

American Folklife Center. Traditional Music and Spoken Word Catalog. Library of Congress, Washington, DC. https://memory.loc.gov/diglib/ihas/html/afccards/afccards-home.html.

American Folklife Center. National Sampler: Florida Audio and Video Samples and Notes. Research Centers, Library of Congress, Washington, DC. https://web.archive.org/web/20210124191108/https://www.loc.gov/folklife/sampler/FLaudio.html.

American Philosophical Society. Ojibwe Interviews. https://www.amphilsoc.org/item-detail/ojibwe-interviews.

Antoine-Mahut, Delphine, and Stephen Gaukroger, eds. 2017. *Descartes' "Treatise on Man" and Its Reception*. Cham: Springer.

Anzaldúa, Gloria. Papers. Nettie Lee Benson Latin American Collection, University of Texas, Austin. https://txarchives.org/utlac/finding_aids/00189.xml.

Anzaldúa, Gloria. 2000. *Interviews / Entrevistas*. New York: Routledge.

Anzaldúa, Gloria. 2007. *Borderlands / La Frontera: The New Mestiza*. 3rd ed. San Francisco: Aunt Lute.

Anzaldúa, Gloria. 2009. *The Gloria Anzaldúa Reader*. Edited by AnaLouise Keating. Durham, NC: Duke University Press.

Anzaldúa, Gloria. 2015. *Light in the Dark / Luz En Lo Oscuro: Rewriting Identity, Spirituality, Reality*. Edited by AnaLouise Keating. Durham, NC: Duke University Press.

Anzaldúa, Gloria. 2021. *Borderlands / La Frontera: The New Mestiza*. Edited by Ricardo F. Vivancos Pérez and Norma E. Cantú. San Francisco: Aunt Lute.

Anzaldúa, Gloria, and AnaLouise Keating, eds. 2002. *This Bridge We Call Home: Radical Visions for Transformation*. New York: Routledge.

Archaeological Institute of America. 2003. "The Tulsa Race Riot: A Sight which Can Never Be Forgotten." *Archaeology Magazine Archive*, September 16, 2003. https://archive.archaeology.org/online/features/massacre/tulsa.html.

Askew, Rilla. 2001. *Fire in Beulah*. New York: Penguin.

Askew, Rilla. 2017. *Most American: Notes from a Wounded Place*. Norman: University of Oklahoma Press.

Avery, Cyrus S. Collection. Special Collections and Archives, Oklahoma State University Tulsa Library, Tulsa. https://cdm17279.contentdm.oclc.org/digital/collection/Avery.

Avery, Ruth Sigler. Collection. Special Collections and Archives, Oklahoma State University Tulsa Library, Tulsa. https://osu-tulsa.okstate.edu/library/Archives/Series_1_TulsaRaceRiot.pdf.

Baevski, Alexei, Henry Zhou, Abdelrahman Mohamed, and Michael Auli. 2020. "Wav2vec 2.0: A Framework for Self-Supervised Learning of Speech Representations." In *Proceedings of the 34th International Conference on Neural Information Processing Systems (NIPS '20)*, article 1044, 12449–12460. Red Hook, NY: Curran Associates.

Barad, Karen Michelle. 2007. *Meeting the Universe Halfway: Quantum Physics and the Entanglement of Matter and Meaning*. Durham, NC: Duke University Press.

Bay, Mert, John Ashley Burgoyne, Tim Crawford, David De Roure, J. Stephen Downie, Andreas Ehmann, Benjamin Fields, Ichiro Fujinaga, Kevin Page, and Jordan B. L. Smith. 2009. "Structural Analysis of Large Amounts of Music Information." Digging into Data. https://diggingintodata.org/sites/diggingintodata.org/files/salami11wp5.pdf.

Belsey, Catherine. 1980. *Critical Practice*. London: Methuen.

Benjamin, Ruha. 2019. *Race after Technology: Abolitionist Tools for the New Jim Code*. Cambridge: Polity.

Bernstein, Charles. 1998. *Close Listening: Poetry and the Performed Word*. New York: Oxford University Press.

Bernstein, Charles. 2011. *Attack of the Difficult Poems: Essays and Inventions*. Chicago: University of Chicago Press.

Best, Stephen, and Sharon Marcus. 2009. "Surface Reading: An Introduction." *Representations* 108 (1): 1–21.

Birdsall, Carolyn. 2016. "Sound and Media Studies: Archiving and the Construction of Sonic Heritage." In *Sound as Popular Culture: A Research Companion*, edited by Jens Gerrit Papenburg and Holger Schulze, 133–148. Cambridge, MA: MIT Press.

References

Blair, Sara. 2005. "Ralph Ellison, Photographer." *Raritan* 24 (4): 15–44, 172. https://www.proquest.com/scholarly-journals/ralph-ellison-photographer/docview/203867631/se-2.

Bohr, Niels. 1958. *Atomic Physics and Human Knowledge*. New York: Wiley.

Bolter, J. David, and Richard A. Grusin. 2000. *Remediation: Understanding New Media*. Cambridge, MA: MIT Press.

Bordelon, Pamela. 1999. "Zora Neale Hurston: A Biographical Essay." In *Go Gator and Muddy the Water: Writings*, edited by Zora Neale Hurston, 1–60. New York: Norton.

Bornstein, George. 2001. *Material Modernism: The Politics of the Page*. New York: Cambridge University Press.

Boyd, Nan Alamilla, and Horacio N. Roque Ramírez, eds. 2012. *Bodies of Evidence: The Practice of Queer Oral History*. Oxford: Oxford University Press.

Bradley, Adam. 2010. *Ralph Ellison in Progress: From "Invisible Man" to "Three Days before the Shooting . . ."* New Haven, CT: Yale University Press.

Brathwaite, Kamau. 1984. *History of the Voice: The Development of Nation Language in Anglophone Caribbean Poetry*. London: New Beacon.

Brodber, Erna. 1994. *Louisiana*. Jackson: University Press of Mississippi.

Brooks, Daphne. 2021. *Liner Notes for the Revolution: The Intellectual Life of Black Feminist Sound*. Cambridge, MA: Belknap Press of Harvard University Press.

Brown, Gabriel, Zora Neale Hurston, Alan Lomax, and Mary Elizabeth Barnicle. 1935. *John Henry*. Audio. https://www.loc.gov/item/ihas.200196392/.

Brown, Robert McAfee. 1984. *Unexpected News: Reading the Bible with Third World Eyes*. Louisville, KY: Westminster John Knox.

Brown, Wendy. 2005. *Edgework: Critical Essays on Knowledge and Politics*. Princeton, NJ: Princeton University Press.

Browne, Simone. 2015. *Dark Matters: On the Surveillance of Blackness*. Durham, NC: Duke University Press.

Burgoyne, John Ashley, Ichiro Fujinaga, and J. Stephen Downie. 2016. "Music Information Retrieval." In *A New Companion to Digital Humanities*, edited by Susan Schreibman, Ray Siemens, and John Unsworth, 213–228. Malden, MA: Wiley.

Burke, Edmund. (1790) 1987. *Reflections on the Revolution in France*. Indianapolis, IN: Hackett.

Burrows, David. 1980. "On Hearing Things: Music, the World, and Ourselves." *Musical Quarterly* 46 (2): 180–191.

Butler, Judith. 1993. *Bodies that Matter: On the Discursive Limits of "Sex."* New York: Routledge.

Butler, Judith. 2004. "Performative Acts and Gender Constitution: An Essay in Phenomenology and Feminist Theory." In *The Performance Studies Reader*, edited by Henry Bial, 154–166. New York: Routledge.

Camlot, Jason. 2019. *Phonopoetics: The Making of Early Literary Recordings*. Stanford, CA: Stanford University Press.

Cannon, Christopher, and Matthew Rubery. 2020. "Introduction to 'Aurality and Literacy.'" *PMLA* 135 (2): 350–356.

Cappetti, Carla. 2010. "Defending Hurston against Her Legend: Two Previously Unpublished Letters." *Amerikastudien / American Studies* 55 (4): 602–614.

Carpio, Glenda, and Werner Sollors. 2011. "The Newly Complicated Zora Neale Hurston." *Chronicle of Higher Education*, January 2, 2011. http://www.chronicle.com/article/the-newly-complicated-zora-neale-hurston/.

Carter, Rodney G. S. 2006. "Of Things Said and Unsaid: Power, Archival Silences, and Power in Silence." *Archivaria* 61. https://archivaria.ca/index.php/archivaria/article/view/12541/13687.

Caswell, Michelle. 2014. "Seeing Yourself in History: Community Archives and the Fight against Symbolic Annihilation." *Public Historian* 36 (4): 26–37.

Caswell, Michelle, and Samip Mallick. 2014. "Collecting the Easily Missed Stories: Digital Participatory Microhistory and the South Asian American Digital Archive." *Archives and Manuscripts* 42 (1): 73–86.

Center for Programs in Contemporary Writing. University of Pennsylvania. https://writing.upenn.edu/pennsound/.

Chaves Daza, Maria P. 2015. "Enacting Queer Listening, or When Anzaldúa Laughs." *Sounding Out!*, September 28, 2015. https://soundstudiesblog.com/2015/09/28/15957/.

Chun, Wendy Hui Kyong. 2021. *Discriminating Data: Correlation, Neighborhoods, and the New Politics of Recognition*. Cambridge, MA: MIT Press.

Clement, Tanya E. 2013. "Distant Listening or Playing Visualisations Pleasantly with the Eyes and Ears." *Digital Studies / Le Champ Numérique* 3 (2). https://www.digitalstudies.org/article/id/7237/.

Clement, Tanya E. 2014. "The Ear and the Shunting Yard: Meaning Making as Resonance in Early Information Theory." *Information & Culture: A Journal of History* 49 (4): 401–426.

Clement, Tanya E. 2016. "Towards a Rationale of Audio-Text." *Digital Humanities Quarterly* 10 (3). https://www.digitalhumanities.org/dhq/vol/10/3/000254/000254.html.

References

Clement, Tanya E. 2018. "Word. Spoken. Articulating the Voice for High Performance Sound Technologies for Access and Scholarship (HiPSTAS)." In *Digital Sound Studies*, edited by Mary Caton Lingold, Darren Mueller, and Whitney Trettien, 155–177. Durham, NC: Duke University Press.

Clement, Tanya E. 2020. "Anne Sexton Listening to Anne Sexton." *PMLA* 135 (2): 387–392.

Clement, Tanya E. Forthcoming. "Playback is a Bitch: A Feminist Rationale for Inter-Media Textuality in Digital Humanities." In *Feminist DH*, edited by Susan Schreibman and Lisa Rhody. Champaign: University of Illinois Press.

Clement, Tanya E., Loretta Auvil, and David Tcheng. 2016. "White Paper: High Performance Sound Technologies for Access and Scholarship." White paper, HT-50069-12, National Endowment for the Humanities Office of Digital Humanities, Institutes for Advanced Topics in the Digital Humanities Grant. http://hdl.handle.net/2152/33295.

Clement, Tanya E., Loretta Auvil, David Tcheng, Tony Borries, and Steve McLaughlin. 2018. "High Performance Sound Technologies for Access and Scholarship Research and Development with Repositories." White paper, National Endowment for the Humanities Office of Digital Humanities, Preservation and Access Research and Development Grant. https://hdl.handle.net/2152/119308.

Clement, Tanya E., Ben Brumfield, and Sara Brumfield. 2022. "The AudiAnnotate Project: Four Case Studies in Publishing Annotations for Audio and Video." *Digital Humanities Quarterly* 16 (2). http://digitalhumanities.org:8081/dhq/vol/16/2/000586/000586.html.

Clement, Tanya E., Maria Esteva, and Weijia Xu. Forthcoming. "Labeling This Thing Called Life: Using Machine Learning to Automatically Generate Metadata for Oral History Collections." *Artificial Intelligence and the Humanities*. Anderson, PC: Parlor.

Clement, Tanya, E., and Elizabeth Fischer. 2021 "Audiated Annotation from the Middle Ages to the Open Web." *Digital Humanities Quarterly* 15 (1). http://www.digitalhumanities.org/dhq/vol/15/1/000512/000512.html.

Clement, Tanya E., Andi Gustavson, Allyssa Guzman, Nathan Alexander Moore, and Lauren Walker. 2022. "Good Systems—Humanist-in-the-Loop: Responsible Data Operations and Workforce Development in Libraries, Archives, and Museums." White paper, September 10, 2022. Texas ScholarWorks, University of Texas at Austin. https://hdl.handle.net/2152/115594.

Clement, Tanya E., and Stephen McLaughlin. 2016. "Measured Applause: Toward a Cultural Analysis of Audio Collections." *Journal of Cultural Analytics* 1 (1). https://culturalanalytics.org/article/11058-measured-applause-toward-a-cultural-analysis-of-audio-collections.

Clement, Tanya E., David Tcheng, Loretta Auvil, and Tony Borries. 2014. "High Performance Sound Technologies for Access and Scholarship (HiPSTAS) in the Digital Humanities." *Proceedings of the Association for Information Science* 51 (1): 1–10.

Clement, Tanya E., David Tcheng, Loretta Auvil, Boris Capitanu, and Joao Barbosa. 2013. "Distant Listening to Gertrude Stein's 'Melanctha': Using Similarity Analysis in a Discovery Paradigm to Analyze Prosody and Author Influence." *Literary and Linguistic Computing* 28 (4): 582–602.

Coates, Ta-Nehisi. 2014. "The Case for Reparations." *The Atlantic*, June 2014.

Coleman, John, Greg Kochanski, Sergio Grau, Ladan Baghai-Ravary, Lou Burnard, Mark Liberman, Jiahong Yuan, and Chris Cieri. 2011. "Mining Years and Years of Speech: Final Report of the Digging into Data Project 'Mining a Year of Speech.'" White paper. Digging into Data. https://diggingintodata.org/sites/diggingintodata.org/files/miningayearofspeechwhitepaper.pdf.

Council on Library and Information Resources and the Library of Congress. 2012. *National Recording Preservation Plan*. Washington, DC: Council on Library and Information Resources and the Library of Congress.

Cramer, Aurora Linh, Ho-Hsiang Wu, Justin Salamon, and Juan Pablo Bello. 2019. "Look, Listen, and Learn More: Design Choices for Deep Audio Embeddings." *IEEE International Conference on Acoustics, Speech and Signal Processing (ICASSP)*, 3852–3856. New York: IEEE.

Da, Nan Z. 2019. "The Computational Case against Computational Literary Studies." *Critical Inquiry* 45 (3): 601–639.

Daniel, Dominique. 2010. "Documenting the Immigrant and Ethnic Experience in American Archives." *American Archivist* 73 (1): 82–104. https://meridian.allenpress.com/american-archivist/article/73/1/82/24227/Documenting-the-Immigrant-and-Ethnic-Experience-in.

Delbanco, Andrew. 1997. "The Political Incorrectness of Zora Neale Hurston." *Journal of Blacks in Higher Education* 18: 103–108.

Dingemanse, Mark. 2020. "Between Sound and Speech: Liminal Signs in Interaction." *Research on Language and Social Interaction* 53 (1): 188–96.

Dorst, John. 1987. "Rereading *Mules and Men*: Toward the Death of the Ethnographer." *Cultural Anthropology* 2 (3): 305–318.

Douglas, Susan. 2004. *Listening In: Radio and the American Imagination*. Minneapolis: University of Minnesota Press.

Duarte, Marisa Elena, and Miranda Belarde-Lewis. 2015. "Imagining: Creating Spaces for Indigenous Ontologies." *Cataloging & Classification Quarterly* 53 (5–6): 677–702.

References

Dunjee, Roscoe. 1921. "A White Man's Country." *The Black Dispatch* 6 (26), June 3, 1921.

Dunn, Jon W., Juliet L. Hardesty, Tanya Clement, Chris Lacinak, and Amy Rudersdorf. 2018. "Audiovisual Metadata Platform (AMP) Planning Project: Progress Report and Next Steps." AMP Planning Report, March. https://scholarworks.iu.edu/dspace/handle/2022/21982.

Dust, Drought, and Dreams Gone Dry: Oklahoma Women in the Dust Bowl Oral History Project. Edmon Low Library, Oklahoma State University, Stillwater, Oklahoma. https://library.okstate.edu/search-and-find/collections/digital-collections/dustbowl/.

D'Ignazio, Catherine, and Lauren F. Klein. 2020. *Data Feminism*. Cambridge, MA: MIT Press.

Du Bois, W. E. B. 2007. *The Souls of Black Folk*. Edited by Brent Hayes Edwards. Oxford: Oxford University Press.

Earhart, Amy, and Toneisha Taylor. 2016. "Pedagogies of Race: Digital Humanities in the Age of Ferguson." In *Debates in the Digital Humanities*, edited by Matthew K. Gold and Lauren F. Klein, 251–264. Minneapolis: University of Minnesota Press.

Ellison, Ralph. Papers. 1890–2005. Part I: Speeches, Lectures, and Interviews, 1945–1993. Manuscript Division, Library of Congress, Washington, DC. https://hdl.loc.gov/loc.mss/eadmss.ms002008.

Ellison, Ralph. 1952. *Invisible Man*. New York: Random House.

Ellison, Ralph. 1995. *The Collected Essays of Ralph Ellison*. Edited by John F. Callahan. New York: Modern Library Giants.

Ellison, Ralph. 2019. *The Selected Letters of Ralph Ellison*. Edited by John F. Callahan and Marc C. Conner. New York: Random House.

Elliston Poetry Collection. Langsam Library, University of Cincinnati, Cincinnati, Ohio. https://www.artsci.uc.edu/departments/english/creative-writing/elliston-collection.html.

Ellsworth, Scott. 1982. *Death in a Promised Land: The Tulsa Race Riot of 1921*. Baton Rouge: Louisiana State University Press.

Embry, Marcus. 1996. "Cholo Angels in Guadalajara: The Politics and Poetics of Anzaldúa's *Borderlands / La Frontera*." *Women & Performance: A Journal of Feminist Theory* 8 (2): 87–108.

Emerson, Lori. 2014. *Reading Writing Interfaces: From the Digital to the Bookbound*. Minneapolis: University of Minnesota Press.

Erlmann, Veit. 2010. *Reason and Resonance: A History of Modern Aurality*. New York: Zone.

Federal Writers' Project of the Work Projects Administration for the State of Florida. "Zora Neale Hurston and The WPA in Florida." Florida Memory Project, State Library and Archives of Florida, Tallahassee, Florida. https://www.floridamemory.com/learn/classroom/learning-units/zora-neale-hurston/documents/audio/.

Feghali, Zalfa. 2011. "Re-Articulating the New Mestiza." *Journal of International Women's Studies* 12 (2): 61–75.

Feinberg, Melanie. 2022. *Everyday Adventures with Unruly Data*. Cambridge, MA: MIT Press.

Florida Folk Festival. Audio recordings of performances and other folk events, 1935–2001, 2017, 2019. State Archives of Florida, Tallahassee, Florida. http://archivescatalog.info.florida.gov/default.asp?IDCFile=/fsa/detailss.idc,SPECIFIC=514,DATABASE=SERIES.

Foucault, Michel. 1977. *Discipline and Punish: The Birth of the Prison*. Translated by Alan Sheridan. New York: Pantheon.

Foucault, Michel. 1978. *The History of Sexuality*. Vol. 1, *An Introduction*. Translated by Robert Hurley. New York: Pantheon.

Francis, Hartwell, Tanya E. Clement, Gena Peone, Brian Carpenter, and Kristen Suagee-Beauduy. 2016. "Accessing Sound at Libraries, Archives, and Museums." In *Indigenous Notions of Ownership and Libraries, Archives and Museums*, edited by Camille Callison, Loriene Roy, and Gretchen Alice LeCheminant, 344–368. Boston, MA: De Gruyter Saur.

Freund, Alexander. 2016. "Toward an Ethics of Silence? Negotiating Off-the-Record Events and Identity in Oral History." In *The Oral History Reader*, edited by Robert Perks and Alistair Thomson, 253–266. 3rd ed. London: Routledge.

Furlonge, Nicole Brittingham. 2011. "'To Hear the Silence of Sound': Making Sense of Listening in Ralph Ellison's Invisible Man." *Interference Journal* 1. http://www.interferencejournal.org/to-hear-the-silence-of-sound/.

Furlonge, Nicole Brittingham. 2018. *Race Sounds: The Art of Listening in African American Literature*. Iowa City: University of Iowa Press.

Gates, Eddie Faye. 2003. *Riot on Greenwood: The Total Destruction of Black Wall Street*. Austin, TX: Eakin.

Gearhart, Sally, and Susan Rennie. 1977. *A Feminist Tarot*. Watertown, MA: Persephone.

Gemmeke, Jort F., Daniel P. W. Ellis, Dylan Freedman, Aren Jansen, Wade Lawrence, R. Channing Moore, Manoj Plakal, and Marvin Ritter. 2017. "Audio Set: An Ontology and Human-Labeled Dataset for Audio Events." In *2017 IEEE International Conference on Acoustics, Speech and Signal Processing (ICASSP)*, 776–780. New York: IEEE.

References

Genette, Gérard. 1997. *Paratexts: Thresholds of Interpretation*. Translated by Jane E. Lewin. New York: Cambridge University Press.

Gilbert, Sophie. 2019. "'Watchmen' Is a Blistering Modern Allegory." *The Atlantic*, October 21, 2019. https://www.theatlantic.com/entertainment/archive/2019/10/review-what-makes-hbos-watchmen-so-timely/600394/.

Gill, Loren. 1946. "Tulsa Race Riot." Master's thesis, University of Tulsa, Oklahoma.

Gilroy, Paul. 1993. *The Black Atlantic: Modernity and Double Consciousness*. Cambridge, MA: Harvard University Press.

Gitelman, Lisa. 1999. *Scripts, Grooves, and Writing Machines: Representing Technology in the Edison Era*. Stanford, CA: Stanford University Press.

Gitelman, Lisa. 2008. *Always Already New: Media, History, and the Data of Culture*. Cambridge, MA: MIT Press.

Gitelman, Lisa. 2014. *Paper Knowledge: Toward a Media History of Documents*. Durham, NC: Duke University Press.

Gold, Ben, Nelson Morgan, and Dan Ellis. 2011. *Speech and Audio Signal Processing: Processing and Perception of Speech and Music*. 2nd ed. Hoboken, NJ: Wiley.

Gref, Michael, Joachim Köhler, and Almut Leh. 2018. "Improved Transcription and Indexing of Oral History Interviews for Digital Humanities Research." In *Proceedings of the Eleventh International Conference on Language Resources and Evaluation (LREC 2018)*, edited by Nicoletta Calzolari, Khalid Choukri, Christopher Cieri, Thierry Declerck, Sara Goggi, Koiti Hasida, Hitoshi Isahara, et al. Miyazaki, Japan: European Language Resources Association (ELRA).

Halliburton, Rudia. 1972. "The Tulsa Race War of 1921." *Journal of Black Studies* 2: 333–357.

Halliburton, Rudia. 1975. *The Tulsa Race War of 1921*. San Francisco: R and E Research Associates.

Haraway, Donna. 1988. "Situated Knowledges: The Science Question in Feminism and the Privilege of Partial Perspective." *Feminist Studies* 14 (3): 575–599.

Haraway, Donna. 2016. *Staying with the Trouble: Making Kin in the Chthulucene*. Durham, NC: Duke University Press.

Harding, Sandra G. 1986. *The Science Question in Feminism*. Ithaca, NY: Cornell University Press.

Harney, Daniel. 2015. "Scholarship and the Modernist Public: Zora Neale Hurston and the Limitations of Art and Disciplinary Anthropology." *Modernism/Modernity* 22 (3): 471–492.

Harrington, Patrick. 2019. "Generating Geographic Terms for Streaming Videos Using Python: A Comparative Analysis." *Code4Lib Journal* 45 (August 9, 2019). https://journal.code4lib.org/articles/14676.

Harris, Verne. 2002. "The Archival Sliver: Power, Memory, and Archives in South Africa." *Archival Science* 2: 63–86.

Harris, Verne, and Sello Hatang. 2001. "Archives, Identity, and Place: A Dialogue on What It (Might) Mean(s) to Be an African Archivist." *Canadian Journal of Information and Library Science* 25 (2/3): 41.

Hartman, Saidiya V. 1997. *Scenes of Subjection: Terror, Slavery, and Self-Making in Nineteenth-Century America*. New York: Oxford University Press.

Harvard Summer School Conference on the Contemporary Novel. August 3–5, 1953. Woodberry Poetry Room, Houghton Library, Harvard University.

Hayles, N. Katherine. 1997. "Voices out of Bodies, Bodies out of Voices: Audiotape and the Production of Subjectivity." In *Sound States: Innovative Poetics and Acoustical Technologies*, edited by Adalaide Kirby Morris, 74–96. Chapel Hill: University of North Carolina Press.

Hayles, N. Katherine. 2004. "Print Is Flat, Code Is Deep: The Importance of Media-Specific Analysis." *Poetics Today* 25 (1): 67–90.

Hayles, N. Katherine. 2007. "Intermediation: The Pursuit of a Vision." *New Literary History* 38 (1): 99–125.

Heidegger, Martin. 1962. *Being and Time*. Translated by John Macquarrie and Edward Robinson. Oxford: Blackwell.

Helmreich, Stefan. 2015. "Transduction." In *Keywords in Sound*, edited by David Novak and Matt Sakakeeny, 222–231. Durham, NC: Duke University Press.

Hemenway, Robert. 1977. *Zora Neale Hurston: A Literary Biography*. Urbana: University of Illinois Press.

Henderson-Espinoza, Robyn. 2013. "Gloria Anzaldúa's El Mundo Zurdo: Exploring a Relational Feminist Theology of Interconnectedness." *Journal for the Study of Religion* 26 (2): 107–118.

Higginbotham, Evelyn Brooks. 1992. "African-American Women's History and the Metalanguage of Race." *Signs* 17 (2): 251–274.

Higgins, Dick. 2001. "Intermedia." *Leonardo* 34 (1): 49–54.

Hill, Lynda Marion. 1996. *Social Rituals and the Verbal Art of Zora Neale Hurston*. Washington, DC: Howard University Press.

Hilmes, Michele. 2014. "The Lost Critical History of Radio." *Australian Journalism Review* 36 (2): 11–22.

References

Hilmes, Michele. 2018. "Interpreting Radio: Culture in Sound and the Role of Media Studies." *New Review of Film and Television Studies* 16 (4): 420–425.

Hine, Darlene C. 1986. "Lifting the Veil, Shattering the Silence: Black Women's History in Slavery and Freedom." In *The State of Afro-American History: Past, Present, and Future*, 224–249. Baton Rouge: Louisiana State University Press.

Hirschkind, Charles. 2006. *The Ethical Soundscape Cassette Sermons and Islamic Counterpublics*. New York: Columbia University Press.

Hochman, Brian. 2014. *Savage Preservation: The Ethnographic Origins of Modern Media Technology*. Minneapolis: University of Minnesota Press.

Hogan, Mél. 2015. "Data Flows and Water Woes: The Utah Data Center." *Big Data and Society* 2 (2).

hooks, bell. 1986. "Talking Back." *Discourse* 8: 123–128.

hooks, bell. 2004. *The Will to Change: Men, Masculinity, and Love*. New York: Atria.

hooks, bell. 2014. *Talking Back: Thinking Feminist, Thinking Black*. 2nd ed. New York: Routledge.

Huggins, Nathan Irvin. 1971. *Harlem Renaissance*. New York: Oxford University Press.

Hurston, Zora Neale. "Dust Tracks: The Complete Performances of Zora Neale Hurston from the Florida Folklife Collection." Florida Memory Project, State Library and Archives of Florida, Tallahassee. https://www.floridamemory.com/discover/audio/playlists/dust_tracks.php.

Hurston, Zora Neale. Papers. George A. Smathers Libraries, University of Florida, Gainesville, Florida. http://findingaids.uflib.ufl.edu//repositories/2/resources/587.

Hurston, Zora Neale. 1934. *Jonah's Gourd Vine*. Philadelphia, PA: Lippincott.

Hurston, Zora Neale. 1935. *Mules and Men*. Philadelphia, PA: Lippincott.

Hurston, Zora Neale. (1937) 2006. *Their Eyes Were Watching God*. New York: Amistad.

Hurston, Zora Neale. 1938. *Tell My Horse*. Philadelphia, PA: Lippincott.

Hurston, Zora Neale. 1942. *Dust Tracks on a Road: An Autobiography*. Philadelphia, PA: Lippincott.

Hurston, Zora Neale. 1979. *I Love Myself When I Am Laughing . . . and Then again When I Am Looking Mean and Impressive: A Zora Neale Hurston Reader*. Edited by Alice Walker. Old Westbury, NY: Feminist Press.

Hurston, Zora Neale. 1981. *The Sanctified Church*. Berkeley, CA: Turtle Island.

Hurston, Zora Neale. 1999. *Go Gator and Muddy the Water: Writings*. Edited by Pamela Bordelon. New York: Norton.

Hurston, Zora Neale. 2001. *Every Tongue Got to Confess: Negro Folk-Tales from the Gulf States*. New York: HarperCollins.

Hurston, Zora Neale. 2002. *Zora Neale Hurston: A Life in Letters*. Edited by Carla Kaplan. New York: Doubleday.

Hurston, Zora Neale. 2008. *Zora Neale Hurston: Collected Plays*. Edited by Jean Lee Cole and Charles Mitchell. New Brunswick, NJ: Rutgers University Press.

Hurston, Zora Neale. 2018. *Barracoon: The Story of the Last "Black Cargo."* New York: Amistad.

Hurston, Zora Neale, Alan Lomax, and Mary Elizabeth Barnicle. 1935. "Interview with Wallace Quarterman, Fort Frederica, St. Simons Island, Georgia," June 1935 (part 1). Alan Lomax, Zora Neale Hurston, and Mary Elizabeth Barnicle Expedition Collection, AFC 1935/001, American Folklife Center, Library of Congress, Washington, DC. https://www.loc.gov/item/afc1935001_afs00342a/.

Ireland, Corydon. 2014. "Lost Voices of 1953." *Harvard Gazette* (blog). August 26, 2014. https://news.harvard.edu/gazette/story/2014/08/lost-voices-of-1953/.

Isaacson, Walter. 1992. *Kissinger: A Biography*. New York: Simon and Schuster.

Jagoda, Patrick. 2019. "Computational Literary Studies: A Critical Inquiry Online Forum." *In the Moment* (blog). March 31, 2019. https://critinq.wordpress.com/2019/03/31/computational-literary-studies-a-critical-inquiry-online-forum/.

Jessee, Erin. 2016. "The Limits of Oral History: Ethics and Methodology amid Highly Politicized Research Settings." In *The Oral History Reader*, edited by Robert Perks and Alistair Thomson, 674–688. 3rd ed. London: Routledge.

Johnson, Hannibal B. 2007. *Black Wall Street: From Riot to Renaissance in Tulsa's Historic Greenwood District*. Austin, TX: Eakin.

Johnson, James Weldon. Memorial Collection, Yale Collection of American Literature, Beinecke Rare Book and Manuscript Library, Yale University. https://beinecke.library.yale.edu/collections/curatorial-areas/james-weldon-johnson-memorial-collection.

Joudrey, Daniel N., Arlene G. Taylor, and Katherine M. Wisser. 2018. *The Organization of Information*. 4th ed. Santa Barbara, CA: Libraries Unlimited.

Kane, Denise. 2014. "'Fightin' long atter I is gone': Opposing Agendas in the Georgia Federal Writers' Project Slave Narratives." MA thesis, California State University San Marcos.

Keating, AnaLouise. 1996. *Women Reading Women Writing: Self-Invention in Paula Gunn Allen, Gloria Anzaldúa, and Audre Lorde*. Philadelphia, PA: Temple University Press.

References

Keating, AnaLouise. 2005. "Shifting Perspectives: Spiritual Activism, Social Transformation, and the Politics of Spirit." In *EntreMundos / AmongWorlds: New Perspectives on Gloria E. Anzaldúa*, edited by AnaLouise Keating, 241–254. New York: Palgrave Macmillan.

Keating, AnaLouise. 2007. Afterword to *Borderlands / La Frontera: The New Mestiza*, by Gloria Anzaldúa. 3rd ed. San Francisco: Aunt Lute.

Keating, AnaLouise. 2008. "'I'm a Citizen of the Universe': Gloria Anzaldúa's Spiritual Activism as Catalyst for Social Change." *Feminist Studies* 34 (1/2): 53–69.

Keating, AnaLouise. 2009. "Introduction: Reading Gloria Anzaldúa, Reading Ourselves . . . Complex Intimacies, Intricate Connections." In *The Gloria Anzaldúa Reader*, edited by AnaLouise Keating, 1–15. Durham, NC: Duke University Press.

Keating, AnaLouise. 2015. Introduction, "Re-envisioning Coyolxauhqui, Decolonizing Reality Anzaldúa's Twenty-First-Century Imperative," in *Light in the Dark / Luz En Lo Oscuro: Rewriting Identity, Spirituality, Reality*, by Gloria Anzaldúa, ix–xxi. Durham, NC: Duke University Press.

Keating, AnaLouise. 2022. *The Anzaldúan Theory Handbook*. Durham, NC: Duke University Press.

Kirschenbaum, Matthew G. 2016. *Track Changes: A Literary History of Word Processing*. Cambridge, MA: Belknap Press of Harvard University Press.

Kirschenbaum, Matthew G. 2021. *Bitstreams: The Future of Digital Literary Heritage*. Philadelphia: University of Pennsylvania Press.

Kittler, Friedrich A. 1999. *Gramophone, Film, Typewriter*. Stanford, CA: Stanford University Press.

Krehbiel, Randy. 2020. "1921 Race Riot: Tribune Mystery Unsolved." *Tulsa World*, May 21, 2020. https://tulsaworld.com/archive/1921-race-riot-tribune-mystery-unsolved/article_81f8ac0b-01bd-56a8-97ba-851961c400be.html.

LaBelle, Brandon. 2010. *Acoustic Territories: Sound Culture and Everyday Life*. New York: Continuum.

Lacan, Jacques. 2008. *My Teaching*. Translated by David Macey. London: Verso.

Library of Congress. Catalog. https://catalog.loc.gov/.

Lieberman, Jennifer L. 2015. "Ralph Ellison's Technological Humanism." *MELUS* 40 (4): 8–27.

Locke, Alain. Papers. Collection 164. Moorland-Spingarn Research Center, Howard University, Washington, DC. https://huaspace.wrlc.org/public/repositories/2/resources/449.

Locke, Alain. 1938. "Jingo, Counter-Jingo and Us: A Retrospective Review of Negro Literature." *Opportunity* 26 (January and February): 8.

Lomax, Alan. Collection. American Folklife Center, Library of Congress, Washington, DC.

Lomax, Alan, Zora Neale Hurston, and Mary Elizabeth Barnicle. Expedition Collection, AFC 1935/001, Archive of Folk Culture, American Folklife Center, Library of Congress, Washington, DC. https://lccn.loc.gov/2008700301.

Lomax, John A., and Alan Lomax. Papers. American Folklife Center, Library of Congress, Washington, DC. https://www.loc.gov/collections/john-a-lomax-and-alan-lomax-papers/.

MacArthur, Marit, Georgia Zellou, and Lee Miller. 2018. "Beyond Poet Voice: Sampling the (Non-) Performance Styles of 100 American Poets." *Journal of Cultural Analytics* 3 (1). https://culturalanalytics.org/article/11039.

Madigan, Tim. 2001. *The Burning: Massacre, Destruction, and the Tulsa Race Riot of 1921*. Middletown, DE: St. Martin's Griffin.

Manovich, Lev. 2001. "Post-Media Aesthetics." http://manovich.net/content/04-projects/032-post-media-aesthetics/29_article_2001.pdf.

Maringanti, Harish. 2017. "A Decision Making Paradigm for Software Development in Libraries." In *Developing In-House Digital Tools in Library Spaces*, 59–75. Hershey, PA: IGI Global.

Martinez-Keel, Nuria. 2021. "'A Conspiracy of Silence': Tulsa Race Massacre Was Absent from Schools for Generations." *The Oklahoman*, May 26, 2021. https://www.oklahoman.com/story/news/education/2021/05/26/oklahoma-history-black-wall-street-left-out-public-schools-tulsa-massacre-education/4875340001/.

Mascaro, Michelle. 2011. "Controlled Access Headings in EAD Finding Aids: Current Practices in Number of and Types of Headings Assigned." *Journal of Archival Organization* 9 (3–4): 208–225.

Mattern, Shannon. 2015. "Deep Time of Media Infrastructure." In *Signal Traffic: Critical Studies of Media Infrastructures*, 94–114. Champaign: University of Illinois Press.

Mazin, Craig, and Damon Lindelof. *The Official Watchmen Podcast*. HBO. https://www.hbo.com/watchmen/article/the-official-watchmen-podcast.

McCarthy, Jesse, Cheryl Alison, and Paul Devlin. 2020. "Ralph Ellison at Harvard." Woodberry Poetry Room, Zoom recording, October 7, 2020. YouTube video, 1:24:26. https://www.youtube.com/watch?v=8SIwmV8USpw.

McCarty, Willard. 2004. "Modeling: A Study in Words and Meanings." In *Companion to Digital Humanities*, edited by Susan Schreibman, Ray Siemens, and John Unsworth.

References

Oxford: Blackwell. https://companions.digitalhumanities.org/DH/?chapter=content/9781405103213_chapter_19.html.

McEnaney, Tom. 2020. "'Rigoberta's Listener': The Significance of Sound in *Testimonio*." *PMLA* 135 (2): 393–400.

McFee, Brian. 2020a. "Digital Sampling." *Digital Signals Theory*. https://brianmcfee.net/dstbook-site/content/ch02-sampling/intro.html.

McFee, Brian. 2020b. "Signals." *Digital Signals Theory*. https://brianmcfee.net/dstbook-site/content/ch01-signals/Intro.html.

McGann, Jerome J. 2001. *Radiant Textuality: Literature after the World Wide Web*. New York: Palgrave.

McGowan, Paul. 2014. "Jitter's Audible Effects." Paul McGowan, PS Audio, January 26, 2014. YouTube video, 4:21. https://www.youtube.com/watch?v=ZT_1UATci3c.

McKinney, Cait. 2020. *Information Activism: A Queer History of Lesbian Media Technologies*. Information Activism. Durham, NC: Duke University Press.

McKittrick, Katherine. 2021. *Dear Science and Other Stories*. Durham, NC: Duke University Press.

McLuhan, Marshall, and Eric McLuhan. 1992. *Laws of Media: The New Science*. Toronto: University of Toronto Press.

Meisenhelder, Susan. 1996. "Conflict and Resistance in Zora Neale Hurston's Mules and Men." *Journal of American Folklore* 109 (433): 267–288.

Melville, Herman. 1849. *Redburn, His First Voyage Being the Sailor-Boy Confessions and Reminiscences of the Son-of-a-Gentleman, in the Merchant Service*. New York: Harper.

Messer, Chris M. 2011. "The Tulsa Race Riot of 1921: Toward an Integrative Theory of Collective Violence." *Journal of Social History* 44 (4): 1217–1232.

Middlebrook, Diane. 1991a. *Anne Sexton: A Biography*. New York: Vintage.

Middlebrook, Diane. 1991b. "The Poet's Art Mined the Patient's Anguish." *New York Times*, July 26, 1991, sec. Opinion. https://www.nytimes.com/1991/07/26/opinion/l-the-poet-s-art-mined-the-patient-s-anguish-536091.html.

Mills, Mara. 2010. "Deaf Jam: From Inscription to Reproduction to Information." *Social Text* 28 (1 [102]): 35–58.

Mills, Mara. 2011. "Hearing Aids and the History of Electronics Miniaturization." *IEEE Annals of the History of Computing* 33 (2): 24–45.

Moore, Alan, Dave Gibbons, and John Higgins. 1987. *Watchmen*. New York: DC Comics.

Moraga, Cherríe, and Gloria Anzaldúa, eds. 1981. *This Bridge Called My Back: Writings by Radical Women of Color*. Watertown, MA: Persephone.

Morris, Jeremy W. 2012. "Making Music Behave: Metadata and the Digital Music Commodity." *New Media & Society* 14 (5): 850–866. https://doi.org/10.1177/1461444811430645.

Morrison, Toni. 1992. *Playing in the Dark: Whiteness and the Literary Imagination*. Cambridge, MA: Harvard University Press.

Morrison, Toni. 2019. *The Source of Self-Regard: Selected Essays, Speeches, and Meditations*. New York: Alfred A. Knopf.

Moten, Fred. 2003. *In the Break: The Aesthetics of the Black Radical Tradition*. Minneapolis: University of Minnesota Press.

Musher, Sharon Ann. 2014. "The Other Slave Narratives: The Works Progress Administration Interviews." In *The Oxford Handbook of the African American Slave Narrative*, edited by John Ernest, 101–118. Oxford: Oxford University Press.

Mustazza, Chris. 2014. "Provenance Report: William Carlos Williams's 1942 Reading for the NCTE." *Jacket2*. https://jacket2.org/article/provenance-report.

Mustazza, Chris. 2016. "Vachel Lindsay and *The W. Cabell Greet Recordings*." *Chicago Review* 59/60 (4/1): 98–117.

Mustazza, Chris. 2018. "Machine-Aided Close Listening: Prosthetic Synaesthesia and the 3D Phonotext." *Digital Humanities Quarterly* 12 (3). https://www.digitalhumanities.org/dhq/vol/12/3/000397/000397.html.

National Public Radio. 2002. "The Sound of 1930s Florida Folk Life." *All Things Considered*, February 28, 2002. NPR. https://www.npr.org/2002/02/28/1138968/the-sound-of-1930s-florida-folk-life.

National Public Radio. 2005. "StoryCorps and Stetson Kennedy." *Talk of the Nation*, May 23, 2005. NPR. https://www.npr.org/templates/story/story.php?storyId=4663544.

Network Development and MARC Standards Office. 2021. *MARC Code List for Relators*. Washington, DC: Library of Congress. https://www.loc.gov/marc/relators/relaterm.html.

1921 Tulsa Race Massacre Centennial Commission. "Our History." Accessed May 17, 2021. https://web.archive.org/web/20210727215239/https://www.tulsa2021.org/history.

Noble, Safiya Umoja. 2018. *Algorithms of Oppression: How Search Engines Reinforce Racism*. New York: University Press.

Nussbaum, Emily. 2019. "The Incendiary Aims of HBO's 'Watchmen.'" *New Yorker*, December 2, 2019. https://www.newyorker.com/magazine/2019/12/09/the-incendiary-aims-of-hbos-watchmen.

References

Oard, Doug. 2012. "Can Automatic Speech Recognition Replace Manual Transcription?" In *Oral History in the Digital Age*, edited by Doug Boyd, Steve Cohen, Brad Rakerd, and Dean Rehberger. Washington, DC: Institute of Museum and Library Services. https://ohda.matrix.msu.edu/2012/06/automatic-speech-recognition/.

Ochoa Gautier, Ana María. 2006. "Sonic Transculturation, Epistemologies of Purification and the Aural Public Sphere in Latin America." *Social Identities* 12 (6): 803–825.

Ochoa Gautier, Ana María. 2014. *Aurality: Listening and Knowledge in Nineteenth-Century Colombia*. Durham, NC: Duke University Press.

Odum, Howard Washington, and Guy Benton Johnson, eds. 1926. *Negro Workaday Songs*. Chapel Hill: University of North Carolina Press.

Oklahoma Commission to Study the Tulsa Race Riot of 1921. 2001. "Tulsa Race Riot: A Report by the Oklahoma Commission to Study the Tulsa Race Riot of 1921." *Oklahoma Historical Society*. https://www.okhistory.org/research/forms/freport.pdf.

Olson, Gary A. 1994. "bell hooks and the Politics of Literacy: A Conversation." *Journal of Advanced Composition* 14 (1): 1–19.

Olson, Gary A., and Elizabeth Hirsh. 1995. *Women Writing Culture*. Albany: State University of New York Press.

Olson, Gary A., and bell hooks. 1994. "JAC Audio Interview: bell hooks." Audio recording. University of North Texas Libraries, UNT Digital Library. https://digital.library.unt.edu/ark:/67531/metadc40375/.

Orne, Martin T. 1991. "The Sexton Tapes." *New York Times*, July 23, 1991, sec. Opinion. https://www.nytimes.com/1991/07/23/opinion/the-sexton-tapes.html.

Padilla, Thomas. 2019. *Responsible Operations: Data Science, Machine Learning, and AI in Libraries*. Dublin, OH: OCLC.

Padilla, Thomas. 2021. "Workshop 1: Thomas Padilla, 'Keep True: Three Strategies to Guide AI Engagement'—AEOLIAN Network." AEOLIAN Network: Artificial Intelligence for Cultural Organisations. July 15, 2021. https://www.aeolian-network.net/workshop-1-thomas-padilla-keep-true-three-strategies-to-guide-ai-engagement/.

Parrish, Mary E. Jones. [1922] 2021. *Events of the Tulsa Disaster*. Independently published. https://lib.utulsa.edu/speccoll/collections/F704T92P37%201922_Events/Events1.pdf.

Parshina-Kottas, Yuliya, Anjali Singhvi, Audra D. S. Burch, Troy Griggs, Mika Gröndahl, Lingdong Huang, Tim Wallace, Jeremy White, and Josh Williams. 2021. "What the Tulsa Race Massacre Destroyed." *New York Times*, May 24, 2021, sec. U.S. https://www.nytimes.com/interactive/2021/05/24/us/tulsa-race-massacre.html.

Perez, Domino Renee. 2014. "New Tribalism and Chicana/o Indigeneity in the Work of Gloria Anzaldúa." In *The Oxford Handbook of Indigenous American Literature*, edited by James H. Cox and Daniel Heath Justice, 489–504. Oxford: Oxford University Press.

Perks, Robert, and Alistair Thomson, eds. 2016. *The Oral History Reader*. 3rd ed. London: Routledge.

Pias, Claus, ed. 2016. *Cybernetics: The Macy Conferences 1946–1953. The Complete Transactions*. Zurich: Diaphanes.

Pizzolato, Nicola. 2018. "Harvests of Shame: Enduring Unfree Labour in the Twentieth-Century United States, 1933–1964." *Labor History* 59 (4): 472–490.

Plant, Deborah G. 2018. "Afterword." In *Barracoon: The Story of the Last "Black Cargo."* Edited by Zora Neal Hurston. New York: Amistad.

Portelli, Alessandro. 2016. "What Makes Oral History Different." In *The Oral History Reader*, edited by Robert Perks and Alistair Thomson, 48–58. 3rd ed. London: Routledge.

Prentice, Frances W. 1939. "Oklahoma Race Riot." In *Tellers of Tales: 100 Short Stories from the United States, England, France, Russia and Germany*, edited by W. Somerset Maugham, 1519–1526. New York: Doubleday, Doran. Originally published August 1931 in *Scribner's Magazine* 90 (2): 151–157.

Primus, V. 2002. "'I Love My Vincent Baby . . .'" *Harvard Magazine*, September 1, 2002. https://www.harvardmagazine.com/2002/09/i-love-my-vincent-baby-html.

Rampersad, Arnold. 2007. *Ralph Ellison: A Biography*. New York: Alfred A. Knopf.

Rhodes, Jewell Parker. 1998. *Magic City*. New York: HarperCollins.

Rhodes, Jewell Parker. 2017. "How I Came to Write Magic City." *Jewell Parker Rhodes* (blog). https://jewellparkerrhodes.com/adult/books/magic-city/how-i-came-to-write-magic-city/.

Risam, Roopika, and Alex Gil. 2022. "Introduction: The Questions of Minimal Computing." *Digital Humanities Quarterly* 16 (2). http://www.digitalhumanities.org/dhq/vol/16/2/000646/000646.html.

Robinson-Sweet, Anna. 2018. "Truth and Reconciliation: Archivists as Reparations Activists." *American Archivist* 81 (1): 23–37.

Rooth, Mats, Jonathan Howell, and Michael Wagner. 2013. "Harvesting Speech Datasets for Linguistic Research on the Web." White paper, Cornell University Library. https://ecommons.cornell.edu/handle/1813/34477.

Roulston, Kathryn. 2019. "Using Archival Data to Examine Interview Methods: The Case of the Former Slave Project." *International Journal of Qualitative Methods* 18 (January): 1609406919867003.

Sayers, Jentery. 2011. "How Text Lost Its Source: Magnetic Recording Cultures." PhD diss., University of Washington.

Schröter, Jens. 2010. "The Politics of Intermediality." *Film and Media Studies: Scientific Journal of Sapientia University* 2: 107–124.

Schröter, Jens. 2011. "Discourses and Models of Intermediality." *CLCWeb: Comparative Literature & Culture: A WWWeb Journal* 13 (3). https://docs.lib.purdue.edu/cgi/viewcontent.cgi?article=1790&context=clcweb.

Schwartz, Marie Jenkins. 2014. "The WPA Narratives as Historical Sources." In *The Oxford Handbook of the African American Slave Narrative*, edited by John Ernest, 89–100. Oxford: Oxford University Press.

Sexton, Anne (HRC). Papers. Harry Ransom Center, University of Texas, Austin.

Sexton, Anne (AESL). Audiotapes and Papers of Anne Sexton, 1956–1988. Arthur and Elizabeth Schlesinger Library on the History of Women in America, Radcliffe Institute, Harvard University, Cambridge, MA.

Sexton, Anne. 1962. *All My Pretty Ones*. Boston, MA: Houghton Mifflin.

Sexton, Anne. 1965. "For the Year of the Insane." *Harper's Monthly*, June 1965, 231: 68.

Sexton, Anne. 1966. *Live or Die*. Boston, MA: Houghton Mifflin.

Sexton, Anne. 1999. *The Complete Poems*. Boston, MA: Mariner.

Sexton, Anne, Linda Gray Sexton, and Lois Ames. 1977. *Anne Sexton: A Self-Portrait in Letters*. Boston, MA: Houghton Mifflin.

Sharpe, Jenny. 2020. *Immaterial Archives: An African Diaspora Poetics of Loss*. Evanston, IL: Northwestern University Press.

Shepperd, Josh. 2018. "Media Archival Studies: Library of Congress's Radio Preservation Task Force as a Memory Advocacy Project." *New Review of Film and Television Studies* 16 (4): 426–433.

Showalter, Elaine. 1993. "On Hysterical Narrative." *Narrative* 1 (1): 24–35.

Siegert, Bernhard. 2013. "Mineral Sound or Missing Fundamental: Cultural History as Signal Analysis." *Osiris* 28 (1): 105–118.

Skorczewski, Dawn. 2012. *An Accident of Hope: The Therapy Tapes of Anne Sexton*. New York: Routledge.

Smith, Jacob. 2012. "Laughing Machines." In *The Sound Studies Reader*, edited by Jonathan Sterne, 533–538. New York: Routledge.

Smith, Mark M. 2001. *Listening to Nineteenth-Century America*. Chapel Hill: University of North Carolina Press.

Smith, Mark M. 2006. *How Race Is Made: Slavery, Segregation, and the Senses*. Chapel Hill: University of North Carolina Press.

Society of American Archivists. 2013. *Describing Archives: A Content Standard*. DACS 2019.0.3. Chicago: Society of American Archivists. https://files.archivists.org/pubs/DACS_2019.0.3_Version.pdf.

Southern Christian Leadership Conference Records. Stuart A. Rose Manuscript, Archives, and Rare Book Library, Emory University, Atlanta, GA. https://findingaids.library.emory.edu/documents/sclc1083/.

Star, Susan Leigh. 1999. "The Ethnography of Infrastructure." *American Behavioral Scientist* 43 (3): 377–391.

Steege, Benjamin. 2012. *Helmholtz and the Modern Listener*. Cambridge: Cambridge University Press.

Stein, Murray. 1983. *In Midlife*. Dallas, TX: Spring.

Sterne, Jonathan. 2003. *The Audible Past: Cultural Origins of Sound Reproduction*. Durham, NC: Duke University Press.

Sterne, Jonathan. 2012. *MP3: The Meaning of a Format*. Durham, NC: Duke University Press.

Sterne, Jonathan. 2015. "Compression: A Loose History." In *Signal Traffic: Critical Studies of Media Infrastructures*, edited by Lisa Parks and Nicole Starosielski, 31–52. Urbana: University of Illinois Press.

Sterne, Jonathan, and Tara Rodgers. 2011. "The Poetics of Signal Processing." *Differences* 22 (2–3): 31–53.

Stoever, Jennifer Lynn. 2016. *The Sonic Color Line: Race and the Cultural Politics of Listening*. New York: New York University Press.

Stoler, Ann Laura. 2009. *Along the Archival Grain: Epistemic Anxieties and Colonial Common Sense*. Princeton, NJ: Princeton University Press.

Strong, William Duncan. Papers. National Anthropological Archives, Smithsonian Institution, Washington, DC.

Sulzberger, A. G. 2011. "90 Years after a Bloody Race Riot, Tulsa Confronts Its Past." *New York Times*, June 20, 2011. https://www.nytimes.com/2011/06/20/us/20tulsa.html.

Svenonius, Elaine, and Dorothy McGarry. 1993. "Objectivity in Evaluating Subject Heading Assignment." *Cataloging & Classification Quarterly* 16 (2): 5–40.

Szwed, John. 2011. *The Man Who Recorded the World: A Biography of Alan Lomax*. Reprint edition. London: Arrow.

Taylor, Diana. 2003. *The Archive and the Repertoire: Performing Cultural Memory in the Americas*. Durham, NC: Duke University Press.

References

Texas Advanced Computing Center. Stampede. University of Texas at Austin. https://web.archive.org/web/20150406093430/https://www.tacc.utexas.edu/stampede/.

Thompson, Emily Ann. 2002. *The Soundscape of Modernity: Architectural Acoustics and the Culture of Listening in America, 1900–1933*. Cambridge, MA: MIT Press.

Toop, David. 1999. *Exotica: Fabricated Soundscapes in a Real World*. London: Serpent's Tail.

Trouillot, Michel-Rolph. 1995. *Silencing the Past: Power and the Production of History*. Boston, MA: Beacon.

Tulsa Race Massacre of 1921 Archive. Department of Special Collections and University Archives, McFarlin Library, University of Tulsa, Oklahoma.

Underwood, Ted. 2017. "A Genealogy of Distant Reading." *Digital Humanities Quarterly* 11 (2). http://www.digitalhumanities.org/dhq/vol/11/2/000317/000317.html.

Urch, Kakie, Michael Dorn, and J. Abraham. 1995. "Working the Borderlands, Becoming *Mestiza*: An Interview with Gloria Anzaldúa." *DisClosure: A Journal of Social Theory* 4 (1). https://uknowledge.uky.edu/disclosure/vol4/iss1/8/.

UT Folklore Center Archives. Dolph Briscoe Center for American History, University of Texas at Austin. https://txarchives.org/utcah/finding_aids/00385.xml.

Vazquez, Alexandra T. 2013. *Listening in Detail: Performances of Cuban Music*. Durham, NC: Duke University Press.

Visweswaran, Kamala. 1994. *Fictions of Feminist Ethnography*. Minneapolis: University of Minnesota Press.

Vivancos Pérez, Ricardo F. 2021. "Introduction." In *Borderlands: The New Mestiza / La Frontera*, edited by Ricardo F. Vivancos Pérez and Norma E. Cantú. San Francisco: Aunt Lute.

Xu, Weijia, Maria Esteva, Peter Cui, Eugene Castillo, Kewen Wang, Hanna-Robbins Hopkins, Tanya Clement, Aaron Choate, and Ruizhu Huang. December 2020. "A Study of Spoken Audio Processing Using Machine Learning for Libraries, Archives and Museums (LAM)." In *2020 IEEE International Conference on Big Data*, 1939–1948. New York: IEEE.

W3C. 2017. *Web Annotation Data Model*. Edited by Robert Sanderson, Paolo Ciccarese, and Benjamin Young. https://www.w3.org/TR/annotation-model/.

Wagner, Laura. 2017. "*Nou Toujou La!* The Digital (After-)Life of Radio Haïti-Inter." *Archipelagos* 2 (July). https://archipelagosjournal.org/issue02/nou-toujou-la.html.

Walker, Alice. 1975. "In Search of Zora Neale Hurston." *Ms. Magazine*, March 1975, 74–79.

Walker, Alice. 1979. "Looking for Zora." In *I Love Myself when I Am Laughing and Then again When I Am Looking Mean and Impressive*, edited by Zora Neale Hurston, 297–312. New York: Feminist Press.

Walker, Malea. 2021. "Tulsa Race Massacre: Newspaper Complicity and Coverage." *Headlines & Heroes: Newspapers, Comics, and More Fine Print* (blog), Library of Congress, Washington, DC, May 27, 2021. https://blogs.loc.gov/headlinesandheroes/2021/05/tulsa-race-massacre-newspaper-complicity-and-coverage/.

Wallace, Irving, David Wallechinsky, and Amy Wallace. 1983. *Significa*. New York: Dutton.

Ward, Cynthia. 2012. "Truths, Lies, Mules and Men: Through the 'Spy-Glass of Anthropology' and What Zora Saw There." *Western Journal of Black Studies* 36 (4): 301–313.

Weisbard, Eric. 2014. *Top 40 Democracy: The Rival Mainstreams of American Music / Eric Weisbard*. Chicago: University of Chicago Press.

Weheliye, Alexander G. 2005. *Phonographies: Grooves in Sonic Afro-Modernity*. Durham, NC: Duke University Press.

Wernimont, Jacqueline. 2019. *Numbered Lives: Life and Death in Quantum Media*. Cambridge, MA: MIT Press.

West, Anthony. (1955) 2010. *Heritage*. New York: Gallery.

Wheeler, Ed. 1971. "Profile of a Race Riot." *Impact*, July 1971.

White, Sara. 2012. "Crippling the Archives: Negotiating Notions of Disability in Appraisal and Arrangement and Description." *American Archivist* 75 (1): 109–124. https://doi.org/10.17723/aarc.75.1.c53h4712017n4728.

Wilcox, Johnnie. 2007. "Black Power: Minstrelsy and Electricity in Ralph Ellison's 'Invisible Man.'" *Callaloo* 30 (4): 987–1009.

Williams, Lee E., and Lee E. Williams II. 2008. *Anatomy of Four Race Riots: Racial Conflict in Knoxville, Elaine (Arkansas), Tulsa, and Chicago, 1919–1921*. Jackson: University Press of Mississippi.

Williford, Christa, and Charles Henry. 2012. *One Culture: Computationally Intensive Research in the Humanities and Social Sciences*. Alexandria, VA: Council on Library and Information Resources. https://www.clir.org/pubs/reports/pub151/.

Winick, Stephen. 2017. "Ralph Ellison, Invisible Folklorist." *Folklife Today: American Folklife Center & Veterans History* (blog), Library of Congress, Washington, DC, June 2, 2017. https://blogs.loc.gov/folklife/2017/06/ralph-ellison-invisible-folklorist/.

Woodward, C. Vann. 1985. "History From Slave Sources". In *The Slave's Narrative*, edited by Charles T. Davis and Henry Louis Gates Jr., 48–59. Oxford: Oxford University Press.

References

WPA field recordings in Calhoun County and Raiford (the 1935, and the 1936–1937 recording expeditions). 1935. State Archives of Florida, Florida Memory. https://www.floridamemory.com/items/show/238002.

WPA field recordings in Jacksonville and Ybor City (1939 recording expedition: Herbert Halpert). 1939. State Archives of Florida, Florida Memory. https://www.floridamemory.com/.

Wright, Richard. 1937. "Between Laughter and Tears." *New Masses*, October 5, 1937, 22–23.

Wright, John S. 2003. "'Jack-the-Bear' Dreaming: Ellison's Spiritual Technologies." *Boundary 2* 30 (2): 175–194.

Yeo, Geoffrey. 2007. "Concepts of Record (1): Evidence, Information, and Persistent Representations." *American Archivist* 70 (2): 315–343. https://doi.org/10.17723/aarc.70.2.u327764v1036756q.

Yeo, Geoffrey. 2008. "Concepts of Record (2): Prototypes and Boundary Objects." *American Archivist* 71 (1): 118–143. https://doi.org/10.17723/aarc.71.1.p0675v40tr14q6w2.

Index

Adaptive Recognition with Layered Optimization (ARLO), 150
Agency, 166n30
  aurality and, 13
  intermedia and, 41
  listening and, 11–13
  in *Magic City*, 39
  of Sexton, Anne, 98–99
  silence and, 78
  talking back and, 11
Allan, Jeffner, 114
Along the Archival Grain (Stoler), 162n2
Always Already Computational, 188n11
"America's Biggest Race War" (Avery, R.), 173n36
Amplify, xv, 3
  close listening to, 17, 43, 60
  context to, 78
  dissonance to, 16–17
  distortion and, 43, 65–66
  through fiction, 42
  identity and, 108
  interference to, 84, 88
  key scenes, 36–37
  laughter, 117
  microphones to, 43, 77
  ordinary lives, 39
  reception and, 133
  for resonance, 20–21
  silencing and, 25, 30, 78, 88
  as technical, 152–153
  voices, 5
Anne Sexton (Middlebrook), 184n7
Anzaldúa, Gloria Evangelina, xiv. *See also* Conocimiento
  acts of love by, 145–147
  audio recordings of, 20, 168n45
  on authority, 146–147
  Borderlands by, 113, 121–122, 132–133
  catalysts for, 127
  criticisms of, 122
  Gearhart session with, 145–146
  guidance for, 127
  identities of, 114, 117, 120–121
  on indigenous spirituality, 125, 186n13
  juxtaposition by, 120–121
  Keating interview with, 131–132
  on language and gender, 121–122
  La Prieta, 124–125, 185n10
  laughter of, 117–118
  Levin recording with, 133–145
  liminal sounds of, 117–119
  on listening, 115
  marginalization and, 113
  mislistening by, 118
  occult tools of, 110, 127–128
  omissions about, 129–131
  process of, 111, 185n1

Anzaldúa, Gloria Evangelina (cont.)
"Reading LP" by, 124–125, 185n10
on reception, 112, 114–115, 117, 130
on return, 132
on sound, 123–125
on spiritual receptivity, 122–123
spiritual recordings of, 16–17, 111, 129
subliminal persuasion tapes used by, 128–129, 186n18
tarot reading by, 20, 111, 117–118, 127–128, 133–146
"Using Meditation and Occult Tools" by, 115
on white women, 121
Archival recordings, xi–xiii, 3–4
ARLO. *See* Adaptive Recognition with Layered Optimization
Askew, Rilla, 35, 173n37. *See also Fire in Beulah*
AudiAnnotate Audiovisual Extensible Workflow (AWE), 189n18. *See also* AVAnnotate
Audible Past, The (Sterne), 161n6
Audience, 182n14
  as little man, 81–82, 86, 182n15
  reception by, 82, 117, 121, 131, 147
  truth and, 81–82, 182n16
Audio data, 152
AudioSet, 158
Audio signal processing, 152
Audio technology terms, 3
Aurality, 13, 166n31
Aurality (Gautier), 161n6
AVAnnotate, xvi, 159–160, 189nn18–19
Avery, Cyrus Stevens, 167n36
Avery, Ruth Sigler, 15, 17, 167n36
  "America's Biggest Race War" by, 173n36
  "Fear, the Fifth Horseman" by, 26–27, 34, 170n12

gendered politics and, 28, 171n22
Holway and Clinton interviews with, 32–33
on participants, 28–29
Prince interview with, 30–31, 33
AWE. *See* AudiAnnotate Audiovisual Extensible Workflow

Barad, Karen, 166n26
  on agency, 166n30
  on mattering, xv, 8, 151
  on physics, 165n18
Barnicle, Mary Elizabeth, 46, 50–51, 54–55
Belarde-Lewis, Miranda, 162n6
Bernstein, Charles, 161n6, 174n49
Birdsall, Carolyn, 167n34
Black Dispatch, 26, 82–83, 169n10
Black music, 14, 165n17, 167n34
Bodies of Evidence (Boyd & Ramírez), 162n6
Bohr, Niels, 165n18
Borderlands (Anzaldúa), 113, 121–122, 132–133
Boyd, Nan Alamilla, 162n6
Brodber, Erna, 126
Brooks, Daphne, 21, 167n34
Brown, Martin, 169n10
Brown, Wendy, 17, 40, 169n6, 173n38
Browne, Simone, 18, 51
Brown v. Board of Education, 16, 18–19, 69–70, 72, 78
Burke, Edmund, 180n3
Burrows, David, 126
Butler, Judith, 165n18

Camlot, Jason, 161n6
Cannon, Christopher, 166n31
Carter, Rodney, 162n6
CDs, xii, 161n3
Clement, Tanya E., 149, 185n15, 188n12
Clinton, Walton, 32–33

Index

Close listening
  access and, 46
  to amplify, 17, 43, 60
  close reading and, 25, 43, 174n49
  compression and, 19–20
  conocimiento and, 111–112
  deep listening *vs.*, 174n49
  as difficult, 46
  in dissonant records, 17, 43
  distant listening *vs.*, 159
  for distortion, 18
  to "For the Year of the Insane," 19–20
  to intermedia, 17, 43, 115
  as methodology, xv, 3, 159–160
  silencing and, 70
Close Listening (Bernstein), 161n6
Close reading, 25, 43, 174n49
Collins, Carvel, 71, 77
Community activism, 168n40, 170n17
Compression, 3
  anxiety and, 92, 183n4
  close listening and, 19–20
  in dissonant records, 19–20, 152–153
  in intermedia, 19–20, 151
  for resonance, 20–21
  Sexton, Anne, and, 19–20, 91–92, 95, 97–100, 106–107
  Sterne on, 91–92, 183nn3–4
Computational models, 151, 187n6
Conocimiento, 20
  close listening and, 111–112
  nepantla in, 113–114, 116
  reception and, 111–113, 129
  step five of, 126–128
  step four of, 122–125
  step one of, 113–115
  step seven of, 132–145
  step six of, 128–132
  step three of, 120–122
  step two of, 115–120
  tape recording and, 112
  theory of, 112, 185n3

Corse, Carita Doggett, 46, 59
  on influences, 61
  on purpose, 62–63
Council on Library and Information Resources, xi
Cultural analytics, 150–151, 187n4

Daniel, Dominique, 162n6
Dark sousveillance, 18, 51, 53
Data, 149–150. *See also* Audio data
Davis, Christina, 69, 180n2
Daza, Maria P. Chaves, 114, 117
Death in a Promised Land (Ellsworth), 28, 171n22
Debt slavery, 60, 179n28
Deep listening, 174n49
Degener, Cindy, 102
Digging into Data Challenge, 153–154, 156, 187n8
Digital Public Library of America, xi
Dingemanse, Mark, 116
Dissonance, 13–14
  to amplify, 16–17
  in intermedia, 16
  resonance and, 14, 21
Dissonant records
  audio recordings in, 20–21
  close listening in, 17, 43
  compression in, 19–20, 152–153
  distortions in, 18
  interference in, 18–19
  intermedia and, 6–7, 16
  in libraries, 15–16, 167n35
  voyeurism in, 17
Distant listening
  accuracy thresholds in, 157
  analysis tools in, 156–157
  audio data curation in, 156
  close listening *vs.*, 159
  definitions of, 149–150, 187n1
  dialogic meaning making in, 153–155, 188n10

Distant listening (cont.)
  entelechic and agential meaning making in, 155–160
  interference and, 155, 159
  material and apparatus in, 152–153
  resonance and, 151–152
  scalability in, 157–158
  sustainability in, 158
"Distant Listening or Playing Visualisations Pleasantly with the Eyes and Ears" (Clement), 149
Distortion, 3
  amplify and, 43, 65–66
  close listening for, 18
  dark sousveillance and, 18, 53
  digital editing and, 58
  in dissonant records, 18
  meanings of, 53
  on records, 46, 53, 151
  for resonance, 20–21
  social, 56
  technical, 57–59, 65, 152, 178n23
  in writing, 98
Dreams, 100
Duarte, Marisa Elena, 162n6
Dunjee, Roscoe, 82–83
"Dust Tracks," 60–61, 178n27
Dust Tracks on a Road (Hurston), 45, 52, 178n27

"Ear and the Shunting Yard, The" (Clement), 165n17
Easter egg, 41–42, 174n46
Ellis, Dan, 155
Ellison, Ralph, xiv, 5–6, 8, 166n29. See also Harvard Summer School Conference; *Invisible Man*
  on audience, 81–82
  Brown v. Board of Education influencing, 16, 18–19, 69–70, 72, 78
  on dehumanization, 121
  on desegregation, 74–75
  on discrepancies, 87
  "Going to the Territory" by, 22, 34
  on identification, 79–80
  interference and, 77–87
  "Living with Music" by, 78–80
  on moral imagination, 72–73
  morality and, 18–19
  on motivations, 85–86, 182n18
  on Page, 87–88
  pronouns used by, 73–74, 83
  on reportage, 35
  on Rushing, 84–85
  on segregation, 72–75, 78, 83, 181n6, 181n10
  on slavery, 82–83
  on stereotypes, 25, 169n8
  on technology, 79, 181n13
  on Tulsa Race Massacre, 83, 85, 88, 182n17
  "Twentieth-Century Fiction and the Black Mask of Humanity" by, 72–73, 84, 180n5
Ellsworth, Scott, 24, 169n11
  archives for, 171n20
  on community activism, 170n17
  Death in a Promised Land by, 28, 171n22
  on participants, 29
  process for, 30
  as reference, 174n41
Erlmann, Veit, 13
Europeana, xi

Farrell, Dennis, 101, 104
"Fear, the Fifth Horseman" (Avery, R.), 26–27
Federal Writers' Project, 59–60, 172n26
Feinberg, Melanie, 149
Feminist Tarot, A (Gearhart & Rennie), 186n17
Fire in Beulah (Askew), 17, 42
  inspiration for, 35, 174n41
  narratives in, 37–38
  nationalist discourse in, 173n39
  racial identities in, 37
  scenes in, 36–37

Index

"Flee on Your Donkey" (Sexton, Anne), 185n15
Former Slave Project, 172n26
"For the Year of the Insane" (Sexton, Anne), 90
   close listening to, 19–20
   dreams in, 100
   faith and, 101–102
   limits and, 108
   liturgy and, 102–104
   in *Live or Die*, 184n14
   motivation for, 91–92, 182n1
   performance of, 102, 184n13
   time and, 104–107
Fourier transform, 152, 187n7
Franklin, John Hope, 169n11
Freund, Alexander, 169n7
Frohock, Wilbur Merrill, 71–72, 75–76, 77
Fulton, Maggie, 60, 62–63
Furlonge, Nicole Brittingham, 149, 161n6, 174n42, 181n9

Gates, Eddie Faye, 24, 27–28, 172n33
Gautier, Ana María Ochoa, 161n6, 162n6, 165n24, 166n28, 177n13
Gearhart, Sally, 118, 127
   Anzaldúa session with, 145–146
   A Feminist Tarot by, 186n17
   on tarot readings, 127–128, 146, 186n17
Gil, Alex, 189n19
Gilroy, Paul, 53, 177n17
Gitelman, Lisa, 163n11, 164n14
"Going to the Territory" (Ellison), 22, 34
Gold, Ben, 155
Good Systems, 150–151
Google, 158
Graphics processing units (GPUs), 158
Gray Sexton, Linda, 16, 92, 167n38, 183n5

Halliburton, R., Jr., 170n16
Halpert, Herbert, 59–60, 61–63
Haraway, Donna, 162n4
Harding, Sandra, 9
Harney, Daniel, 177n9
Hartman, Saidiya, 33, 121
   on audience, 182n14
   on institutionalized dehumanization, 169n8
   on scenes of subjection, 48, 176n8
   on slavery narratives, 173n40
   on truth, 182n16
Harvard Summer School Conference, 15, 18–19
   current politics and, 73–75
   introduction to, 71
   microphones at, 71, 76–77
   participants at, 71–72, 180n2
   recordings from, 69–70, 180n1
   silences in, 70, 75–77
Harvesting Speech Datasets for Linguistic Research on the Web project, 154–155
Hayles, N. Katherine, 6, 163n12
Heidegger, Martin, 13
Helmreich, Stefan, 174n48
Hemenway, Robert, 49–50
Henry, Charles, 154, 156
Higgins, Dick, 166n32
High Performance Sound Technologies for Access and Scholarship (HiPSTAS), 150, 153, 157–158, 187n3
Hill, Lynda Marion, 61–62, 177n9
HiPSTAS. *See* High Performance Sound Technologies for Access and Scholarship
Hirsh, Elizabeth, 2, 7, 10–11
Hochman, Brian, 5, 164n14, 166n27
Holway, William R., 32–33
hooks, bell, xii, 1–2, 7, 10–12, 21
   on agency, 12
   Olson interview with, 1–2, 7, 10–12
   on resonance, 12
   on talking back, 11–12

Hughes, Langston, 49–50
Humes, Harold L., 72, 180n4
Hurston, Zora Neale, xiv, 15–16, 44
  archives for, 45–46, 175nn4–5
  background of, 45
  on between-story conversation and business, 60, 179n30
  direction by, 55–56
  on "Dust Tracks," 60–61, 178n27
  Dust Tracks on a Road by, 45, 52, 178n27
  equivocation by, 52, 177n13
  on folklore, 149, 153
  frustrations of, 47–48
  as indispensable, 51–52
  jook songs by, 63–64
  in June 1935, 54–59
  in June 1939, 59–65
  laugh of, 63–64
  listening for, 53–65
  Lomax log of, 52, 54–57
  as polarizing, 45, 48, 175n3
  process of, 48–50
  publications by, 18, 168n43
  reading of, 47–50
  reviews of, 48–50, 177n9
  sousveillance by, 18, 51, 53
  technical distortions of, 57–59, 65, 178n23
  tracks by, 18, 46, 54–58, 168n41, 175n6
  as unnamed, 66, 179n38
  Walker on, 45, 175n2
  watching of, 50–52
Hyman, Stanley Edgar, 71
Hysteria, 92–93, 102, 183n6

Identification
  in fiction, 80
  through listening, 79, 181n12
  technology and, 79, 181n13
IIIF. *See* International Image Interoperability Framework

Interference, 3
  absences through, 152
  to amplify, 82–83, 85, 88
  audience and, 82
  as constructive, 78–79, 83–85, 86, 88, 155
  definition of, 78
  as destructive, 78–80, 83, 85–86, 88, 155
  in dissonant records, 18–19
  distant listening and, 155, 159
  Ellison and, 77–87
  in *Invisible Man*, 83–87
  for resonance, 20–21
  silence as, 70, 81–82
Intermedia, xiv, 3, 163n12
  agency and, 41
  along the archival grain, 25
  as central, 166n32
  close listening to, 17, 43, 115
  compression in, 19–20, 151
  dissonance in, 16
  dissonant records and, 6–7, 16
  five primary theories in, 164n13
  occult tools as, 127–128
  in poetry, 107–108
  spirituality and, 128–129
  variety in, 6–7, 164nn14–15
International Image Interoperability Framework (IIIF), 158, 188n16
Internet Archive, xi, 161n1
Invisible Man (Ellison), 8
  award for, 69
  critique of, 75–77
  inspiration for, 85–86, 182n18
  interference in, 83–87
  moral imagination of, 72, 180n3
  narrator in, 70, 77
  Tulsa Race Massacre in, 88

Jackson, Irene, 60, 62–63
Johnson, Charles E., 34, 173n34
Johnson, Guy, 47

Index

Jook houses, 63
Jook songs, 63–64

Kayo. *See* Sexton, Alfred Muller, II
Keating, AnaLouise, 122, 185n1
  Anzaldúa interview with, 131–132
  on Anzaldúa spirituality, 113–114
  as biographer, 113, 119
  omissions by, 119, 130–131
Kennedy, Stetson, 50, 52, 59
Kissinger, Henry, 181n6
Kittler, Friedrich, 126, 164n14

LAMs. *See* Libraries, Archives, and Museums
Lange, Beatrice, 60, 62
Learning interfaces, 157
Levin, Lisa, 133. *See also* Anzaldúa, Gloria Evangelina
Libraries, Archives, and Museums (LAMs), 158, 160, 188n11
Library of Congress, xi
Liminality, 127, 129, 186n16
Liminal sounds, 20, 115–117
  of Anzaldúa, 117–119
  reception of, 117, 119, 133
  significance of, 130
  transcription of, 119–120
Lindelof, Damon, 174n41. See also *Watchmen*
Listening, xii–xiii, 161n6. *See also* Close listening
  agency and, 11–13
  identification through, 79, 181n12
  mislistening in, xiii–xiv, 161n5
  as receptive, 115, 121
  resonance and, 7, 11
Listening in Detail (Vazquez), 161n4
"Little Girl, My Stringbean, My Lovely Woman" (Sexton, Anne), 184n13
"Little Uncomplicated Hymn, A" (Sexton, Anne), 184n14
Live or Die (Sexton, Anne), 184n14, 186n16

"Living with Music" (Ellison), 78–80
Locke, Alain, 47
Lomax, Alan, 46, 47, 50, 51–52, 54–56, 176n6. *See also* Hurston, Zora Neale
Lunsford, Andrea, 146
Lytle, Andrew Nelson, 71–72

Machine-learning, 21, 150, 153–154, 157
Machine-Readable Cataloging (MARC) standard, 56
Macy Conferences, 9, 166n25
Madigan, Tim, 28, 36, 171n25
Magic City (Rhodes), 17
  agency in, 39
  inspiration for, 35, 38
  scenes in, 36–37
Manovich, Lev, 164n15
MARC. *See* Machine-Readable Cataloging standard
McEnaney, Tom, 163n8
McGann, Jerome, 168n44
McKinney, Cait, 162n6
McKittrick, Katherine, 14, 165n17
McNulty Park detainments, 31–32, 172n32
Mead, Margaret, 9, 166n25
Media, 6–7, 8, 163n12, 165n21
Melville, Herman, 64–65
Metadata, xii, 161n3
Metaphors, 3, 162n3
Microphones
  for amplification, 43, 77
  as analogy, 77–78, 181n9
  at Harvard Summer School Conference, 71, 76–77
Middlebrook, Diane, 92, 184n7, 184n10
Mills, Mara, 5
Minimal computing, 160, 189n19
Mining a Year of Speech project, 154–155
Mislistening, xiii–xiv, 118, 161n5
Modality, 163n12
Moral imagination, 72–73, 75–76, 180n3
Morgan, Nelson, 155

Morris, Jeremy, 161n3
Morrison, Toni, 84, 87, 121, 169n8

National Association for the Advancement of Colored People (NAACP), 48, 176n7
Negro Workaday Songs (Odum & Johnson, G.), 47
Nepantla, 113–114, 116, 133

Occult tools, 110, 127–128
O'Connor, Frank, 71–72
Odum, Howard, 47
Olson, Gary, 1–2, 7, 10–11
Orne, Martin, 91, 184nn7–8. *See also* Sexton, Anne
    control of, 95, 100
    diagnosis by, 92–93
    identity of, 107–108
    letter to, 100, 184n12
    as male auditor, 184n10
    method of, 96–100
    nonverbal communication by, 103
    photograph of, 107–108
    trance reactions by, 94

Page, Inman, 87–88, 173n35
Parrish, Mary Elizabeth Jones, 27, 169nn9–10, 170n16, 172n32
Persephone Press, 186n17
Phonopoetics (Camlot), 161n6
Pizzolato, Nicola, 179n28
"Playback is a Bitch" (Clement), 188n12
"Poetics of Signal Processing, The" (Sterne & Rodgers), 162n5
Portelli, Alessandro, 163n7, 163n10, 169n7
Prayer, 101–102
Prentice, Frances W., 27
Prince, Verna, 30–31, 33
"Protestant Easter" (Sexton, Anne), 184n14

Race Sounds, 161n6
Ramírez, Horacio N. Roque, 162n6
"Reading LP" (Anzaldúa), 124–125, 185n10
Reception, 3, 7
    amplify and, 133
    Anzaldúa on, 112, 114–115, 117, 130
    by audience, 82, 117, 121, 131, 147
    conocimiento and, 111–113, 129
    of liminal sounds, 117, 119, 133
    listening as, 115, 121
    mishearing and, 122
    nepantla and, 114
    of new ideas, 120–121
    resistance and, 146
    for resonance, 20–21
    spiritual, 122–123
    technology and, 151–152
    vibration and, 124
Records, 7
    audiovisual media in, 5
    misrepresentation in, 4, 162n6
    selectivity in, 5–6
    as written text, 3–4
Redburn (Melville), 64–65
Registers, 7
Rennie, Susan, 186n17
Resonance, 3, 165n17
    amplify for, 20–21
    dialogism in, 8–9, 165n24
    dissonance and, 14, 21
    distant listening and, 151–152
    entelechy in, 9–11, 166nn26–30
    hooks on, 12
    listening and, 7, 11
    materiality in, 8, 165nn19–21
    properties of, 8–11, 165n18
    reception for, 20–21
Rhodes, Jewell Parker, 171n23, 174n43. See also *Magic City*
Risam, Roopika, 189n19

Index

Rodgers, Tara, 162n5
Roulston, Kathryn, 172n26
Rowland, Dick, 23, 27–28
Rubery, Matthew, 166n31
Rushing, Jimmy, 84–86

SALAMI. *See* Structural Analysis of Large Amounts of Music Information
Sampling, 152–153
Sawyer, Jim, 169n4
Schröter, Jens, 164n13, 164n15
Sea shanty, 64–65
Segregation, 69–70
    desegregation and, 74–75
    Ellison on, 72–73, 78, 83, 181n6, 181n10
Sexton, Alfred Muller, II (Kayo), 92–93, 100, 184n8
Sexton, Anne, xiv, 90, 161n5. *See also* "For the Year of the Insane"; Gray Sexton, Linda
    agency of, 98–99
    biography about, 92, 184n7
    compression and, 19–20, 91–92, 95, 97–100, 106–107
    on dreams, 100
    on faith, 101–102
    "Flee on Your Donkey" by, 185n15
    frustrations of, 93–94
    hysteria diagnosis for, 92–93, 102, 183n6
    identity and, 107–108
    journals of, 94–95, 184n9
    on liminal state, 186n16
    Live or Die by, 184n14, 186n16
    memories of, 105–106
    mental health issues of, 92–94, 183nn5–6
    on mother figure, 106
    motivations of, 92
    Orne letter from, 100, 184n12
    Orne photograph by, 107–108
    poetry of, 16, 101–107, 184nn13–14
    poetry as liturgy by, 102–104
    recording of, 95–97
    resistance by, 100
    in therapy, 92–95
    therapy recordings of, 16–17, 19–20, 167n38
    therapy text of, 19–20, 92–100
    time and, 104–107
    trance tapes of, 94–95, 97–98, 101, 103–105
    writing process of, 92
Sharpe, Jenny, 174n44
Silence, xi, 21
    agency and, 78
    in Harvard Summer School Conference, 70, 75–77
    as interference, 70, 81–82
    modalities of, 25, 169n6
    off the record, 25, 169n7
    of Page, 87–88
    in US literature, 87
Simenon, Georges, 71
Singleton, Alabama, 60, 62–63
Slavery, 82–83, 173n40. *See also* Debt slavery
Smith, Jacob, 126
Sonic Color Line, The (Stoever), 161n6
Sound technologies, 152–153
Sousveillance, 18, 51, 53
Southworth, Rolla, 66
Speech transmission, 155
Stampede, 157–158, 188n14
Steege, Benjamin, 165n17
Stein, Murray, 127
Stereotypes, 25, 169n8
Sterne, Jonathan, xiv, 126, 164n14
    The Audible Past by, 161n6
    on compression, 91–92, 183nn3–4
    on privilege, 5
    on signal processing, 162n5
Stoever, Jennifer Lynn, xiv, 161n6
Stoler, Ann Laura, 162n2

Structural Analysis of Large Amounts of Music Information (SALAMI), 154–155
Surveillance culture, 52
  singing in, 50
  sousveillance in, 51
Swann v. Charlotte-Mecklenburg Board of Education, 30–31
"Sylvia's Death" (Sexton, Anne), 184n14

Talking back, 11
Tarot
  Anzaldúa readings of, 20, 111, 117–118, 127–128, 133–147
  bells and, 145–146
  Gearhart on, 127–128, 145–146, 186n17
Taylor, Diana, 5–6, 177n10
Tcheng, David, 150
Text, 168n44
Trouillot, Michel-Rolph, 10
Truth, 42, 81–82, 182n16
Tulsa Race Massacre, 15, 17, 182n19
  in archives, 29–35, 171n20, 172n33
  Ellison on, 83, 85, 88, 182n17
  erasure of, 24, 169n4
  in fiction, 28, 35–42, 171n21
  freedom and, 36–37
  historiography process for, 30, 172n26
  instigation of, 23–24, 168n1, 169n4
  McNulty Park detainments in, 31–32, 172n32
  in print, 26–29, 169n10
  racist editorials about, 26, 169n9
  renaming of, 29
  silencing of, 24–27, 169n11, 170n13, 170n17
  Tulsa Tribune editorial about, 23–24, 26, 169n4
"Twentieth-Century Fiction and the Black Mask of Humanity" (Ellison), 72–73, 180n5

"Using Meditation and Occult Tools" (Anzaldúa), 115

Vazquez, Alexandra, 161n4
Vibration, 123–124, 165n24
Visweswaran, Kamala, 177n9, 177n13, 178n23, 179n38
Voices, xiii

Wagner, Laura, 161n2
Walker, Alice, 45, 175n2
Walker, Malea, 169n11
Watchmen, 17, 174n41
  comic series origin for, 39–40, 174n45
  Easter egg in, 41–42, 174n46
  inspiration for, 28, 36
  resonant truths in, 42
  scenes in, 36–37
  untold futures in, 39–40
WC3 Web Annotation Data Model standard (W3C 2017), 158
Weheliye, Alexander, 14, 126, 164n14, 165n21
Weiland, Christine, 123
Werner, Evelyn, 60, 62
West, Anthony, 71, 75–77
Wheeler, Ed, 27–28, 170n13, 170n18
White, Sara, 162n6
Williams, William D., 24
Williford, Christa, 154, 156
Wolf, John B., 22, 34–35, 173n35
Women Writing Culture (Hirsh & Olson), 2, 10
Work Projects Administration (WPA), 18, 168n42
Wright, Richard, 48, 60

Yeo, Geoffrey, 4